WOMEN IN GRASSROOTS COMMUNICATION

COMMUNICATION AND HUMAN VALUES

SERIES EDITORS

Robert A. White, Editor, *The Centre of Interdisciplinary Studies in Communication, The Gregorian University, Rome, Italy*
Michael Traber, Associate Editor, *World Association for Christian Communication, London, UK*

INTERNATIONAL EDITORIAL ADVISORY BOARD

Binod C. Agrawal, *Development and Educational Communication, Space Applications Centre, Ahmedabad, India*
Luis Ramiro Beltrán, *Caracas, Venezuela*
S. T. Kwame Boafo, *African Council on Communication Education, Nairobi, Kenya*
James W. Carey, *University of Illinois, USA*
Marlene Cuthbert, *University of Windsor, Canada*
William F. Fore, *Yale Divinity School, USA*
George Gerbner, *University of Pennsylvania, USA*
James D. Halloran, *University of Leicester, UK*
Cees Hamelink, *Institute of Social Studies, The Hague, The Netherlands*
Neville D. Jayaweera, *Stockholm, Sweden*
Emile G. McAnany, *University of Texas, USA*
Walter J. Ong, *St. Louis University, USA*
Breda Pavlic, *Culture and Communication Sector, UNESCO, Paris*
Miquel de Moragas Spa, *Autonomous University of Barcelona, Spain*
Anabelle Sreberny-Mohammadi, *Centre for Mass Communication Research, University of Leicester, UK*

WOMEN IN GRASSROOTS COMMUNICATION

Furthering Social Change

edited by Pilar Riaño

SAGE Publications
International Educational and Professional Publisher
Thousand Oaks   London   New Delhi

For information address:

 SAGE Publications, Inc.
2455 Teller Road
Thousand Oaks, California 91320

SAGE Publications Ltd.
6 Bonhill Street
London EC2A 4PU
United Kingdom

SAGE Publications India Pvt. Ltd.
M-32 Market
Greater Kailash I
New Delhi 110 048 India

Printed in the United States of America

Library of Congress Cataloging-in-Publication Data

Main entry under title:

Women in grassroots communication: Furthering social change/
edited by Pilar Riaño.
p. cm. — (Communication and human values.)
Includes bibliographical references and index.
ISBN 0-8039-4905-7. — ISBN 0-8039-4906-5 (pbk.)
1. Women in development. 2. Communication in community development. 3. Women in communication. 4. Women—Communication. 5. Social change. I. Riaño, Pilar. II. Series.
HQ1240.W6613 1994
305.42—dc20 94-4487

94 95 96 97 98 10 9 8 7 6 5 4 3 2 1

Sage Production Editor: Astrid Virding

Contents

Acknowledgments

Editing this book would not have been possible if I had not received exceptional intellectual, emotional, and practical support from a number of people. Dorothy Kidd provided me with the opportunity to discuss and exchange ideas throughout the entire editing process. Her criticisms, information, and editorial assistance have been most relevant to this effort. Dean Brown volunteered to do the translations from Spanish to English. I am very grateful for the dedication, time, and excellence of his work and for his unconditional friendship. Ann Mackleam's editorial comments challenged me and provided invaluable suggestions. Pat Howard's review of earlier drafts of the introduction and framework were very helpful. Thanks to Francisco Ibañez for his suggestions and willingness to read the manuscript.

Contacting contributors was not an easy task. I am most thankful to Jhothy Ghadham, Nancy George, Bruce Giroux, Vanessa Marmentini, Mary E. Brown, Patricia Ardila, Harry E. Brown, and Louise Ettling who provided me with contacts and excellent ideas.

The support I received from Les Abreo with photocopies, faxes, and transcripts is very much appreciated. Garth Manning provided much needed help in typing and Ita Margalit and Mario Lee with computer time.

I am especially grateful to Bob White, editor of this series, for his unique guidance, critical comments, and understanding. The World Association for Christian Communication provided a grant that made my initial engagement in the editing task possible. Special thanks to Michael Traber and Philip Lee in WACC for their help and to Intermedia in the United States.

I want to express my deepest appreciation to all the contributors in this book. Their works have influenced my thinking and provided intellectual stimulation and challenge. I appreciate the hard work put into writing the chapters despite the authors' personal and national difficulties, and their lack of resources and time. Special thanks to Maria Protz who made special efforts in identifying contributors and for her enthusiasm and feedback.

During the time I spent in Colombia working on this manuscript, I had the opportunity to discuss its main ideas with my sister Ivonne Riaño. Thanks also to the Urban Circle of Anthropology (URBANOS) for their discussion and comments. And to my parents, Jaime and Cecilia, who have encouraged and supported me throughout this time. Finally, I express my deepest thanks to my children, Andrea, Raphaelle, Gabriel, and Sebastian, who had to suffer my tension, stress, and lack of time because I was finishing the manuscript on my "free time" away from a full-time job. To my son Sebastian who became the first user of this book, finding difficult words for his spelling assignments and who so early in life has become aware that his mother is a "feminist." My friend and husband, Barry Wright, has been a great assistant in the editing task, but most important, his emotional and practical support were fundamental for finishing this book. Thanks.

Preface

This book documents the diversity of grassroots communication experiments carried out by **Third World women:** These women come together to voice their concerns, name who they are, share and build projects of change. These women create communication spaces that involve speaking, writing, dancing, meeting, story telling, media production, and networking. Communication spaces represent a terrain for expression and collective action for transformation. Yet they are also alternative spaces for promoting the processes of transforming the individual subject and the collective "we": spaces for organizing across differences and/or around commonalities of gender, **class, race,** and sexual orientation.

The term *grassroots communication* is used here not as a conceptual framework but as a descriptive category that encompasses a variety of communication processes, practices, and systems that are distinguished by their grassroots origin. Falling into this general category are women's informal communication practices, networks and associations, interpersonal and group communication, performing arts, cultural and artistic artifacts, writing, media produced in a group setting, folk and community media, and indigenous communication systems and practices.[1] Along the same lines, the term *participatory communication* is used here as a descriptive category that refers to the active involvement of a community or group in using media or group communication to produce their own messages and to engage audiences in critical reception (Riaño, 1990). At the end of this book is a glossary that contains the definition, or definitions, of the key concepts used here. The concepts defined in the glossary appear in boldface type at first use.

The women who have contributed to this book constitute a very special group, as they all are or have been participants or facilitators in participatory communication processes and/or in social and women's movements. Their contributions introduce regional frameworks and concerns from Africa, Asia, Latin America, and North America. Although most of them are linked to universities or research centers, their writing and communication pursuits extend beyond academic research to the articulation of their commitment to change and to the development of new forms of grassroots communication. Their contributions offer the freshness and creativity inherent in their practical experiences as well as the critical analysis and perceptiveness generated from their organizational and research links.

Although the contributors are from different regions, this book does not offer a complete and balanced coverage of grassroots communication experiences of women in all regions of the world. There are significant geographical gaps, particularly contributions from Europe, the Baltics, and the former USSR countries. Disproportionately more articles come from Latin America. This reflects in part my limited access to and knowledge of literature and peoples from other regions and my closer ties and familiarity with Latin America. The emphasis here is to cover the various analytical dimensions of grassroots communication while acknowledging the regional-geographical contributions and variations.

This collection of chapters is a dialogue about women's grassroots communication experiences with two main sets of goals: an analysis of the contribution women are making to processes of social change and the role communication plays in activating women's alternatives for social change. Two sets of questions guide this dialogue:

1. The role of women in communication and grassroots participation: How and to what extent are Third World women with grassroots communication creating communication avenues for the democratization of communications and for the construction of alternatives that foster social change? What does the evidence reveal about the nature, dynamics, and operationalization of such participation in grassroots communication?

2. The role communication plays in activating women's alternatives for change: How are grassroots communication processes consolidating women's views and perspectives on gender subordination and social change? How are these connections and social identities being built through communication by women? To what extent do these processes reveal a growing sense of identity based on pluralism and the acknowledgment of differences of gender, race, and class identities?

This book's contributors connect the discussions emerging from their experiences in the field with those originating in communication, development, and feminist scholarship. They describe principles and concerns that link this dialogue to the debate on the **democratization of communications**. These principles and concerns constitute the connecting ideas of the book and the guiding concepts of our framework. They refer to (a) the conception of women as social actors in communication, as subjects active in directing the cultural orientation of their social actions; (b) the rooting of their communication experiences and ways of communicating in the local, daily reality of their social environment (neighborhood, village, community, or nation); (c) the definition of communication enterprises as acts of naming and reframing histories of oppression and their articulation in larger movements that seek change (i.e., the women's movement and national liberation movements); (d) the consideration of grassroots participation as a condition and foundation for processes of communication rooted in democratic principles of the horizontal circulation of ideas and continuous redistribution of power; and (e) the identification of **women** from a multiplicity of angles that shape their perceptions and identities— as subjects of struggles, as partners of communication, as mothers, as workers, as activists, as citizens.

Although the various cases examined focus on women, the analyses are not just concerned with gender. More important, they address broader issues that connect questions of gender and communication with the various ways in which race, class, culture, sexual orientation, age, generation, history, colonialism, and the social division of labor intersect and shape women's communication experiences, social participation, and identities. Our approach to the subject emphasizes variables of diversity and complexity: the diversity contained in the category *woman* and the complexity of the communication strategies and processes of media production.

Initially, the book was going to focus exclusively on women from Third World countries, arguing that one of the important dimensions in the emancipation of women is their significant role in grassroots development and their ability to make this more participatory. However, the review of experiences in North America revealed that the **social movements** and communication perspectives of marginalized groups such as women of Color, Aboriginal women, immigrant women, and lesbians have some commonalities with the liberation goals of women from the Third World and with the concerns that guide various communicative strategies and methods. Furthermore, a concept of Third World based not only in geographical location but in sociohistorical conjunctures (such as among the poor and marginalized of the North) provided the framework within which the contributions from North America are included.

My task as editor of the book has also been influenced by many of the same concerns and commitments as its contributors. I am a Colombian anthropologist and communicator who has been living in Canada for the last seven years. Editing this book provided the opportunity to place several years of training and research experience in a broader perspective. This experience is in the use of popular communication tools and the development of communication strategies for community development and mobilization with Colombian unions, women's and youth groups, cultural and neighborhood associations or with victims of violence. My interest in this book developed from these years but has been furthered by my research work on Latin American popular culture and participatory communication in development programs with women in Third World countries. My reflection on women's grassroots communication and alternative communication strategies has been enriched by my work in Canada with immigrants and refugees, and by my "location" as a Latina and a woman of Color who alternates between academia, research, activism, and training and between Latin America and North America.

As my work on the book advanced, my analysis and approach to the subject matter became more and more influenced by the analyses developed by the book's contributors and their regional frameworks. I have been particularly inspired by the pioneering work on popular communication and culture that is being developed in Latin America. This special relationship allowed me to establish a connection between my daily life as a researcher and community activist and my writing. My writing style reflects such a background, distancing itself from a mere linear structure of thought, including a variety of concepts from Latin America.

I would like to make explicit some of the key concepts that originate in this Latin American approach as they underscore many of the discussions included in this book. In particular, the analysis of communication processes from the perspective of social movements and the multifaceted characteristics of everyday life. The notion of social movements recognizes nontraditional forms of participation and organized social expressions that, lead by **social actors** such as women or youth, have opened new spaces for political action. These new ways of political action are largely rooted in everyday concerns (i.e., access to urban facilities, improvement of living standards, and impact of everyday violence on families) and on experiences of oppression as members of marginalized groups. The analysis of women's leadership in urban and regional social movements, for example, recognizes that the role played by Third World women in the community and the domestic realm is wide and three tiered: reproductive (childbearing and child rearing), productive (as secondary income earners through informal activities or agricultural work), and community management work (allocation of limited resources to ensure the survival of the household)

(Moser, 1989). The existence of a collective memory that despite historical attempts to subordinate and silence popular classes[2] has evolved as a positive underground and silent process is a key concept in understanding the construction of oppositional identities and the vitality of women's grassroots communication. The concept of identity is grounded in notions of change and **mestizaje**. Individual and group identities are continuously recreated with new cultural and sectorial fusions (the rural and the urban, the massive and the traditional, the ethnic and the generational). Mestizaje recalls the processes of cultural fusion that characterizes any Latin American cultural expression.

Organization of the Book

The book is divided into four related parts. While the first part of the book provides a general framework on gender and participation in communication, the following parts present the three fundamental dimensions of women's grassroots communication processes: the social and community dimension, the media dimension, and the organizational and networking dimension.

Part I reviews the various frameworks for addressing the relationship among women, participation, and communication, looking both at the ways women have been perceived and at discourses on participation and communication framed around women's issues. As we cannot discuss and compare grassroots communication practices in different countries without understanding the societal context in which they evolved, this part introduces an analysis of the societies of reference. Furthermore, I elaborate on the definitions of participation and empowerment present in the collection and introduce the key descriptors of grassroots communication with women.

This part also reviews gender issues in communication by highlighting key elements from the chapters and establishing a critical dialogue with the literature in this field. The review reveals a tendency to define women in monolithic terms and to associate women with notions of passivity, victimization, and isolation. On the contrary, the contributors to this collection view women as diverse subjects and social actors, as subjects of their collective histories, as heterogeneous groups with different experiences of subordination. By placing our examination at the grassroots level and by identifying the various dimensions of women as community, social, and public communicators, a more holistic picture emerges. Issues of women's representation and access to communication resources are linked with their social **roles** and their participation in the exercise of community democracy and transformation. In this view, we move beyond a communication-based perspective to include dimensions of human and community development; social, economic, and cultural struggles; and organizational dynamics and change.

The three subsequent parts of the book discuss the social and community dimensions, the media dimension, and the organizational dimension in grassroots communication. Correspondingly, women are identified as (a) social and community communicators, (b) media producers, and (c) political and collective actors.

Part II deals with the social roles of women in their communities, their capabilities to communicate, and their informal networks at the local and community levels. Women are seen as developing their own forms of communication and skills in specific social and cultural settings. By looking at the interpersonal and collective level in women's communication practices and at the development of women's **communicative competence** in **indigenous knowledge** and informal networks, the authors introduce the foundations and dynamics at play in grassroots communication processes.

This section presents analytical clues for understanding individual and collective levels of women's communication practices, looking at the tensions and dynamics intrinsic to the social community dimension. Thus the context and reasons for the emergence of grassroots and participatory processes, the factors hindering these movements, and the tensions arising from these processes are reviewed. The other social and community dimension considered here is that of the consumer. We look at the competencies women develop as consumers of media, the relationship to their social/community networks, and the ways women use media in their daily life.

Part III focuses on the process of media production and issues of media competency, identity, representation, evaluation, and group process. Here the guiding issues are elaborated on for understanding group processes of media production and the skills developed in activities as consumers. The chapters present a rich variety of local and national experiences in video, radio, writing, and print production, raising issues key to understanding the potential of media production to activate women's identity processes and to support group dialogue and women's processes of coming to voice.

Part IV is concerned with women as sociopolitical and collective actors. By looking at the connections between women's participatory practices and wider sociopolitical initiatives (coalitions, networks, social movements, liberation, and antiracist struggles), this part examines issues of organization, leadership, and communication strategies. The implications of women's communication and media production experiences in relation to the overall organizing and community-building efforts are discussed. The chapters offer a critical evaluation of communication processes that have been used in support of women's social movements and within other social movements and raise a number of issues regarding their communication strategies.

Notes

1. Grassroots communication is identified in some of the works in this book as those communication processes that encourage grassroots participation in processes of media production. In a more conceptual definition, grassroots communication is described as those communication processes guided by the goals of education for liberation that "help the poor and underprivileged acquire a critical understanding of social reality" (Calda, 1988, p. 2).

2. In Latin America the *popular* is identified with people (as arising from the people) and their cultural practices and spaces.

PART I

Framework

1

Women's Participation in Communication: Elements for a Framework

PILAR RIAÑO

While there have been advances in the raising of women's issues in the movement for the democratization of communications, the debate has ignored the widespread women's social movements that are building class, race, and cultural alliances as well as new communication alternatives and propositions for change at the grassroots. The omission is significant: These alliances not only speak to the advances of social movements in opening democratic spaces for people's communication but also address many of the same concerns raised by international communication agendas such as the New World International Communications Order (NWICO) and current debates about the democratization of communications.[1] This book explores this omission by looking at the analytical, practical, and evaluative dimensions of women's grassroots (participatory) communication in a broader societal framework.

This chapter focuses on **participation** in communication, introducing four central elements of our framework: a reassessment of the various frameworks that have in one way or another affected communication activities with women, an analysis of the broader societal context in which women's grassroots communication takes place, a definition of the alternative principles of this framework, and a description of the issues of process and method in the implementation of grassroots communications. The first part of this chapter reviews the various frameworks that address the relationships among women, participation, and communication. The discussion of this relationship is situated within a societal context. I do this by mapping the types of societies the communication experiences analyzed in this book refer to, the alternative societal discourses and conceptions of participation they are based on, and the principles guiding their proposals for societal change. It is in this context that the importance of the grassroots level of action in participatory communication is discussed.

A Typology of Women's Participation in Communication

The following typology reviews the various frameworks that address the relationships among women, participation, and communication. I have placed participation at the very center of my discussion, as this concept encompasses a point of reference in the discourses and practices of states, institutions, and social movements about women. The typology identifies the discourses and practices of four major frameworks: **development communications,** participatory communications, **alternative** communications, and feminist communications (see Table 1.1). The order of presentation introduces critical elements developed by each framework about the others. However, the discussion does not necessarily follow a sequence.

Sénécal (1991) argued that in every aspect of social communication—from the control of the media to public perceptions, social representations, and even the definition of technological choices—each social actor possesses his or her own specific practice or discourse. For example, development communications and to some extent participatory communication frameworks respond to the logic of the state and to institutions in seeking consent and support. The logic underlying alternative communications and feminist communications is that of social movements, or the identification of a social project in which "a variety of social actors seeks to create a new social reality, a new culture, a new logic for all aspects of life, including the technology and skills of audio-visual communications" (Sénécal, 1991, p. 213). Women's participation in communication initiatives constitutes a tool of struggle and a meaningful space in which to develop women's own discourses.

Development Communications:
Participation as a Development Tool

Development communication interventions are those that originated from outside the control of the community or target group and are delivered through government or international development institutions and non-governmental organizations (NGO) (Bernard, 1991). Traditionally, development communications have overlooked barriers faced by women in accessing development information and, therefore, have failed to benefit women. More recently developed communication programs have revised their approach to women.[2]

In India, Indonesia, Cameroon, and Swaziland, the goal of programs directed to child survival and nutrition is to develop the mother's sense of self-confidence in child rearing and decision making. These programs rely on the use of interpersonal communication between experts or extension workers and poor urban and rural mothers. Focus groups, photostories, photographs, and radio soaps produced by professionals reinforce the educational strategy that conceives the development of the mother's self-esteem as a condition for behavioral change (Griffiths, 1990).

Women as farmers, mothers, wives, agents of environmental protection, and managers of households constitute subjects of information in development interventions. Women's participation is encouraged in regard to three specific goals: (a) to change current critical practices, (b) to encourage active support, and (c) to mobilize the community for mass campaigns.

Change Current Critical Practices. This refers to the attempt to convince a target population to change critical practices, for example, risk behaviors such as sexual practices, smoking, and drinking. This model implements communication strategies that encourage public awareness and consensus, including public health campaigns for family planning, breast feeding, reduction of smoking and drinking, and AIDS prevention. Participation of women is conceived as cooperation with planners, administrators, and power elites and as a willingness to change critical behaviors (Deshler & Sock, 1985).

Encourage Active Support. Communication campaigns are used to encourage the active support of women and their communities for national or regional programs of nutrition, child vaccination, agricultural extension, water supply, and sanitation. International support programs are commonly concerned with disseminating development messages in a way that encourages support for specific programs. In these projects participation describes women's input or voluntary contribution of time and effort to the development program (Protz, 1991), for example, water supply and sanitation projects have ensured that women participate in workshops on the theme and that extension workers include women who are familiar with the local language and culture (Yacoob, 1990). Participation is used as a tool to activate the acceptance of the program by the intended beneficiaries.

TABLE 1.1　A Typology of Women, Participation, and Communication

Type	*Goals*	*Context*
Development communication (women as subjects of information)	Change critical practices Encourage support for development campaigns Mobilize the community	International/national development campaigns Development support communication programs Extension work Social marketing
Participatory communication (women as participants)	Enable people to take control of their lives Reduce knowledge gap Encourage organizational and sociocultural change Influence public policies	Development of communication programs Participatory communication programs Policy making
Alternative communication (women as subjects of change)	Support social struggles Advocacy and defense of rights Promote group reflection Awake consciousness of subordination	Social movements Popular communication Civil and human rights Community communication Group communication Media education
Feminist communication (women as producers of meaning)	Naming oppressions of race, class, gender, sexual orientation, and disability Negotiate fair representation and equity of access Construction of individual and collective identities Production of alternative meanings	Feminist and women's movements Advocacy Feminist communication in scholarship

Mobilize the Community. This seeks the participation of women in the dissemination of development messages and mobilization of the community through a variety of communicative strategies. An example of this type of program is the Facts for Life, which was launched by UNICEF, UNESCO, and the World Health Organization (WHO) to diffuse child health messages to poor families in the so-called developing countries. Forms of participation include mass mobilization of information (mass media); intercultural communication (translated information and the use of religious leaders or elders to diffuse messages); and folk media such as traditional drama, folk songs, puppetry, and indigenous dances. This approach en-

TABLE 1.1   Continued

Participation	Empowerment	Message
Participations as a **means** Public cooperation with planners Public feedback	Empowerment as acquiring information Learning new facts Engaging in discussion	One way: expert to target Diffusion of information
Participation as **transaction** Interaction between receivers and information source	Empowerment as enabling Acquiring knowledge and status to take control of their lives Capacity to benefit from involvement	Participatory message development Interface of top-down and bottom-up information flow Two ways
Participation as a process of **control** As a condition for social change As a capacity of actively producing meaning	Empowerment as developing individual and collective capacity to impact on change Increased control and ownership of process	Multidimensional flow of messages Horizontal message delivery Activity of both sender and receiver
Participation as **ownership, inclusion, and accountability** Developing a sense of community Ownership of collective experiences/identities	Empowerment as transformation of social subjects and the acts of naming Coming to voice Breaking the silence	Communication as exchange Circularity of meaning of messages Horizontal messages Network of meanings

visions participation of the community as an instrument to further a more community-oriented development. Promotion of participation will also improve the appeal and reach of development programs and campaigns by directing their messages in a culturally appropriate language (in the local language, with actors such as popular artists, who are recognized by the local community) and by increasing the feedback from the public to the experts (Moore, 1986).

These three types of participation are meant to maximize the success of a development intervention, which is designed from the principles discussed above. Participation and communication strategies are reduced to a set of techniques that are used to implement some of the stages of the development program or to a methodological choice of doing "better development." Women constitute either the target group, the subjects of the information, or the active listeners, who through participation will embrace the development message.

The community's input is considered mostly in the early stages of the program design. Usually developed as a cursory consultation, it is a way to gain knowledge about the living conditions, sources of income, local hierarchies, and customs of the target audience. In the final stages of dissemination and implementation, community participation is regarded as public cooperation and acceptance of the development campaign. In terms of the communication strategy, participation is seen as public feedback (i.e., filling out surveys that measure information learned) or, sometimes, interactive viewing (carrying out a discussion immediately after the program is broadcast). Participants do not formulate the message or use the communications equipment.

These programs rely on the mass media and on a growing use of indigenous communication networks such as women's informal associations, folk media (puppets, theater, and dance), interpersonal communication between experts and community, and small-format media (including educational illustrations and texts displayed in areas of community gathering and photographs used as references for discussion). This use of indigenous channels reflects a belief that the interpersonal and informal levels are central when it comes to persuading people to change. Media function in this context to legitimize the centrality of the issue for public attention, to act as loudspeakers of the expert messages, and to assist in reinforcing the project's messages (Hornik, 1988).

Strategies aimed at empowering people to control the programs rarely appear in these discourses. Eventually, empowerment is seen as the capacity of the individual to grasp the information learned (nutritional foods, value of breast feeding, and child immunization) and actively to seek more information (going to the local health clinic and talking to others).

Overall, this approach to participation in communication does not change or even question linear modes of information diffusion or the hierarchical position between the sender/expert's and receiver/target group's approaches to this type of communication. The scanty interest in the public's perception underlines a conception of participation as a means or "element" within a program rather than as an approach to its design and implementation.

Participatory Communication:
Participation as Development

In Nepal, rural women received training in video production as part of the communication strategy of a project on credit to rural women. Video was used in community development, to engage women in assessing needs and in elaborating plans for video production and recording. Videos produced by women were shown to other women in workshops. Women responded very positively to seeing other women using this medium. They felt confident, and realized they also could do it. Showing the videos to the community fostered discussion and negotiation with policy makers and government representatives (see Belbase, 1988, 1989; Burkert, 1989a, 1989b).

The Nepali example illustrates the principles of the participatory communications framework. In this framework *women are seen as participants* in a process that enables them to take control of their lives, develop their confidence and learning and information skills, and influence public policies through the media production process.

This approach arose out of the critique of the diffusionist and one-way tendencies of many development programs. It pointed out the importance of conceiving development communications as a participatory process (Nair & White, 1987b; Servaes, 1989; Williamson, 1991; White, 1989). In this view, participation is seen as bringing a more people-centered, rather than market-centered, perspective to development.

Media and overall development communication are used to motivate, educate, and mobilize the target population to respond to planned programs (Kulakow quoted in Nair & White, 1987a). The focus of participatory communication strategies is to allow an interface of information flow from the top down (institutions and development experts) and the bottom up (women and their communities). The communication message then is defined in a two-way interaction but is controlled by the information source. Participation is a transaction between grassroots receivers and information sources:

the process is on altering communication processes and strategies. We are not talking about social movements at the grassroots, a la Freire, but communication processes that take into account indigenous knowledge and self-reliance gained through increased information, access and acquisition. (Nair & White, 1987c, p. 6)

Nair and White have applied this framework to video production programs with village women in Poona, India, and with farmers in Washington County (New York), in the United States. Participants are trained in the use of video machines and in the production of videos around community issues. This participation is conceived as a continuum; the different levels of interaction of the group varies by the degree activity or passivity of each member as well as by their level of dialogue and engagement in the production of messages (Nair & White, 1987a). The target group is more or less involved in the process of building a participatory message, from needs assessment through media production to final evaluation and effectiveness. People's, or popular, participation represents a driving force for the determination of development processes and the materialization of a right to participate in the decisions that affect their lives (African Charter for Popular Participation in Development and Transformation, quoted in Ansah, 1992).

If information access is placed at the very center, empowerment is conceived in this approach "as the process through which individuals acquire knowledge and skills to take control of their lives" (Nair & White, 1987c, p. 16). Empowerment is thought of as a process of enabling individuals to benefit from involvement in the development program, as a means to bring about people's control over economic and political forces (Kindervatter, 1979). However, this view fails to analyze the differences in power and access to resources in the context in which people's relations with the larger social environment occur. Furthermore, by placing the emphasis on the individual's self-reliance and capacity to deal with the problems, the larger structural condition of dependency and domination of Third World societies is disregarded.

Another missing element in this approach is the multitude of power differences hidden behind the concepts of target population and people. The question has already been posed: Who benefits from participation? Failure to account for differences of class, **ethnicity,** patterns of organization, age, or gender can mean unequal distribution of benefits, violation of traditional practices, and creation of conflict (Jurmo, 1980; McKee, 1988; Pigozzi, 1982).

Alternative Communication:
Participation for Social Change

In the *pueblos jovenes* of Lima, Peru, most market vendors are women. They are members of the association of public markets; nevertheless, until 1985, the association's executive group consisted almost entirely of men.

At that time, a member of the board concerned with the weak interaction and diffusion of communication among association members invited women of the market to use the loudspeakers. A group of women, assisted by a local institution of communication, decided to use the market's loudspeakers to communicate problems such as tax payments, selling permits, and legalization of land. Through radio soaps, which were completely created and narrated by the women, personal stories were recreated and broadcast in the market; the stories were about migration to the cities, the barrio's lack of urban facilities, working conditions, and the association's internal conflicts.

The popular weekly programs began reaching many other barrios of Lima. Women's programs provided community services and support to organizational activities. Women assumed a leadership role in their communities, and by 1985, the elected board of the association consisted entirely of women (for a detailed description see Alfaro, 1988b, and Chapter 18).

Women in a variety of social movements (for the improvement of living conditions, reproductive rights, environmental issues, peace, and human rights) have sought alternative ways of communication to support their social struggles, advocate and defend their rights, promote group reflection, awaken women's consciousness to their subordinate position in society, and diffuse their own forms of representation. Women in this framework constitute subjects of struggle and change.

The framework is built around an oppositional and a proactive communication alternative that influences language, representations, and communication technologies used by women. Alternative communication encourages the development of alternatives to commercial media and to the vertical, one-way, dominant communication system, while it supports the creation of local group participatory processes of solidarity and identity and the active production of cultural meanings from oppressed groups (Puntel, 1992; Roncagliolo, 1991). The horizontal communication model proposed in the alternative approach is based on the principles of community access to media production and decision making. It is intended to promote dialogue and a cyclical communication that does not distinguish between senders and receivers. Consequently, the communication process is seen as generating a multidirectional flow of messages.

In these approaches, participation is viewed as both a dimension of and a condition for social change. Women's participation in communication activities is seen as a way of empowering them to struggle and defend their rights. Participation constitutes a measure of a group's control over the process and their involvement in most, if not all, the stages of planning, design, production, and diffusion.

Empowerment refers to the individual and collective capacity and right to transform and affect change. The recognition of power differences in society implies that empowerment is not a matter of individuals controlling economic and political conditions, but rather of their joining social movements and struggles for the transformation of these conditions. The cases presented in this book largely follow this view.

A common denominator that defines alternative communication practices is the struggle for **democracy** (Ambrosi, 1991). Ambrosi defines democracy as a practice of freedom to define one's own present and future history. In the context of social movements this conception of democracy is seen as a collective project; a collective practice of freedom and government by the people. Democracy in communications involves the right to acquire and produce information (Gómez, 1990) and the opening of spaces for the construction of people's (popular) cultural spaces (Alfaro, 1988a). From this understanding of democracy, alternative communication approaches see the democratization of communication as a crucial struggle that will respond to the needs of all to transmit and receive information and to see their views and groups represented in the media.

The Latin American view that the democratization of information would not succeed without a democratization of societies is particularly relevant here. Latin Americans have argued that to achieve the desired levels of democratization, communication activities would have to be implemented within those spheres of society where the control of information rests with the people and their organizations. The democratization views contained in the MacBride report[3] would never be reached if systems of political repression, censorship, and coercion of expression were prevalent. They emphasized that information and communication were not separate from the global social context and that their democratization was part of the struggle against oppressive structures (Kaplún, 1984; Roncagliolo, 1982).

There are a number of regional frameworks that can be identified here: popular communication, group communication, critical consciousness approaches, and political community action. These frameworks, besides encouraging the development of original participatory communication experiences at the regional or local level, share an assessment of the inequalities and imbalances inherent in national and international information and communication orders. The views contained in the MacBride report regarding the changes in the international information and communication order needed to guarantee democratic, horizontal communication and information exchange are shared and advocated by these approaches.

Popular Communication

Popular Communication developed in the **South** and particularly in Latin America. Popular communication initiatives aim at providing a language and an infrastructure of communication that are owned and controlled by the people. This communicative strategy fosters women's organization and mobilization to create their own expressive channels, manifesting their nonconformity and demands (Moore, 1986). The Popular Women's Union of Loja, Ecuador, is a grassroots organization working to improve the living conditions of its 1,500 members. The union promotes the organization of women to defend their rights and to develop skills and nonformal education activities. The popular communication promoted among women starts from the analysis of their own reality and leads to involvement in struggles to change their situation (Puntel, 1992). Popular communication refers not only to media but to the communication that occurs among popular groups (peasants, women, and workers).

Popular media are those produced, owned, and operated by nonprofessionals (White, 1987). Initiatives with women have used a variety of communication media such as the cassette forum to present material of community interest. Participants are encouraged to interact with the tape and to share their views with the forum. Other communication media used are cartoons, which provide material for reflection and discussion, and sound slides, which involve women in theme identification, research and script development, photography, and editing. Radio and video production of informational programs, documentaries, dramas, and forums that are concerned with women's issues (health, violence against women, and human rights), local information, and conflicts are widely used.

Popular communication processes are seen as participatory processes committed to social organization and mobilization. Popular communication methodology starts at the local level from an analysis of the individual's historical situation. Analysis of the historical reality brings and transforms individual awareness and consciousness leading to action and, therefore, involvement in social struggles and movements. These approaches are used by grassroots organizations such as Christian-based communities, unions, peasant associations, women's groups, citizens associations, social movements, and progressive NGOs.

Group Media

The concept of **group media** has been actively used in Latin America, Africa, and Asia, particularly in the Philippines and India. Group media refers to the use of posters, sound slide productions, cartoons, audio cassette productions, and rural newspapers developed by small groups. The main goal of group media is to foster group interaction through media production and communication around the life situations of group members and the sharing of personal experiences. This sharing helps group media to identify common endeavors and actions (Ambroise, 1987; Muller, 1987). In the Philippines, for example, community and group media have been used to offer alternative systems by bringing the information disseminated by mass media several steps further by explaining the relevance of the information to the lives of the people (Muller, 1987). For this process to happen, small, cohesive, and active groups need to be in place.

Group media and critical consciousness approaches apply similar strategies and methods based on the goals of individual and group liberation from their oppressed condition. They evolved from the method of **conscientization** that is described as the bringing of the individual to critical reflection about his or her life conditions and situation. Based on the framework of Freire and liberation theology, communication and educational work are seen as awakening the individual's consciousness to his or her situation of oppression, by community animation and activation or organizational process and social change (Freire, 1970; Muller, 1987). The recognition of oppression leads the individual and group to become agents of change, breaking the culture of silence and engaging in social actions and group initiatives.

Deza (1989) described this process within a Philippine fishing community. As part of a community organizing strategy, a local communication center used group media such as posters and sound slides to support community organizing and to provide tools for reflection. The fishing community, which was facing a degeneration of its living conditions, was invited to produce the sound slides with the support of the local center. Deza (1989) described how the process of media production became a process of consciousness raising. From an initial stage of apathy, the group moved to an involvement in the identification of the community problems that would be raised by the sound slides. Participants became precritical when they identified themselves as part of the problem as well as its solution, moving then to a liberation stage, at which they expressed commitment to community organization. This growth process ran parallel to the process by which the group developed the message and final media product.

These approaches have been very common among Christian-based communities, adult education groups, literacy campaigns, and community organizing efforts led by Marxist and social democratic activists. The emphasis, however, is on the use of participation in communication for raising individual and group consciousness and encouraging critical analysis and skills. Communication practices are characterized in this context as *oppositional;* they contribute to the articulation of a consciousness of the individual's oppressed realities and silence and toward people's mobilization. These processes facilitate the learning of a language that liberates the word and world of the oppressed.

Community Media

Participatory communication for political-community action aims to provide the means to express the claims and protests of communities and the advocacy of their rights. In 1981, residents from the small town of Cardedeu created the first local television in Catalunya. Today there are 94 television stations created by citizens groups that act as networks linking the various community groups, providing alternative information and promoting and developing the Catalan language and cultural identity. Based on the principles of flexibility, informality, and pluralism, the television stations are used by a variety of social groups: senior citizens, women, children, artists, political and environment activists, and Latin American and African immigrants (see Rodríguez, 1990).

Community media have been developed mainly in North America and Europe. The concept of community media was defined by Lewis (1984) as "communication for the democratic exercise, respecting the rights of the people as subjects and participants in the actions and processes in which communication media are involved" (p. 235). Lewis also noted that the notion of **community** used in this approach originated in the mid-1960s in the industrialized West when capitalist states "could afford to tolerate and contain decentralized initiatives" (p. 235).

Community media offer an alternative to and an expansion of the services of the mass commercial media or state. Access and participation are the two main tenets of community media production, and they are specifically related to the concept of citizens in the **public** sphere and their capacity and right to access a public resource of media systems.

Participation in this framework is largely associated with access to media and is seen as a form of democracy. Participation implies the public's involvement in the production and management of these communication systems, including decision making and planning (Kennedy, 1989; Lewis,

1984). However, this understanding of access and participation implies that the possible publics will have equal conditions of access to media. This assumption disregards the specific and marginal conditions of many social groups, their little knowledge of media organizations and economic and social power, and their lack of media skills and required professional competencies. Jankowski, Vos, and Brouwer (1989) presented the notion of affirmative access to counterbalance this view. This notion recognizes imbalances of access and focuses on identifying, giving priority to, and training marginalized groups.

The experiences reviewed in this book formulate a number of questions to the alternative communications framework, identifying some gaps and limitations in addressing gender, cultural, race, and class issues. For example, the enthusiasm for the empowering potential of participatory communication practices has fostered a view of participation as a salvation strategy that operationalizes communication alternatives and activates consciousness. The danger with this view is that it instrumentalizes participation and reduces empowerment to an end in itself, while disregarding the power and conflict dimensions in which processes of participation take place and are negotiated (Lozare, 1989).

Another problem arises from the main goals of these approaches, which are defined in terms of nontangible outcomes such as learning, consciousness raising, and so on. These experiences tend to be weak in fostering social action for the improvement of economic conditions and for obtaining tangible changes (La Belle, 1987). In light of worsening living conditions and social crises in many parts of the Third World and for poor and working-class people in the North, this disconnection between educational goals and tangible changes can reduce the trust that participants or communities have in the benefits of a participatory process. The worldwide crisis that marks an increased gap between the rich and the poor, increased state repression of social movements, the inability of states to respond to their constituencies, the magnitude of the environmental and health crisis, the increase of conflicts around ethnic and territorial issues, and the rapidly changing conditions of daily life continuously challenges simplistic associations and formulates new dilemmas for the use of concepts such as **empowerment** and participation.

As group processes of media and communication production develop and evolve, uses and potentials of participation are further problematized. For example, Alfaro (Chapter 18) argues that the development of grassroots leadership skills and the appearance in the public discourse of the voices of the powerless are not necessarily indicators of effective grassroots participation. There is a need to look further to the models of leadership reproduced—to look at, for example, whether the women's movement's exercise of leadership is a democratic one, what the content of the popular discourses is, the nature of the representations held by women in their communication productions, the ways leaders and movements use and control communication media, and the ways the facilitators intervene and assume or manage their differences (of gender, race, class, and status) in the process.

Feminist Communication:
Gender in Participatory Communication

Gender has not been considered an analytical dimension in the frameworks mentioned above (see McAnany & Storey, 1989; Nair & White, 1987a, 1987b, 1987c; O'Connor, 1989; Riaño, 1990, 1991). References to gender are limited to identifying the gender of the participants and to describing the subordinate position of women in their communities and societies. Neither the ways in which gender influences the nature of participation and communication production nor the mediation of gender in women's and men's experiences of subordination have been taken into serious consideration.

Although much of the communication work of women's groups and feminists is inspired by the principles of alternative communications (Steiner, 1992), their works are distinguished by the inclusion of a gender perspective. This perspective influences not only their goals and agendas but also their communication strategies and methodologies. Among others, this includes the valorization of the personal experience of each individual involved in a participatory process, the questioning of the objectivity attached to the communication and academic exercise, and the acknowledgment that all individual participants (including the facilitator) bring their subjectivities and experiences of oppression and discrimination to any communicative interaction.

Periodicals by women of Color in the United States offer an analysis of racism, class, and gender oppression from the perspective of Black, Hispanic, Asian-American, American Indian, Alaska Native and Pacific-Islander. Working under a collective structure and using a variety of formats such as newsletters, magazines, and bulletins, the women who run these periodicals are women of Color who publish for women of Color (Kranich, 1989). Women's participation in this framework is attached to the goals of enhancing processes of speaking about gender, race, class, and other oppressions. It also involves the negotiation of fair representation and equal participation of women, the recognition of the many voices of women and the defense and building of identity.

In these approaches, participation in communication projects and media production is seen as a project of naming their own experiences and identities. Participation enhances the process of coming out, of speaking about the oppression faced as individuals and as members of a group, and the carrying out of actions designed to achieve social change (Kidd, 1992). Participation also names a project of inclusion that acknowledges differences of race, gender, class, and sexual orientation. Empowerment involves the transformation of women as social subjects of struggle and as active producers of meaning. The next chapter, which focuses on gender and communication, further elaborates this approach.

The typology presented here is an attempt to map out the field and to raise critical issues regarding myths of participation, empowerment, and democratization while challenging how differences are silenced in current proposals of participatory communication. It is a map that cannot completely identify all the corners and paths to be taken. It is left to the reader to identify or deduce them through the darkness of the journey. Many of the experiences referred to in this book will belong to these various frameworks or may be difficult to place in any of them. The typology offers a basis for the discourses and perception of women, participation, empowerment, and communication.

The Societal Context

The formation of independent women's media and communication networks has been seen as a crucial component of feminist politics and an important contribution to the development of grassroots communication alternatives (Gallagher, 1992). However, a number of questions have been raised regarding the marginal space and reach in which these alternatives evolve. Gallagher (1992) spoke of the dilemma posed between the control over the content and narratives offered by alternative media and the power to reach larger audiences offered by mainstream media. The dilemma is certainly important to discuss, but there is a risk of reducing the discussion to an issue of choosing between the two.

Grassroots communication processes have been seen as embryonic versions of a new order that is working to achieve both its own successes and to demonstrate the potential of new ways of ordering communication (Golding, 1991). Although this view validates the creative and democratic orientation of these processes, it tends to reduce them to experimental formats while deactivating their political and social potential of acting as interlocutors of larger global issues.

Our attempt is to explore these dilemmas in a relational perspective that connects the local or micro view to a larger societal context. Although at the marginal and local levels,[4] grassroots processes of communication dialogue with and challenge larger societal issues, because they contain specific ideas about society and democratization. This section begins the exercise of mapping grassroots participation. The key markers are drawn from the contributors' definitions of their own societies of reference and of their alternative principles and ideals. The discussion starts by analyzing how the "grassroots" constitutes a key component in the framing of a proposal for participation in society.

At the Grassroots

At the very center of our discussion of participation is the consideration of the grassroots level of action as a condition and foundation of "real" participatory processes and democratization. This consideration not only contains issues of equity of access and fair representation but addresses strategies, methods, and processes of participation. In particular, I suggest that it is at the level of the grassroots where women's competencies, capabilities, and **community communication** roles are generated and that it is in the realm of everyday life where people's communication systems are elaborated. From a methodological perspective in communication production (media or networking), to place the grassroots at the center implies the dissolution of the control exercised by "the maker" in message construction and narrative language. Instead, the conception of the communication process as a circular process, activating understandings and perceptions at the grassroots, is introduced.

The Societies of Reference

The spontaneous and peaceful protest actions of thousands of Filipino men and women in 1986 marked the end of the Marcos dictatorship. The revolt in which people gathered in the streets, stopped soldiers' tanks, and crowded into the gates of two military camps demonstrated the potential of peoples' power. It is an example of grassroots mobilization, for which mass and group media were crucial in mobilizing people, sharing the message of a peaceful protest, and informing them about the evolution of events. The crystallization of Filipino goals of emancipation and change was made possible by a specific combination of political, social, and economic factors.

The educational and supportive role that group media played in the Philippines was the result of long-standing sociopastoral work and community and other forms of organization.[5] This work, combined with the leadership of mass media and the importance given to the symbolic and cultural worldview of the Filipino people, fostered a certain maturity that led people to make decisions and take actions.[6]

The presentation of the Filipino example is an illustration of how we will analyze local processes of women's participation as part of broader processes. A specific set of political conditions (e.g., censorship, media regulations, the role of the state, the police, the legislature, the media, and control of civil life) in connection with the degree of maturity in grassroots participation (informal and formal levels of organization and development of social movements) and a specific economic, social, and political context (deterioration of the standards of living, civil strife, lack of political representation, corruption, and poverty) shape group or community communication strategies and practices. Participatory communication practices at the local level are framed by these external conditions. However, the strategies developed at the local level constitute grassroots responses or ways to dialogue with the societies in which they are located. This reference to the national and regional contexts in which these practices emerge is fundamental. As Sénécal (1991) argued we cannot compare practices from Africa, Latin America, North America, and Asia without referring to the context in which they emerged and to the role that media plays in their respective social dynamics.

The chapters from Latin America included here, for example, describe societies affected by deep economic, social, and political crises and the consequent change of social roles and public participation of women. The imposition of neo-liberal models that promote privatization and decentralization of the state has had particular impact on the communication industries. Media ownership has become much more concentrated in many of the cultural industries in Latin America. The trend toward the transnationalization of communications and the homogenization of messages favor such a concentration (Uribe, 1992), as does the restructuring of the state and society according to neo-liberal models and privatization. As Rodríguez and Muñoz explain in their chapters, mass media reach almost the entire Latin American territory, including both rural and marginal populations. The complex articulation of social policies, armed responses, and civil and everyday violence (occurring in several Latin American countries) has drastically affected the agendas and communication alternatives of women's groups and the overall efforts for access, equity, and the exercise of democratic practices of communication.

In Africa, since the 1970s, the massive foreign debt and the deteriorating standard of living have created a number of economic and political constraints that limit the reach of the mass media to poor and rural populations (Boafo, 1992; Mlama, 1989a). This situation is especially aggravated by the politics of state control and ownership of the media: Many African communicators have concluded that the media are simply unable to reach larger audiences and reflect their views (Ansah, 1992; Boafo, 1989, 1992). The financial weight of development programs based on Western models, communication, media and funds constitutes one of the most serious obstacles to the implementation of grassroots participatory alternatives. While a number of countries are engaged in democratic transitions (South Africa, Benin, Cameroon, and Zambia), a larger number are facing acute social instability and civil war (Nigeria, Somalia, and Rwanda). In particular, the widespread movement to restructure and reconceptualize public communication (e.g., the South African campaign to free the air waves) offers an important space to rethink and articulate participatory communication proposals. The chapters by Mlama, Mensah-Kutin, and Lloyd name some of the challenges that participatory grassroots communication face: how to use indigenous communication forms in a horizontal format and how to integrate them within endogenous development strategies.

The 1992 riots in the United States and the subsequent series of racial protests by African-Americans and Latinos in various cities revealed the critical fissures and deep conflicts affecting this country. The chapters from Canada and the United States address some of these fissures and the issues of social injustice, economic disempowerment, racism, sexism, and lack of political representation that affect large numbers of **people of Color,** immigrants, Aboriginals, and the poor: the Third World in the First World. The neo-conservative trend of these societies to reduce social and health services and their movement toward a regional free trade pact are having significant repercussions on the working class, the poor, and the disempowered **minorities.** Many of these groups have used a variety of participatory media to articulate and mobilize their dissent on these issues and discontent with a society that denies conflict while emptying the issues of multiculturalism and power imbalance of their meaning. The social movements of the First World, of people of Color, of welfare rights activists, of women, and of peace and environmental leaders have acquired a central place in articulating dissent. The chapters by Dyer-Bennem,

Kawaja, Kidd, and Taylor document the struggles and communication strategies of these social movements in North America.

Overall, the chapters of this book identify the tension between the modernizing projects attributed to the media industries (as instruments of development and **modernization**) and the traditional—or call it indigenous media, popular culture, or folklore. This tension is not manifested as one of either total imposition or total resistance but as a complex set of "entrances and exits," of mixing and overlapping between tradition and modernity (García-Canclini, 1989). In the context of the grassroots communication processes examined here, this aspect is critical, as it emphasizes the complexity of the societies of reference as well as the commonality of these conflicts in both the so-called developed and underdeveloped societies.

Closely connected to the larger social context, the communication strategies and processes we are examining emerge as a response to a number of specific junctures. There are, for example, grassroots communication responses to institutional and repressive practices implemented within the societies (racism, homophobia, sex discrimination, and violence) and to issues of critical social and cultural concern (the AIDS epidemic, the cost of living, and the regulation of working conditions). These participatory processes are not just those that use media. Any development or community process designed with educational, organizational, or information goals requires communication strategies in order to carry it out.

Once the connection between the grassroots and the larger societal context is made explicit, it is important to clarify that this connection is initially established at the ideological and communication level. There is still the need to look at the connection from a more operational and strategic perspective. The question that must still be asked is formulated by Kidd (1992) in her review of alternate media: What is the potential of grassroots (participatory) communication in articulating social issues and in mobilizing action effectively to transform power relations?

Alternative Concepts of Participation and Empowerment

Participation, in the view of many of the projects included here, is seen as a set of practices working for the liberation of the individual and collective subject. This is part of a "much larger process, that of the historic collective building of a participative society" (Diaz-Bordenave, 1989, p. 1). The group or community engages itself in identifying a project of social transformation and a way to exercise democracy through specific grassroots projects. Social participation in this regard goes beyond the communication enterprise to constitute a mediated process of decision making, production of cultural meanings, and facilitation of transformation (Goulet, 1989; Protz, 1991).

For these types of participatory processes to be achieved, individual and collective empowerment are seen as fundamental goals. Empowerment in this light is not just individual achievements or accessing certain power positions, but the energizing of individual and collective subjects to participate in social movements and processes of emancipation. Empowerment constitutes the process of working to bring about individual and collective transformation.

The contribution that grassroots experiences with women bring to this framework is that for participation to become an instrument of transformation for social subjects, differences of race, class, gender, social roles, and sexual orientation must be acknowledged and the power dimension they embody recognized. Furthermore, the individual and collective dimensions of the processes of empowerment and change and the differences in styles of leadership and democracy have to be taken into account.

Participation, therefore, will only be a real instrument of change if differences in subordination and the diversity of women's experiences are acknowledged. Any program or community process implementing goals of participation must acknowledge the cultural and social forces underlying the dynamics of interaction in the community or group involved. Participation is referred to in specific terms: The meaning, form, and implementation of participatory forms depend on the larger social, economic, and political forces in which such a process is carried out, but they also depend on the cultural and community processes of decision making, power, and resource distribution.

Communication—especially participatory communication—is more than just a technology or set of methodologies, resources, or media; it is a set of exchanges comprising a collective "word" for naming people's realities—a word that by naming a denied and fragmented reality makes it visible, identifiable, and meaningful (see Chapter 13).

A last important component of these alternative societal discourses is the idea of democratization as a continual process of redistribution of social power. Closely related is the concept of social and cultural democracy that points to the connection of communication as a form of expression and interrelation among the members of a society. This principle of democracy challenges the logic of the market and economic domination under which transnational corporation and media structure operate (Gómez, 1990).

Social change is the ultimate goal of these processes, viewed as the trans-formation of power structures into a more egalitarian model in which participation, empowerment, and democratization can take place. Many of the chapters view such change as the reclaiming of a humanitarian process in which the very individuality of each of the participant members of a community is acknowledged and also as a discourse that looks at differences as the motor for building group identities and projects of change.

Grassroots Communication in Practice: Strategizing Participation

This section examines some of the guiding elements for the implemen-tation of grassroots participatory communication processes. It focuses on the description of the process and methods of communication production, providing a practical illustration of the proposals of participation and em-powerment surrounding grassroots communication practices and strategies.

Participatory Communication as Process

Focus on the process rather than on its product defines the main objec-tive of participatory communication: Participants learn through doing. The emphasis is on the process of communication production as an em-powering strategy of the community or group of women. The end product nevertheless plays an important role within the process as a communica-tive tool that invites critical reflection or provides useful and meaningful information to participants, their peers, and communities.

An important conclusion emerging from some of the chapters in this book is the understanding that the communication process does not end with the construction of the message, as participants' empowerment through communication is not a fixed outcome expressed by the emergence of women as leaders and public actors. The authors take issue with the idea that consciousness, empowerment, or liberation constitutes the final stage or end product of these processes. On the contrary, these chapters em-phasize that it is at this level that a new set of more complex problems arises, requiring that new processes be developed and new issues addressed. These issues concern the role of communication in the exercise of leader-ship and democracy, the relationships between grassroots leaders and their communities, and the process of message construction and decision making (see Chapter 18). In conclusion, participation and empowerment are seen as part of a continuum that poses different challenges at different points in the process.

Issues of Process and Method

The concepts of participation, empowerment, and democracy introduced can be further understood by looking at the process followed and the methods used in the implementation of grassroots (participatory) communication experiences with women. This section describes some of the key issues of method and process that guide communication activities with women. They do not refer to a particular communication means or to its visual or narrative language but to the *overall* process and methods of production and reception.

Issues of Process

The Community/Group as the Main Actor in the Communicative Process. Rural women in Nepal received training in video production as part of the communication program of a project to extend credit to rural women. Video was used in community development to engage women in assessing needs and in planning video production and recording. A strong group of women communicators emerged. The videos produced were shown to other women in workshops, where the audiences responded very positively to seeing other women using video. They felt confident and realized that they could also do it. Showing the videos to the community fostered discussion and negotiation with policy makers and government representatives (see Belbase, 1988, 1989; Burkert, 1989a).

In Zimbabwe, emerging leadership in the villages and community development are being supported through a community publishing project in which books are collectively produced by more than 1,000 people. In 1990, production began on a book about women and development. Hundreds of community workers traveled throughout the country listening to what the local people wanted to include in the book. This visit was followed by correspondence that motivated people to write, draw, or express any idea they wanted included. The team then put together a first draft that was presented at workshops, with the objective of acquiring national consensus. Once the book is printed, it will be translated into all five Zimbabwean languages, and workshops will discuss its possible uses ("Building Zimbawe Together," 1989).

As these examples suggest, women must have control over the processes of decision making, planning, access to resources, production, and distribution. In theater, radio, and video, participants decide the content, narrative structure, and creative treatment. They also engage in dramatic representation, manipulation of equipment, broadcasting, interactive viewing, and promotion.

The Social and Cultural Dynamics as the Communication Context. In Nicaragua, the Women's Secretariat of the Nicaraguan Association of Rural Workers organized workshops (get-togethers) to assist women in communicating about their difficult working conditions to the general assemblies on work norms. The workshops used photostories as an educative means. The combination of a visual and dramatic language was seen as particularly suited to the workshop's participants, because they could not easily read. The written and visual languages of the photostories were carefully reviewed by the women workers themselves to ensure that they matched their vernacular uses of the language and popular narrative forms. The photostories were collectively read and analyzed in the workshop sessions, producing a very enthusiastic response. Workshops facilitated a firm integration of women in the discussion of work norms (see International Council for Adult Education [ICAE], 1989).

Empower, a Thai NGO in Bangkok, offers sex workers programs of English-language classes, continuing education, and health and AIDS education. Health education programs use drama and humor inspired by the dramatic and performing traditions of Thai cultures. Performances are presented by the sex workers themselves, with the philosophy that drama "encourages people to take their role and respect the roles of others" (quoted from Empower's calendar). Using humor and drama to educate people about health and AIDS issues is seen as providing a safe communication space for the sex workers while enhancing equality and respect among sex workers, customers, and business owners.

These examples demonstrate the fundamental need, when implementing a participatory strategy, to recognize that engagement in a communication process is mediated by individual's social and cultural concerns and backgrounds. This characteristic of participatory processes also includes narrative forms and visual codes that recognize indigenous knowledge, communication forms, and cultural traditions.

Issues of Method

Incorporating Participatory Research Methods. Chapter 4 examines the use of popular theater and dance for the development of programs for women and communication in Tanzania. Mlama explains how participatory research methodologies are incorporated into theater-training workshops. In these workshops, the dramatic content is decided after participants identify villagers' perceptions of problems. Through the theater workshop and acting, women have rediscovered their dramatic potential to represent specific problems and the situations in which these problems emerge (see Lihamba & Mlama, 1986; Mlama, 1989b). Chapter 4 shows how information gathering and problem identification are both the result of a participatory process. The power of the message relies on its collective production and validation at several levels: first, at the internal level of the group in sessions of discussion, exchange, and brainstorming; and second, at the external level with the community through the active involvement of participants in collecting information, interviewing the community and local authorities, seeking and collecting necessary information, and selecting the appropriate places to shoot or broadcast or stage a dramatic presentation.

The Participants as Producers. The conventional description of communication technologies identifies them as inaccessible, expensive, and complex technologies that require professional expertise and male-gendered technological abilities. Women's participatory communication experiences question this idea, promoting participants' use and manipulation of the technology. The process helps participants become critical of the technology instead of accepting it or taking its content for granted. In theater, for example, the star aura of the theater crew is demystified by acknowledging the dramatic potential of each participant. Video and radio training stresses the easy manipulation of each medium and the importance of creative skills that do not require literacy.

The experience of the Self-Employed Women's Association (SEWA) in Ahmedabad, India, illustrates this. The association assists its members (20,000 home-based workers, vendors, and providers of labor and services) with skills training, social services, cooperative mechanisms, and advocacy of their rights. SEWA received training in video production and formed a cooperative—Video SEWA—to support the organizational activities of the association. The participants are all women, some of whom are illiterate. Since they received the training, they have been using the cameras to produce community videos. Their videos treat themes such as child labor, the struggle for better working conditions, and the demands of the weaving and block printing workers. The association travels from village to village producing videos and involving each community in recording the programs. They also use video to influence policy decisions such as getting licenses for vegetable and other street market vendors (see Jumani, 1988; Stuart 1987, 1989a, 1989b).

Interactive Reception as a New Communication Process. *Club Mencia* is a women's radio program in the southern region of the Dominican Republic. Women from the area participate in the program, which is structured as a listener's club. Women join the club by sending in their name, address, and other information. Audience participation is the most important element of the program, and it relies on such formats as on-air discussions and letters. The producers invented a pirate station called Radio Macho ("the radio station for men who wear the pants") to introduce the problem of machismo with a combination of humor and critical reflection. Radio Macho's interruptions of the women's program are discussed on the air (see Mata, 1989; O'Connor, 1989).

Participatory uses of media conceive the stage of reception as an interactive communicative moment between image and viewer, play and audience, producers and receptors. Audience participation and the perception and meaning listeners make of messages that have been disseminated by others "like them" are key to the problem of sensitization and the development of a new process of communication production.

The framework suggested in this chapter focused on participation in communication. The next chapter focuses on gender in communication as the other key component of the framework.

Notes

1. In the 1990s, reformulating the democratization debate has become a necessity in the light of global economic, social, and political changes; the shift of UNESCO's communication policies; and the critical evaluation of the previous decade's small advances toward the democratization of communications. Such a reformulation requires first and foremost that the debate be moved away from institutional agendas concerned with state-related communication policies and be situated in a grassroots perspective. Basically, what is implied by this shift is the emergence of an alternative view of communications and democracy in society. A view in which democracy is generated in the active and dynamic interaction of the people, the social movements, the institutions, and the cultural industries.

2. In McAnany and Storey's (1989) discussion of the guiding issues for the research and practice of development communication, they argued that participation is synthetic because it encompasses individuals and the social systems in which they live and interact with one another. In the review here, this understanding of participation is applied: I recognize individual and group practices as part of larger social processes not as isolated actions.

3. In 1977, UNESCO established a commission to address problems of communication and information flow. This commission produced the MacBride report, which identified the

unbalanced distribution of information flow, the concentration of ownership in media industries, and the need to promote a more balanced and free flow of information. The report argued for the need to create a new world information and communication order and called on state and media institutions to enable its development by instituting democratic policies and creating national news agencies (see Puntel, 1992; Roncagliolo, 1992).

4. Relevant to this discussion is hooks's (1990) differentiation between "that marginality which is imposed by oppressive structures and that marginality one chooses as site of resistance, as location of radical openness and possibility" (p. 22). The grassroots and local processes I am referring to here might be affected by historical circumstances and particular state policies oriented to marginalize specific groups, but they are also affected by the attempts of these groups to redefine their marginalization as a site of transformation.

5. For a detailed analysis of the Philippine experience, see "Communication and Social Change" (1986).

6. Beltran (1986) argues that the February Revolt was a display of a popular culture expressing their consciousness of the need for change. Beltran showed how the work that group media had done with theater, radio, and sound slides was based on a reconceptualization of traditional and popular cultural forms (oral and theatrical traditions). The ways in which radio and street symbols were used during the revolt were for Beltran the continuation of the popular forms of expression and suggested the transformational power that popular culture might have when put in a social context of people's needs for change.

2

Gender in Communication:
Women's Contributions

PILAR RIAÑO

This chapter focuses on the gender variable in **communication** and its interconnection with other variables of race, class, sexual orientation, and ability. I discuss the key issues of grassroots communication processes that challenge existing frameworks and suggest instead a framework based on the principles of pluralism, diversity, and social change.

In the last two decades, women's movements and feminist scholarship have raised the issue of the subordinate position of women in the structure, organization, and programming output of the communication industries (Dervin, 1987; International Women's Tribune Centre, 1984). This issue includes the lack of women's participation and representation in mainstream media (e.g., their lack of control over communication channels), the sexist portrayal of women, the absence of women in the news and current affairs, and women's disadvantaged access to new communication technologies (Moraga & Anzaldúa, 1981).[1]

During the 1960s and 1970s women's groups in the Third World responded to their negative portrayal in the mainstream media by establishing media monitoring and social action groups (Bhasin & Agarwal, 1984). From an initial period of denouncing biases and demanding equity, the field now emphasizes the qualitative differences women are making in democratizing communication. In spite of this recognition, a number of issues remain largely unresolved. Women's demands for democratization have not been reflected in any structural changes in the media industries. Women continue to be underrepresented in the cultural industries, and little improvement has been seen in terms of employment in media organizations (Mahoney, 1991).

Advances are more significant in the creation of coalitions among women. A growing number of women's information networks, linking researchers, journalists, and activists across countries and regions, are starting to break down the barriers of communication and information. This increasing "connectedness" is granting new democratic spaces and allowing information exchange at the grassroots (Annis, 1990).[2] At the publishing level, the creation of alternative presses such as the Long Haul Press, Third World Women Press, and Kitchen Table Books (the United States); Kali for Women Press (India), Sister Vision Press (Canada); and the Sechata publishers (South Africa) has opened new publishing opportunities for women. The work published by these companies belongs to a varied group of women who use writing as a way of voicing and validating their experiences as individual writers, as members of a community, and as a form of power that challenges silence and articulates other visions of women (Anzaldúa, 1990a; Charnley, 1990).

Worldwide networks of independent video makers and filmmakers are developing a variety of visual alternatives and narratives. Film festivals distribute this work through alternative formats for exhibition that privilege interaction with the makers. New song movements such as the *Nueva Canción* in Latin America and the work of feminist songwriters and record producers in Europe and North America provide examples of group communication. Women's growing participation in journalism schools and in the mainstream media is introducing new views to the world information order and mass communication. Women researchers in the fields of media and cultural studies have contributed significantly to analyzing how the media constructs definitions of femininity and masculinity and how women consume mass-mediated cultural products. Analyses of **consumption** and pleasure and their political dimensions stress the active reception and use of these products by women. Feminist works in communication studies have explored women as meaning makers: creators of new and resistant meanings through research, narratives, writing, or political activism (Rakow, 1992).

The significance of these contributions and movements is largely political, but as Mahoney (1991) has argued, these movements are constrained by international political and economic realities (e.g., the unrestricted operation of transnational media enterprises) in the cultural industries and by the weakening of the United Nations. The demands of the women's and social movements have not been met by significant structural changes in the communication industries. Their significance instead has been in consolidating information and communication networks of exchange among women's groups and other social movements of women and men.[3]

The political weight and democratizing potential contained in grass-roots communication processes and overall class, gender, race, and cultural alliances underscore some of the missing points of the international debate (Roach, 1990). These movements reveal some of the key contributions women are making as media and communication producers, at both the discursive and political levels, and the ways they are making possible the presence of the feminine and popular subjects in the public/collective scene. While emerging literature on feminist communication scholarship has started to address such contributions (Rakow, 1992), literature and reviews on grassroots processes have failed to evaluate these contributions. Until now, the reviews of group media or grassroots communication experiments at the local level have been criticized for a celebratory tone that ignores critical issues (see Riaño, 1991). Developments from feminist communication work, emphasizing the activity of women as meaning makers, have remained ignored by most of the literature on women, participation, and communication. What does exist has focused on assessing women's lack of control and access to media industries or on psychological analysis of sex and language differences, thereby disregarding women's roles as communicative subjects and as producers of communication.[4] This view affects the field of not only mass media but also alternative media. As Alfaro (1988a) noted,

> Unconsciously, we considered our female recipients as objects, and not as human subjects of communication who are producers of contents of real life, capable of interpreting and using communication. We even regarded them as mute and intellectually limited, simply listening to us and observing our efforts without thinking over our proposals. (p. 10)

Challenges Posed:
Rethinking Women and Communication

This section raises some of the key issues to consider in assessing the contributions that women's grassroots (participatory) processes are making not only to the international democratization agendas but also at local, regional and national levels. This section introduces a multidisciplinary perspective used to explore the relationship between gender and communication.

A critical reading of the outcomes and constraints in women's participatory experiences reveals their contributions: the integration of issues of diversity, power, and privilege linked with issues of personal and group selfhood and the dialogue and movement between the individual and collective spheres (issues of race, class, and gender identity). These issues emerged not just from the successes and advances in women's organizations but from the criticism of the neglect and silences of the women's and feminist movements. Acknowledging that women are effective communicators at the community and social levels, I ask to what extent their abilities as media producers and as social and political actors reside in their communication skills.

The stereotypical representations of women as passive and silent abound in dominant discourses on women. However, assumptions regarding passivity, instrumentalization, and objectification of women are also embedded in alternative or participatory proposals that vest themselves with the power to speak on behalf of oppressed groups, women included. The lack of careful consideration of these representations—and furthermore of the aspects they silence—has had an impact on communication strategies by generating proposals that instrumentalize, fragment, or deny women's reality. It is precisely in the encounter between the critical proposal of participation for liberation or empowerment and the everyday experiences of the group's participants where a number of tensions and silences emerge. This encounter tends to privilege the institutional, rationalistic (goal-based, time-lined, and preset), target-oriented agendas (of the NGO, political group, or women's movement) over the participant's experiences and goals. It is precisely in this realm where some of the gaps in existing frameworks are identified. The guiding question here is, "How do existing frameworks obscure or silence the experiences of women in the various life contexts of race, class, sexual orientation, and ability?"

The attempt in this book is to address the ideological and discursive level in which most of the programs for women have operated by including gender as a human variable and by addressing questions of political and linguistic representation. Thus a link is established between the material and practical level at which grassroots communication occurs and the discourse within which it operates (the community, social struggle, home, and sexuality).[5] The issues are as follows.

The Multifaceted Experience of Subordination

Kawaja maintains in Chapter 9 that bringing individuals together as a group for media production must cross class, race, and cultural boundaries. The experience of media production can foster a sense of collectivity when differences are acknowledged. Paradoxically, this multifaceted view of the individual experience is largely absent in the dominant discourses about women and in proposals for their development. Current proposals for development focus almost exclusively on the identification of a gender factor (e.g., isolation in a household and confinement to a private sphere) as the descriptor of their experience of subordination.

It is my thesis that the acknowledgment of the diversity of experiences of subordination and the various subjectivities, relations of power, and experiences of discrimination that participants bring to a communication process encourages a democratic and participatory process that is meaningful and interactive for the participants. Consequently, the narrative forms and the messages generated will encourage discursive differences.

The construction of gender identities is linked to concepts of self, personhood, and autonomy by reference to sexual identities and to the ways history, class, and race shape the various cultural definitions of women. Until recently, these connections have been disregarded in some Western feminist analyses of the subordinate condition of women, which saw the experience of being a woman as principally defined by gender. This reduction is most dramatically exposed in the affirmation that there is a woman's point of view and a separate model of the world. The problem with this affirmation is that it implies that gender is the main factor defining all women's experiences, with no substantial differences among women. This reductionism universalizes the experiences of specific groups of women and of Western feminist concerns and cultural assumptions.[6]

Thus, for example, in the discussion of gender, communication, and mass media, some Western feminists define "woman's communication patterns and systems" (Rush & Allen, 1989) predominantly by gender. From this perspective, the issue of the democratization of communication is simplistically resolved by women affecting or entering the sphere of mass media. Anzaldúa (1990a), among many others, vividly objects to the idea that gender oppression is the only predominant experience of women:

> Yes, when I go home I have to put up with a lot of heterosexist bullshit from my family and community, from the whole Chicano nation who want to exclude my feminism, my lesbianism. This I have in common with women-of-all-colors. But what really hurts, however, is to be with people that I love, with you *mujeres-de-todos-los colores,* and to *still* feel, after all our dialogues and struggles, that my cultural identity is *still* being pushed off the side, being minimized by some of my so-called allies who unconsciously rank racism a lesser oppression than sexism. (p. 218)

In conclusion, it is important to recognize that women's subordinate condition is connected to race and class oppressions. Women from nondominant groups have continued to raise this issue, indicating "the failure of contemporary feminism to deal productively with race and class diversity, that is their differences based on ethnic culture and socio-economic status" (Houston, 1992, p. 45).

Third World feminism, feminist anthropology, and **gender and development (GAD)** research provide important insights. In these three discourses gender is seen as a core variable of human social life, a socially constructed category that requires specification according to each particular context (Moore, 1988; Stamp, 1989). Feminist anthropology and GAD research have accurately pointed out the mediated experience of gender. The analysis of women's subordination has moved from the earlier feminist tradition, which isolated gender as the main determining factor in shaping women's subordinated experiences, to look at other forms of oppression and difference. The shaping of gender identity and the ways women experience subordination are connected and mediated by other core variables such as race, class, age and generation, sexual orientation, history, culture, and colonialism.

This view of a multifaceted experience of subordination has theoretical implications at the level of communication. Through communication, individuals recognize that they are members of a community, culture, or group. This process of recognition activates specific identities, mediating and shaping gender experiences through verbal and nonverbal communication interactions. Furthermore, communication provides and activates those verbal, nonverbal, visual, and dramatic means that constitute the vehicles of representation and expression of women's perceptions of themselves and their experiences of subordination. An important aspect of this process of collective identification is raised by Mata in Chapter 13. She explores how the discourses created through grassroots communication are not about the Other but about a We. In conclusion, the recognition of the otherness (of gender, race, and class) is achieved in grassroots communication through the dynamic building of group bonds; through identifying a common project, a sense of belonging (ours); and through the recognition of the participants as a collective subject (we).

*Reclaiming Cultural and
Ethnic Concerns*

Grassroots organizations also use group processes of communication to facilitate the recovery of indigenous knowledge and historical memory.

Alternative networks of all kinds have been created to redress the significant omissions by mainstream media and Western feminism of the works of women and people of Color (Mahoney, 1991). In particular, Aboriginal women in the North and South have engaged in collective projects of recovering historical memory. Communication in this context represents a strategic venue for struggling against the silencing of a community's ethnic and cultural dynamics, with memory, speaking, and writing providing the space for the creation of group alternatives and the drafting of an oppositional agency (Green, 1990; Kidd, in this volume).

The dominant representations of Third World women encapsulate them in a poverty-driven and stagnant present that ignores historical rootings or reduces them to folkloric images. Participatory programs have also frequently disregarded history and tradition, have privileged consciousness raising about the current conditions of subordination, and have encouraged a participation that speaks only to the "deprived" present reality or to the alternative future. Dyer-Bennem (in Chapter 5), however, shows that this connection between the past and the present is maintained at the grassroots by African-American communities through a handful of overt communication patterns and activities: their quilts, church ledgers, and oral history projects. These traditions and cultural artifacts have sustained a culturally distinctive African-American tradition and an alternative grassroots communication.

These aspects have been of particular interest to the Asian and Pacific regions. In their critique of the technologist tendency of media analysis of women, Bhasin and Agarwal (1984) clearly stated that

> two crucial—and inter-related—aspects which have particular relevance for many Third World countries are obscured by this perspective. The first is that people rather than technology have traditionally been the mediums of communication when, within a largely oral tradition, songs and story-telling, folk drama and puppetry were commonly used in these societies. Second, the content of such communication was taken essentially from religion and myth. (p. 5)

Consequently, in the region, several indigenous forms and cultural traditions such as rallies, *jalsas* (happenings with a certain amount of celebration, including skits, poems, songs, and speeches), songs, *jatras* (tours), dance drama, and street theater have been used with an alternative perspective.

Participatory communication projects have been critical in identifying legacies of knowledge and thought produced orally and informally and at the local level. The importance of documenting, maintaining, and recovering these legacies goes beyond the communication enterprise to represent a key political strategy in identifying the historical threads of resistance and cohesion among women and their communities.

In the relationship between gender and communication, and particularly in projects of participatory communication, the recovery of the ethnic and the cultural are fundamental reactions to the uprooting—by migration, civil wars, political repression, economic crises, or cultural genocide—that has negated traditions, ethnicities, and identities. Cultural and ethnic concerns are at the forefront in women's movements and particularly influence their grassroots communication. In this context, movements to reconstruct ethnic and cultural identities that do not relate to a past but to a changing present are of central importance in their agendas. Social and community participation for Aboriginal women (South and North) is largely influenced by belief systems with an ethnic content and collective historical consciousness (León, 1990). A consciousness of a past that is recreated in the present transforms historical memory into a social and political tool, "because our historical memory exists into the present, and we act on historical memory; history is for us the living present" (Green, 1990, p. 63).

We also need to identify the changing and transitory nature of gender identities. Women as members of ethnic groups that are constantly redefining themselves (e.g., as *mestizas*, African-Americans, Aborigines, and refugees) perceive multiple realities at once (Blondet, 1990; Green, 1990; Hurtado, 1989) and embrace a shifting and multiple identity that, in the words of Anzaldúa (1990a), contains a state of perpetual transition: a *mestiza* or hybrid identity that tolerates contradictions and ambiguity.

Martín-Barbero (1989), referring to Latin America, points out how questions of ethnicity in the region must be posed in historic terms. Historically, the process of ethnicity has evolved through cultural fusion (*mestizaje*) and the impurity of relations between ethnic groups and classes. In this history of colonization and mestizaje, indigenous systems of knowledge and cultural forms were never completely exterminated. The maintenance of a collective memory provided a strategy and a vital space for remembering silenced indigenous histories and cultural expressions. It is a cultural space that mediates the ways in which popular classes make sense of the world. Culture, in this view is an important mediation between communication practices and the popular (as people's culture).

Questioning the Private/Public Dichotomy

In the communication field, the privileged status that men have gained in public, dominant communication has led to mistaken generalizations about the absence of women from public communication activities. The use of the public/private dichotomy to describe the confinement of women to a subordinate position in the private/domestic domain has been extensively questioned in very different fields.

African studies have shown that the extended family is the public realm and how women, despite colonization and Westernization, have continued to have a measure of control over resources. In particular, women have controlled communication resources in the maintenance of informal associations at the local level, which allows them a control over information flows (March & Taqqu, 1986; Rathgebher, 1989a; Stamp, 1989).

Literature on social movements and popular culture in Latin America has analyzed the social and political dimensions of the domestic realm and of women's activities in their social reproductive roles and motherhood (Alfaro, 1988b; Martín-Barbero, 1989; Muñoz, 1988, 1990). Jelin (1990) and Arizpe (1990), referring to the demands of the social movements of neighborhoods in Latin America, stressed the importance of recovering "the public and political dimensions of the domestic role and also of the social forces that 'create' this private sphere" (p. 187).

Latin American women's organizations such as the Mothers' Clubs in Lima and the Movement of Mothers and Grandmothers in Argentina have emerged, as have many others, from the realm of the so-called private sphere. As mothers, the members of these movements have faced the malnutrition of their children and the deterioration of their living conditions because of the deep economic crisis of their regions. And as mothers, they have adopted strategies for collective distribution of goods and advocacy of community rights (e.g., the glass of milk program in Peru and the collective kitchens in Argentina). Facing political coercion and social and military repression of their children and families, women—as mothers—have organized strategies of defense (e.g., Mothers for the Defense of the Revolution in Nicaragua and Mothers Against the Violence in Colombia). Jelin (1990) concluded that these collective strategies of survival have widened the symbolic context of the private domestic role into a public one.

Examining a variety of grassroots experiences, the contributions in this book further expand on the public/collective dimension of women's informal and grassroots communication activities and the influence of their informal information links. In Chapter 18, for example, Alfaro examines how women have transformed their motherhood (individual level) into a social maternity (the public). Socially and culturally constructed ideas of motherhood are extended to their local sociocultural spaces, such as the poor urban neighborhood. The neighborhood constitutes a symbolic and material space in which their social motherhood is exercised by supporting informal networks of exchange and collective strategies of survival (Alfaro, 1988b: Riaño, 1990).

Women of Color and Aboriginal women in the North have argued that the idea of women's confinement to a private, nonpublic, sphere does not explain their experiences of gender, class, racial, or ethnic minority subordination. The state has intervened at every level of the domestic sphere of these groups, altering their family lives and denying the possibility of a private space. Following this argument, Hurtado (1989) affirmed that "there is no such thing as a private sphere for people of Colour except that which they manage to create and protect in an otherwise hostile environment" (p. 849).

Leacock (1978) concluded that women's dependent status does not rely on a supposed confinement to a domestic sphere and motherhood but that it derives from the lack of control over resources, working conditions, and the distribution of the products of their labor. Whether women control the access to communication resources determines their position and status as communicators in their communities. The analysis of women's position in communication industries and the information order must focus on what women and men do in the communication realm and on the cultural understandings underlying their actions (Rosaldo, 1980).

The political consciousness of the community-based social movements in Latin America, of women in India rallying across the country against dowry murders and many other forms of maltreatment, and of Aboriginal people in North America stems from an awareness that the domestic domain is a social and political space and that the public domain is "personally political." It is precisely this view of the lack of separation between the domestic and the public that connects discourses and political agendas of Western and non-Western feminists, white women and women of Color, and middle-class and working-class/popular women. In Chapter 7, Protz makes a key contribution by revealing the dynamics of negotiation and renegotiation between the personal and the collective experiences attached to any grassroots participatory process.

Issues of Power in Dominant Metaphors:
Re-visioning Women's Silence

Women's silence has been a dominant metaphor used to refer to women's marginal position in public communication and in the communication industries. Third World women have criticized the validity of such a metaphor for explaining their communicative and social situation. Accepting that colonialism and neo-imperialism have tended to exclude women from public communication worldwide, each particular group relates to this marginalization in distinct ways, depending on their history and the roles and social functions women have assumed in their societies.

Moore (1988) described how this denial of women's history is stronger in representations of non-Western societies by Westerners. This research has tended to produce,

> accounts of societies in which women were represented as subordinated to men while not in fact being so as regards their ability to act, speak out and make decisions in the world of day-to-day interaction and living. This situation is sometimes referred to as the "myth of male dominance." (Moore, 1988, p. 35)

Women as communicators within their communities have actively, naturally, and informally shaped their definition of themselves, by their complicity, acceptance, or rejection of dominant definitions. Women's informal communicative interactions at the domestic and local levels provide an autonomous space for the building of such definitions.

The metaphor of women's silence, and its associated assumption of women's passivity, describes a dominant discourse that, according to the specific context, speaks of issues of colonialism, racism, class, or gender oppression. This discourse involves a power dimension that we understand here not just as "control over" but as "a strategy," as a network of relations (Stamp, 1989). The power strategy involved in the promotion of the idea of a public, male-dominated communication has transformed the assessment of the marginal situation of women into a powerful myth: that of silenced women. Recognizing the power dimension is fundamental to our understanding of the dynamic in which any communicative interaction evolves, horizontal communication included. Power influences not only the economic and legal spheres but also the symbolic practices. Communication is located within this symbolic sphere, and therefore, any communicative interaction implies a negotiation of power. In a horizontal communication interaction, for example, power is distributed in the active role assumed by those engaged in the communication act who define and position themselves as active communicators.

This recognition of the power dynamics informs the discussion of the differences in the relationship between white women and women of Color to white men. Hurtado (1989) maintained that identity building and the development of one's own definition of what it is to be a woman differ according to the position that each woman's group has in the allocation of power. The different forms of oppression experienced by white women and women of Color and their different expectations of the roles they should fulfill in society imply different political responses and different communication dynamics. For people of Color, speech and oral expression have constituted an important realm for their expression. Women of Color have historically maintained an oral tradition that celebrates the open and spontaneous exchange of ideas. In expressing opinions freely, they exercise a form of power (see Chapters 4, 5, and 15; hooks, 1989).

This empowering feature of oral communication is contested by women's subordination, which constrains their ability to communicate. In particular, the relations that women of Color have with white men have been mediated by state institutions and state interventions at the reproductive and domestic level. These relations imply not only gender oppression but also racism and class oppression (Mohanty, 1991). hooks (1989) noted in this regard how the context of silence is varied and multidimensional. There are the dimensions of class, race, and sex domination, which suppress and silence, but there are other dimensions that directly and daily concern women as subjects: "less obvious as the inner struggles, the efforts made to gain the necessary confidence to write, re-write, to fully develop craft and skill,—and the extent to which such efforts fail" (hooks, 1989, p. 7).

Studies on popular cultures in South America have documented how oral traditions provide a realm of community resistance that maintain the popular local context but that do not necessarily empower communities to challenge openly their class and race oppression (Martín-Barbero, 1989; Rivera-Cusicanqui & Andean Oral History Workshop, 1990; Watchel, 1973). Their subordinated condition has been internalized in the historical legacy of the community and is individually and collectively maintained as a negative vision that Watchel (1973) referred to as "the tragic view of the defeated." The silence attributed to women in public affairs contrasts with their verbal eloquence in the community realm or family. Rivera-Cusicanqui and Andean Oral History Workshop (1990) suggested in this sense that silence is a deliberate form of anonymity and resistance. Silence is placed here in the context of colonialism and its condemnation of indigenous societies to degradation.

The assessment of the devaluation and subordination of women in society and the weight of dominant metaphors such as women's silence have promoted a view of women as passive recipients of cultural definitions of themselves. The review of frameworks and analyses of women and communication presented previously emphasized the need to shift from this view of women as targets or beneficiaries to a view of women as communicators. The move is from a concern with privileging communication research paradigms, models, and views of Others to acknowledging the subjects and their social and communicative functions.

Interactions of Communication and Development

The traditional strategies of development programs for the Third World have also overlooked women as active participants in communication processes. In addition, programs to foster women's communication in development have misinterpreted the situation of women. The analysis of women in communication is built on an erroneous assessment of women's lack of participation in communication and their marginalization in the private sphere just as women's absence from the male-dominated discourse has been equated with their total absence from community life (Steeves, 1990). Similarly, alternative development strategies encouraged by NGOs or progressive organizations mirror the instrumentalization and objectification of women in their identification of Woman (poor women) as a fighter who devotes herself to the struggle because of her maternal love for the people (Pedersen, 1988).

These misconceptions are articulated within diffusionist and modernizing views of development but are also present in consciousness raising and participatory approaches. The focus, then, is on the position of women as objects of representations or as recipients of development programs, media messages, advertising, and technology. These erroneous foci situate women as passive Others, as problems or issues, or as targets for integration in economic or social processes of modernization.

By introducing a gender and cultural perspective, our attempt is to challenge traditional development approaches by exploring how women's own communication activities question these assumptions. At the grassroots level and through various collective communication initiatives, women are expressing, with their own world of symbols and meaning, their multiple and diverse experiences as individuals and members of oppressed groups.

In Chapter 13, Mata describes the dynamic process in which participatory processes of communication appropriate the feminine word moving between submission and dignity, between alienation and feminine self-identity. Mattelart (1986) elaborated on the orientation and meaning of these actions:

> Women are trying to get across what makes them unique and different on the level of subjective experience and symbolic representation. This is leading them to delve into their age-old memory linked to the space and time of reproduction, and in which today part of their specific sensitivity is still shaped. (p. 18)

The various efforts at promoting exchange and networking among women are facilitating diverse, rich representations and artistic creativity for broader cross-cultural, class, and gender alliances. Our discussion on gender and communication stresses, therefore, the complex interaction between grassroots communication practices, antiracist struggles, and national struggles. Of particular relevance to this view is the thesis that Ruíz (in Chapter 11) puts forward regarding the dialectical relation between the need for transformation of the situation of subordination of women and the need to struggle against poverty. It would be impossible to eradicate poverty if actions to change the situation of subordination of women were not also taken at the same time. It is in this context that the authors in Part IV discuss the various ways in which gender and communication issues are connected to the realm of social struggles and social movements of subordinated classes (Jelin, 1990). In conclusion, the contributors to this volume have identified a common terrain for women's struggles worldwide. This is the terrain associated with the defense of human rights, democracy, and the changing of power relations.

By introducing the key components in the evolution of grassroots communication processes, I have mapped a framework for the development of three central dimensions of participatory communication: the community and group dimension, the media production dimension, and the sociopolitical dimension. The chapters in this book develop these dimensions. The contributors consider the social roles and functions of women as communicators, taking into account three central realms: women as producers of communication, women and their access to and control of communication resources, and women as social and cultural consumers. These three realms actively shape women's communication systems and provide their repertoire of cultural responses.

Notes

1. Because of the establishment of 1975 as International Women's Year and the declaration of the United Nations Decade for Women (1976-1985), women's issues were introduced to the international agenda. Throughout those years, a number of important publications and numerous regional and international meetings addressed women's perspectives for the democratization of communications and their demands for representation, access, control, and participation in the world communication order. The literature in the field of women and mass communication is very extensive; see for example Baehr (1980, 1987), Balarubrahmanyan (1988), Gallagher (1988), Creedon (1989), Douglas (1991), and Mahoney (1991).

2. Some examples of these networks follow. (a) The ISIS international network facilitates networking among women's groups through publications, computer databases, and collaborative action. The network reaches more than 10,000 groups and individuals in 150 countries (see Cottingham, 1989; Karl, 1989). (b) The Special Latin American Women's Service (SEMLA) is part of the Women's Features Service (Interpress Service). The network has 22 correspondents in the region, encouraging the development of a female perspective on information (see Corral, 1990). (c) In Africa, the Federation of African Media Women (FAMW) features services with 16 correspondents from several African countries. The exchange of research results and the definition of common methodologies are oriented toward policy recommendations (see Lardinois & Van Dijk, 1990). (d) The European Network for Women in Communication (NETWIC) aims at developing critical perceptions of the media and increasing the development of women's own media. (e) The Development Alternatives with Women for a New Era (DAWN) was created by Third World women in 1984 with the goal of promoting women alternatives in development.

3. For a discussion of the many efforts by women to connect with one another in the light of the development of alternative communication channels see Baehr (1980), UNESCO (1985), Gallagher (1988), Rush and Allen (1989), and Lent (1991).

4. Thus, for example, those works falling in the category of gender and communication are dominated by analyses of speech and language differences and interpersonal and nonverbal communication among the sexes. The discipline is oriented by a psychological framework that restricts gender and communication to the analysis of the communication behavior of men and women (Pearson, 1985). Absent from this literature are aspects of power, subordination, and the social and cultural beliefs that shape culturally constructed definitions of masculinity and femininity. When power issues are addressed (see Bates, 1988), they are limited to discussing power as one way of understanding men's and women's communication or to the analysis of the power of language to define, order and assign values, and shape stereotypes and behaviors (Wood, 1991). Issues of gender representation and the social and power relations through which gender is built are largely absent from this discourse.

5. Representation, as Butler (1990) has argued, serves, on the one hand, as a political term that legitimizes women as political subjects and, on the other, as the normative function of a language that reveals assumptions about the category of woman.

6. In particular, I am referring to feminist developments in communication issues such as Rush and Allen's (1989) *Communication at the Crossroads,* the framework of which is organized around the relation between gender and communication.

PART II

Women as Communicative Subjects: The Social and Community Dimension

Part II focuses on the social and community dimensions in women's grassroots communication and explores the emergence and dynamics of grassroots (participatory) processes. The chapters in this part identify the foundations of women's communication competencies in the indigenous and cultural realm of their communities and local groups. Such competencies relate to three specific realms: indigenous knowledge, oral traditions, and informal communication practices and networks. The social (communication) roles women and men perform in their communities constitute the context that articulates these realms. Thus the analysis presented identifies socially defined roles and explores the impact of social community roles on women's involvement in participatory communication processes and social movements.

Once the foundations of grassroots communication processes are established, we explore their impact on the emergence and evolution of participatory communication processes. Here are highlighted a number of factors that may affect women's participatory communication processes and that will be fully cemented in the subsequent chapters. A participatory process is seen as one of negotiation and renegotiation between the personal experience, the family experience of each participant, and the collective experience of the group process (Chapter 6). Women engaging in a grassroots communication process bring with them a commonsense knowledge that is based in their daily experiences in their family and with others. This constitutes a sociocultural resource base of communication skills, indigenous knowledge, and communication patterns and competencies.

In contrast, the connection established between commonsense knowledge, women's social roles, and participatory communication is frequently disregarded in development programs or discourses about women. The assumption is that learning and empowerment processes are exogenous to the social community realm and are the direct result of an intervention from outside the community. This view disregards the vitality of women's communication roles and activities, and the interpersonal and social communication level through which women establish relations and develop a concept of self and identity.

Furthermore, communication competencies are grounded in the daily interaction that women, as consumers, establish with mass-mediated cultural products, in particular with the mass media. And, as I emphasized throughout the introductory chapters, these competencies and capabilities are mediated and intersected by women's experiences of race, class, gender, and sexual orientation. It is in this context that this part develops an analysis of the elements for the development of, as Protz describes it, a meaningful communication process. This process is centered around the consideration of women as communicative subjects and of the group interaction as a collective process of meaning generation. The four chapters in this part explore these various realms of women's communication competencies, providing specific descriptions of how such skills and knowledge are maintained through history despite dominant attempts to deny the communicative expression of subordinated groups.

Social Roles and Communication

A gender analysis of women as communicative subjects and of their communicative functions provides our initial framework of analysis. In this perspective, roles are socially ascribed and must be identified in a relational manner: what women do (i.e., in communication) in relation to what others do (Rathgebher, 1989b; Young, 1988). The distribution of social communication roles, functions, and cultural traditions (who does what) according to gender, age, and class divisions are at the center of this analysis. Social and cultural perceptions, or constructions, of gender in terms of heterosexual roles, of the world of everyday life that normalizes them, and of the ideal or stereotypical images of relations between the sexes are also defining elements in this analysis (Strathern, 1990).

At the community level, for example, men have been identified in various cultural contexts, as those in charge of public affairs, holding positions of community leadership. Men's communication roles are tied to tasks of representation, public speaking, and leadership (Stamp, 1989). The communicative role of women is tied to the social roles they perform. Moser (1989) argued that the role of Third World women in the community and the domestic realm is wider and three tiered: reproductive (childbearing and child rearing), productive (as secondary income earners through informal activities or agricultural work), and community management work (allocation of limited resources to ensure the survival of the household). Communication, as exchange and mutual support, is an important facilitator in the execution of this triple role but particularly in the tasks of community work.

Women in Third World societies have assumed the additional responsibility of managing their communities as an extension of their domestic role. In carrying out this role, they require basic infrastructural conditions and facilities that are generally scarce in their impoverished communities. To accomplish their reproductive and productive roles, women shoulder the additional responsibility of forming and organizing local groups to demand services and promote networks of survival and mutual help (Moore, 1988). The local context of the neighborhood or the village thus constitutes an extension of their homes. Within their gender-ascribed roles as wives and mothers, women assume a "social motherhood," appropriating the local social context as a space for oral and feminine expressiveness (Alfaro, 1988b). Throughout this book, we will refer to these roles as the context from which women's communication movements and participation are set off.

It is in the realm of family and community communication, through oral tradition and informal associations, that women have expressed social leadership. This communication role includes the managing of networks of information exchange (i.e., self-help groups, gossip, rumor networks, dance, and songs) that provide socially relevant information (i.e., what is happening locally, regionally, and nationally and social roles and norms) and information necessary for survival (i.e., costs of articles, bargains, news, and conflicts). Social communicative practices and communicative networks complement collective strategies for the allocation of limited resources, ensuring social and economic survival (Moser, 1989; Riaño, 1990) as well as physical and mental health (Chapter 4). Overall, these communication practices reinforce social interaction and a sense of community, providing spaces for resistance, solidarity, and group identity.

Ethnographic research in non-Western societies has largely illustrated the variety of initiatives of women to form local self-help groups, informal associations, and support networks (Lomnitz, 1978; March & Taqqu, 1986; Moore, 1988).[1] These informal networks play a central role of information distribution, allocation of resources, and participation in the life of these societies as a whole, guaranteeing economic and political exchanges among communities (March & Taqqu, 1986; Strathern, 1972). Of particular interest for us are the roles that information distribution and communicative exchange play and that women play in forming the ties that bind separate groups. These are communication roles that have fundamental economic and political implications.

Indigenous media forms such as dance and drama are also key factors that circulate information, promote participation, resolve conflict, and transmit knowledge. Mlama (Chapter 3) discusses the use of indigenous dance and theatrical forms in Tanzania and documents this cultural richness of women's indigenous knowledge and oral traditions. Dance is a cultural tradition with specific social and educative roles and functions that women (in the context of democratic, participatory processes) have reappropriated to encourage participation and express their views on crucial development issues. Mlama discusses the failures of foreign media and Western-based development communication models in understanding the living conditions, access to media, and media literacy of their targeted African populations. Some attempts at using indigenous media for development purposes have failed to recognize the participatory nature of these art forms, their horizontal communication dynamics, and their definition as collective responsibility.

The active role women have in the maintenance of oral communication forms, traditions, and transmission of knowledge is illustrated in Chapter 4 by Dyer-Bennem, who discusses African-American women's grassroots communication activities. Dyer-Bennem shows how African-American women, as quilt makers and as storytellers, have held central power positions and maintained an effective infrastructure of communication and historical memory. As carriers of oral traditions, African-American women have always been at the center of the community, because, as stated by Gunn-Allen (1989), the one who tells the stories rules the world. Dyer-Bennem's historical exploration of quilts, folklore, oral histories, and music provides the elements to understanding contemporary communication patterns and practices of African-American women and their extensive involvement as communicative subjects and cultural bearers. Contemporary writers, song composers, and quilt makers continue a distinctive communication legacy based on polyrhythmic, oral patterns. This distinctive system of communication has maintained oral communication systems as a strategy for survival and continuity. Thus forms of oral communication (such as verbal gaming, calls, and responses) and oral testimony are continued today in cultural manifestations such as rap music. The chapters by Dyer-Bennem and Mlama document how participation is the innate style of audience reception for Africans. The cultural roots of participatory audiences' styles in singing, dancing, and performing are maintained in contemporary dances in the region, as they have survived in African-American communication practices.

Consumers, Interpreters, and Readers

The activity of consumption is examined from the point of view of the consumers. The questions, in this regard, relate to what women do, and how they perceive and use mass-mediated cultural products. Consumption is seen "as a social and cultural process in which products are appropriated and used" (Valles, 1991, p. 29). In Chapter 5, Muñoz focuses on the social practices of consumption by women and elaborates on this view, linking it to everyday culture. Social uses of communication are understood as the ways in which media are integrated into the culture and daily lives of the people, the ways people circulate and re-create the meaning of the messages.

Muñoz's chapter exemplifies the gender differences between consumption and reception. As active consumers, women interpret and read communicative messages, obtain entertainment, and derive relevant information. Their perception of mass media is tempered by their socially ascribed roles in the domestic and community realms. Muñoz (1990) researched the use and ways of seeing *telenovelas* (Latin soap operas) by women of the popular barrios in Colombia and concluded that perceptions and readings are mediated by women's experiences of aesthetic pleasure, their conception of time, and by the ways they articulate indigenous knowledge in the act of consumption. These levels of mediation also define how women consume and use mass-mediated cultural products and the competencies they acquire in relating to media. For poor women in the cities of Colombia, for example, domestic and community responsibilities require a permanent work rhythm and a frequent change of activities. Their uses of media adapt to this rhythm. It is a "distracted" consumption, integrated in daily tasks (cooking, services provision, childbearing, and shopping) and embedded in community communication networks.

Muñoz's chapter shows the interrelation between a feminine orality and the discourse of the media. Specifically, she shows how media's narrative forms appeal to the feminine and how women activate their communication competencies and knowledge in the expectations they hold of specific mass-mediated cultural products such as the soap operas. Long familiarity with the medium has constructed a competency, a taste, a way of listening, and an expectation with respect to other media. These expectations and competencies are part of the cultural resources women bring with them to the participatory process.

Emergence and Tensions

The initiation of a participatory communication process and the decision to use media is commonly promoted by community organizations, or NGOs, to facilitate a group effort and strategy to overcome problems of communication and motivation or to address key social and political issues. Some are the result of an intervention by local, national, and international NGOs. In most of these cases, there is a combined effort of the organization or group, the NGO, and the communication expert (facilitator) in the implementation of a participatory process.

Participatory processes are complex because of the dynamics created in the interaction of the different actors: leaders, participants, and facilitators. Facilitators act as mediators between institutional levels and participants, and between program design and the reality of its implementation. Local leaders and activists represent another level of mediation. Each actor has different interests and goals and, therefore, different expectations and perceptions of participatory experiences.

The last chapter in Part II is by Protz, who shows how participatory communication serves different functions at different stages of women's organizational process. For instance, at the beginning stages of a group's organizational process, common issues are given highest priority. Over time, as the group gains confidence there is a shift to reexamine more personal issues. The chapter explores the factors affecting participatory communication and organizational processes of grassroots women's groups, including the interpersonal and group dynamics and the types of relations, expectations, and tensions that are most likely to occur in these processes. A link is established between the biographical experience of participants and their cultural world as well as the existing level of organization before the communication experience.

By identifying the participatory process as one of negotiation and renegotiation, Protz maps a number of intervening variables. She shows how the combination of commonsense differences due to race, class, culture, and gender involve a number of potential tensions or miscommunication problems within the group of participants as competing goals, racism, elitism, or sexism might emerge. The chapter establishes the grounds in which a participatory process occurs, introducing the discussion of women's manipulation of media, the theme of Part III.

Note

1. Documentation exists for almost all regions of the world about the vitality of these initiatives. Since precolonial times, women's associations, mutual aid networks, rotating credit associations, and women's councils have played a crucial role in community life. In the Middle East as well as in Africa and New Guinea, women's kinship networks are seen as the most important system of linkage among communities and lineage groups. In Asia and Latin America, neighborhood associations of women represent powerful brokers of public opinion (see Banerjee, 1990; Chitnis, 1988; Ghadially, 1988; Jelin, 1990; Martín-Barbero, 1987a; Moore, 1988; Stamp, 1989).

3

Reinforcing Existing
Indigenous Communication Skills:
The Use of Dance in Tanzania

PENINA MLAMA

There is a general belief among development and communication agents that women are inactive in the processes of communication for development. In this view, women constitute mere listeners to development messages imposed on them by people who "talk to" them, rather than engage them in genuine communication. Women are said to be timid, lacking the confidence to speak, especially in public or in the presence of men and even when given the opportunity to communicate (Mascarenhas & Mbilinyi, 1983; Sen & Grown, 1987).

The causes of this communication inactivity have been attached to sociocultural factors that relegate women to an inferior position to men and, therefore, inhibit women from speaking out. However, these approaches have not considered that the nonparticipatory nature of the communication media employed by development strategies curtails the participation of media audiences. The one-way communication characteristic of dominant radio, television, film, or print gives no opportunity for audiences to use the media to communicate responses to the messages received. The inaccessibility of the media for the majority of African populations worsens the situation, especially for the rural poor, the majority of whom are women. Furthermore, the undemocratic character of the dominant development program, which assume that the actors of development have no contributing ideas or views, makes no allowance for peoples' participation in communication for development. In fact, most of the development strategies of the past three decades have shared the arrogance of excluding the people at the grassroots from formulating, discussing, analyzing, or evaluating development programs (Kidd & Colleta, 1980; Kilusang, 1986; UNESCO, 1985).

As a result of the international UN decade of women (1975-1985), women's crucial role in development has been recognized. However, the rhetoric has overshadowed action in the incorporation of meaningful participation of women, especially in communication for development. For example, the imposition of development models from the West has brought foreign economic structures supported by foreign communication media to Africa. The accompanying drive for capitalism has given no place for the role of indigenous thinking in the formulation or implementation of development programs. The colonial legacy has maintained the attitude that sees most things African as backward and, therefore, as not contributing to development (Arnold & Nitecki, 1980).

The lack of participation of the people at the grassroots is also a class issue. Ruling classes in Africa have dominated decision-making processes to maintain their interests. Although for several decades development planners have been criticized for not involving the grassroots, governments have continued to exclude the people, the actors of development, from the decision-making process.

The above-mentioned factors have, therefore, not created fertile ground for grassroots participation in the development process. Nonparticipation in communication for development is thus part of the general lack of involvement of the people in all facets of development. It must also be pointed out that the situation is true for both women and men. However, women are affected more because of their inferior position relative to men.

From a gender perspective, struggles in communication have centered on the accessibility of women to media. Poverty, illiteracy, low levels of education, unfair division of labor, cultural inhibitions, and various forms of gender oppression have kept the majority of women out of reach for the conventional media, both as communicators and audience.

Extensive debate has led to some practical attempts to redress the situation. The mass media have striven to widen their audience through outreach programs in the rural areas. The rural presses, rural radio, mobile films, and other media activities have targeted grassroots audiences not reached by the conventional media (Moemeka, 1981). However, the majority of contributors to rural newspapers have also been men, even though the majority of implementors of the development programs discussed are women (Mlama, 1990). Women have also not been very actively involved in presenting their views on radio, television, or film.

These points of view have created a popular belief that women are shy, unable to speak in public, incapable of presenting their views, and predominately passive. Questioning these popular beliefs, I will explore the extent to which women can be considered passive in communication for development.

Communication for Development

It is necessary first to look critically at what constitutes communication for development. It is obvious that, as is the case with development in general, communication for development has been imposed from above, using foreign communication models that have often completely ignored the existence of indigenous media[1] in Africa. Western mass media are presented as the magic communication media for development. Although it has been shown that the mass media never reach the majority of the African populations, this does not seem to have changed the belief in the magic of radio, television, film, and print.

Another disturbing problem is the assumption that where the mass media are not available, there is a vacuum of communication. Communities, especially rural populations, beyond the reach of radio, television, films, newspapers, and books are considered incapable of communication and, therefore, incapable of developing. It is surprisingly forgotten that these communities without mass media have long histories during which other forms of communication have played a vital part.

As a result of this assumption, no effort goes into determining how, in the absence of the mass media, these communities have survived and what other forms of communication they have employed. Instead, efforts are concentrated on expanding the accessibility of the Western mass media, often without significant success. In Tanzania, for example, rural newspapers have been established in areas with low literacy rates and low income levels. Radio and television have crammed their programs with development messages, although the producers know well that the majority of the population do not own radios or television sets. Development-related films have been made for audiences with no cinema facilities, and most cannot be reached even by mobile film vans because of impassable roads.

Communication for development, therefore, seems to be based on a conceptualization that restricts communication to the foreign mass media: radio, television, film, and print. The media indigenous to African communities do not, therefore, constitute communication for development. A need has long arisen to correct this misconception and to explore the potential of indigenous African media for communication for development. Attempts toward that goal can be seen in some African countries. Tanzania, for example, is extensively using traditional media in communication for development. Of interest to this chapter is the use of indigenous dance.

Dance is a very popular art form in Tanzania. There are more than 500 different types of indigenous dances among the 128 plus ethnic groups in Tanzania. Dance carries a variety of functions, including education, religion, work motivation, and merrymaking—the most significant of these is educational.[2] Throughout history, dance had been used to educate the members of the community into their various roles as adults, parents, in-laws, soldiers, leaders, or simply human beings (Mlama, 1983). The dance song and often the action as well are carriers of messages to the audience about what is expected of an individual in the community. Bad behavior is reproached and corrected while acceptable conduct is praised to motivate emulation. The dance song is also the courier for information on the latest events, spreading the word to viewers who may be from neighboring communities. And, indeed, the dance performance itself, which normally draws a large audience, becomes a forum for people to meet, exchange information, and discuss issues in a relaxing and entertaining atmosphere.

The traditional society of precolonial times used dance very effectively to communicate issues about the welfare of society. The colonial experience, as was the case everywhere else in the world, attempted to blot out the indigenous theater forms in the name of civilization. The crucial function of dance in education was ignored and dance was, together with other indigenous cultural practices such as rituals, ceremonies, and initiation rites, removed from the vocabulary of development. The communication effectiveness of dance was not recognized, and instead, dance was generally seen as belonging to the "uncivilized and backward" peoples.

Because of this colonial legacy, the development strategies of the post-independent period (since 1961) had no place for dance or similar indigenous forms of communication for development. During the colonial period and after independence, radio, films, and print media were introduced and created as the required media for development. Soon, however, it became obvious that despite the magical effectiveness of the mass media, they did not reach the majority of the population (Ngwanakilala, 1981). As mentioned earlier, low income levels, low literacy rates, poor communication infrastructures, and the one-way character of mass media have greatly curtailed accessibility of the mass media for the majority.

By the early 1970s, some indigenous media, especially dance and *ngonjera* (poetic drama) were being used by the party (then the Tanganyika African National Union, TANU) and the government to mobilize people for development action. National campaigns on literacy, nutrition, agriculture, afforestation, health, and so on made extensive use of indigenous dance to pass on messages, especially for rural populations. The party also made great use of dance to propagate the policy of socialism and self-reliance (Lihamba, 1985; Mlama, 1991).

Unfortunately, though, the above-mentioned use of indigenous dance became an extension of the previous approach to the mass media, adopting the same one-way communication character of radio and print. Dance groups were organized at all levels to talk to the people and tell them what the government wanted them to do to bring about development. See for example, the following *Mdundiko*[3] dance song for the Child Survival and Development (CSD) campaign in Morogoro (Mlama, 1990); the original Kiswahili-language version is presented first, followed by an English translation.

Leo uzinduzi kufaduro kizuiwe
Polio izuiwe, surua izuiwe
Kulinda mwili kutia nguvu ili wapate afya bora
Kuzuia utapia mlo
Kujenga mwili wale mayia na maziwa
Kujenga mwili wake mayia nayo nyama
Kulinda mwili mboga za majani
Kutia nguvu chakula wanga
Mtoto huyu na apelekwe kliniki
Kuzuia kifaduro
Kuzuia surua, kuzuia kifua kikuu

Today is the inauguration of the campaign [CSD]
Whooping cough should be prevented
Polio, measles should be prevented
To protect the body to strengthen it
So as to acquire good health
To prevent malnutrition
To develop the body they have to teach eggs and milk
To protect the body, vegetables
For strength, starch
This child should be taken to the clinic
To prevent whooping cough
To prevent measles, to prevent tuberculosis

By the early 1980s, although indigenous dance had been effectively revived and the colonial attitude that dance was backward extensively erased, it was clear that dance was being used for top-down communication only. Even though the messages on literacy, health, and nutrition were necessary for the development of the people, the shortfall was in the treatment of the audience as passive recipients of messages formulated and imposed from above. Indeed, this use of indigenous dance was no different from the imposed Western mass media. The majority remained passive audiences. It is important to stress here, therefore, that the mere adoption of indigenous communication media does not necessarily provide for the active participation of the masses in communication for development.

Africa has seen other more positive attempts at using the indigenous media in communication for development. Of great significance is the Theatre for Development movement dating back to the early 1970s. Theatre for Development stands for a process in which members of a community are engaged in searching what they think are their development problems, discussing and analyzing the problems and presenting them theatrically with a view to eliciting wide discussions with audiences on how to solve these problems. Between 1970 and 1991 many Theatre for Development workshops were conducted in Botswana, Swaziland, Lesotho, Malawi, Zambia, Tanzania, Kenya, Ivory Coast, Cameroon, and Nigeria (Eyoh, 1986; Kidd, 1987; Mda, 1987; Mlama, 1991; Nguni wa, 1982).

Theatre for Development workshops place emphasis on the uses of theatrical media indigenous to the community and on enabling participants to express their views. Dance, recitations, story telling, poetic drama, skits, and drama have been used in the process. Below, I discuss the Theatre for Development work conducted in Tanzania with the specific objective of exploring the potential that indigenous theatrical media have for affecting the active participation of women in communication for development.

Women and Communication for Development

From the above discussion, it becomes clear that the view of women as inactive, passive, and nonparticipating in communication for development stems from both a misconception of communication for development and the misguided use of foreign and indigenous media. An alternative perspective of communication for development, however, suggests women are very active communicators. A look at African women in their developmental roles as mothers, wives, aunts, sisters, society leaders, midwives, and educators show them as vocal, outspoken, firm, confident, and eloquent in speech. A look at public activities such as weddings, initiation ceremonies, artistic performances (such as dances or story telling), and meetings of women's societies reveals high levels of public communication by women (Mlama, 1989).

The notion that women are passive in communication, therefore, seems to represent a misconception of women's communication abilities. There are clear indications that women are active communicators. It seems the problem is not in the inability of women to communicate but in the approach of communication in development and the selection of the media.

The following section outlines the experiences of Theatre for Development in Tanzania between 1986 and 1991, showing that women can be active in communication for development. Various indigenous media were employed in these workshops. However, my focus will be on dance.

Indigenous Dance as Communication
for Development
The department of art, music, and theater at the University of Dar es Salaam has engaged in the Theatre for Development movement since 1980 (Chambulikazi, 1983; Lihamba & Mlama, 1986; Mlama, 1991). Since 1986, some of the work has focused specifically on women's participation in communication for development, including five workshops: Msoga (Bagamoyo district in 1983), Mkambalani (Morogoro region in 1986), Namionga (Mtwara region in 1989), Misalai (Tanga area in 1990), and Mbuyuni (Tanga area in 1991).

The process followed in the workshops involves animators-cum-artists staying in a selected community for a minimum of two weeks. The first several days are spent researching what the community feels are the major problems. Members of the community volunteer to assist the animators in conducting this research. They collect information from individuals and groups through informal discussions and interviews. The local theater artists are also identified at the outset and involved in the research teams. In the evenings, theater performances are staged for general entertainment. The animators use this opportunity to learn how to perform in the local theater by participating in the performances along with the local people.

The next stage involves discussions and analyses of what the community thinks are the root causes of the identified problems. Using the research teams as core groups, the rest of the community is invited and encouraged to join any of the discussion groups, depending on which problem interests them most.

After the analyses, the discussion groups turn into theater groups and put their ideas into any artistic form they choose. This can be song, poetry, dance, recitation, story telling, drama, and so on. The artistic forms selected are from the community. Several days are spent rehearsing the theater piece. The rehearsal process is a continuation of the analysis process whereby the members continue to dig deeply into the problem to present it properly in the performance. The content of the theater piece is designed in a way that not only poses the problem but also suggests possible solutions.

The theater pieces by the different groups are then brought together in a community theater performance. Everyone is encouraged to attend and participate in the show. Participation is possible because Tanzania's indigenous theater is participatory in character. Immediately after the performances the audience is engaged in a discussion that takes up the problems presented, analyzes the solutions suggested, and decides on action to be taken by the community to solve the problems.

The animators participate with the community in all the stages. At least one animator is in every group. The animator, however, only takes the role of catalyst for discussion and action.

In the five workshops, women participated with men to get a community perspective on the problems, not just the women's angle. After information gathering, it was found that there were problems that grossly affected the women and for which women felt very strongly. These included schoolgirl pregnancy, lack of water, poverty, unfair division of labor, unsatisfactory marriages, failing income-generating activities, and general male domination and oppression.

At the information-gathering stage, theater forms by women are also identified. In Tanzania there are many forms, especially dances, which are specifically for women. These are dances traditionally related to education, initiation, wedding ceremonies, and women's entertainment.

When it came to the community members choosing which discussion group to join, women always joined the problem that touched them most, as mentioned above. In Msoga, many women joined the group on schoolgirl pregnancies; in Mkambalani, water; in Namionga, marriage problems; in Misalai, water; and in Mbuyuni, failing income-generating activities. The women were, however, free to join any other group.

In all five workshops, various theater forms were chosen, but all the five women's groups picked women's dances. In Msoga, the *Bigililo* dance was used. The *Bigililo* is a women's dance performed by middle-aged and elderly women for ceremonies related to female initiation rites into adulthood (including marriage). It is a dance of the Wakwere people of Bagamoyo district. In Mkambalani, the *Nzekule* women's dance was used. It is a dance performed for female initiation rites into adulthood by adult women of the Waluguru of Morogoro region. In Namionga, the *Mandelela* dance was performed. This dance is for women beyond child-bearing age, performed for relaxation. It is a dance of the Wamakonde of Mtwara region. In Mkuyuni, women chose the *Nchaila* dance. It is performed for any event calling for celebration by women of ages, but it is mostly for the younger women. The dance is from the Wamakonde of Mtwara region.

The women themselves discussed the problems, created the dance performance, composed the songs, rehearsed and directed the dance, and performed for the community audience. The animators only helped in advising or suggesting alternative angles of discussion of action. Emphasis was placed on the participation of women in all stages.

Women in Msoga used the *Bigililo* dance to communicate their views on schoolgirl pregnancies (Mlama, 1991).[4] A considerable number of girls from the village's primary school were getting pregnant and, therefore, getting expelled from school. In the research and discussions, the women argued strongly that the schoolteachers were responsible for the pregnancies. There had been several cases in the village of schoolteachers having affairs with schoolgirls and/or making them pregnant. Also village adults, especially the well to do, lured the schoolgirls with material gifts and then exploited them sexually. The teachers argued back that the parents were to blame for not being good models of sexual behavior themselves. The girls were also blamed for being unruly and material minded. The women, however, emphasized the fact that the men acted irresponsibly, taking advantage of every situation to sleep with schoolchildren and, in the end, getting away with it. They argued that men who make schoolgirls pregnant must bear the consequences. The following is a song composed and performed by the women using the *Bigililo* dance and dance drama format. The Kiswahili-language version is first, followed by the English translation.

Watoto wa siku hizi kwa uhuni wameshinda
Kutoka hapa nyumbani nadhani kenda shule
Kumbe kapakia daladala
Nimepokea barua inatoka CCM
Eti mwanao kapata mimba
Namuuliza mwanangu anisema niambae we mama usinijue

Namchukua mwanangu safari ya CCM
Nimefika CCM wazee kumwuliza
Mimba ni ya nani
Mimba ni ya upepo
Mambo haya sikubali namshitaki mzazi
Amekwenda mahakama
Kisikia mahakama mtoto kapata woga
Amemtaja Mgweno naye akakataa
Mzazi kasikitika hakimu nipe barua
Namshitaki Mgweno kaniharibia mwanangu
Asha na Mgeweno wote mkafungwe
Chitendo chontendile wote mkafungwe

Children of these days have excelled in being loose
They leave home, I assume they have gone to school
But they have boarded daladala [the public bus]
I have received a letter from CCM [the party]
That my daughter is pregnant
I ask my daughter, she tells me to get lost
"Mother leave me alone"
I take my daughter to CCM
I arrive there, CCM elders ask her who made her pregnant
She says it is the wind
"I don't accept, I will sue your parent"
CCM will go to court
When she hears about going to court she is scared
She mentions Mgweno [the male role] who denies it
Mr. Magistrate, give me an injunction I am taking Mgweno to court
He has destroyed my daughter
Asha and Mgweno, both of you should go to jail
for what you have done, both of you should go to jail.

Analysis of all the five workshops indicated a strikingly high level of participation by women. The report on Mkamalani (Mlama, 1991), for instance, states the following on the *Nzekule* dance:

Nzekule is a dance dominated by women, and this was the most dynamic group during the workshop performances. The women engaged themselves on a variety of issues but especially the scarcity of water in the village. From the first day of the workshop, the women improvised and spontaneously created songs relevant to the issues but they also draw upon a reservoir of old songs. The women who usually sat quiet at meetings and listened to men, expressed their anger, frustration, helplessness and protest through song, while some songs were rehearsed in the group before the performance, many more were improvised on the spot during the performance. (Lihamba & Mlama, 1986)

The *Mandelela* dance of the Namionga project involved women 50 years old and older. Traditionally, it is an older women's dance used to express views on social problems. It became quite appropriate for women in the Namionga workshop who decided to deal with the problems relating to marriage. According to the women, the village was afflicted with a very high rate of divorce caused by and resulting in many problems: unfair division of labor, irresponsible fathers, neglected children, unwanted pregnancies, alcoholism, irresponsible stepparents, and oppression of women. The following are two *Mandelela* songs composed and performed by the women of the group (first in Kimakonde and then in English):

Walumbwe nawo
Ma ga newala
Salimu ga likapakete
Walume mwa chitahuka
Kudumbuka ku vijana
Ku Newala
Kutaza kodi ya maendeleo

The girls of today, many are facing problems
They get married by clerks from Newala [town]
Today they are in Newala, tomorrow they have nothing
They cannot pay the development levy.

Walume wa njoko
Njenjelu njenjelu wondila mwana
Walumi mwana
Ndeke kulumuku na tumu baho

Some men like to produce children
Just to produce but they leave all the child's upbringing and upkeep to the
  women
But when the child is grown up
They ask him/her to bring the fire [for lighting cigarettes].

The women in Misalai used the *Kibwebwe* dance to express their dissatisfaction with the village leadership, which had failed to complete a water project that could have brought water to all parts of the village. They argued that they had volunteered to dig the trenches for the pipes and the women had turned out in higher numbers than men. But when the pipes were finally laid and the water connected, it went only to the part of the village where the government leaders had their houses. The *Kibwebwe* dance lamented the people's, especially the women's, suffering over the lack of tap water. They had to fetch water from unclean water sources. The women were saying that unless the water problem was solved they would not turn up for any more volunteer development work.

The women in Mbuyuni used the *Nchaila* dance to tackle the problem of disunity among women that had led to the failure of their various attempts at establishing income-generating activities. An analysis of the problem put the blame not only on a weak male-dominated village leadership but also on dishonest women leaders of women's economic ventures. The women's organization was said to be ineffective. Apathy had set in and women refused to organize into economic groups any more. The *Nchaila* dance group for women composed and performed other songs. The following song urges women to come together again and try to form income-generating groups to raise their economic abilities (the song is in Kikamonde, followed by the English translation):

Akina mama Nchaila na ider.
Eeh eh ehe
Tuunde vikundi vyetu eee
Eeh eh eh
Tuinue uchumi wetu ee
Eeh eh eh
Nasi tuendelee kweli ee
Akina mama Nchaila na ide

Come all women and dance the Nchaila with us
Come please please
Come let us organize your groups
Please please please
Let us raise our economic ability
Please please please
So that we also develop
Come all women and dance the Nchaila with us.

When we first began the workshops, women did not speak in the conventional meetings conducted in each village, but once the workshops started, they became very active in all stages. They were vocal in airing their views on village problems during the research stage, especially when interviewed as individuals or in groups. They became quite animated in group discussions and analysis of the problems, especially because they—as women—suffered most through problems relating to marriage, water, or the division of labor. The women became even extra active when dance was employed.

There are a number of factors explaining this active participation by women in dance in the Theatre for Development workshops. One is the fact that dance is a familiar medium of communication for the women. They have used dance all their lives to communicate about various aspects of life. The women, therefore, possess the skills to use dance as a medium of communication. Through constant participation, the women have acquired the ability to compose dance songs, to perform the dance movements, and to respond to the dance as audience. Dancing, singing, and composing comes naturally to the majority of them. The few with a talent for art normally excel through practice and become leading artists.

Second, Tanzanian indigenous dance is participatory in character. Women and men go to a dance performance not just to watch but to take part. The audience joins the performance and leaves it at will. Using dance as a medium, therefore, means courting those present to participate. The women are thus naturally drawn into the dance performance and into expressing what they think through dance. The dance audience is also not passive. It participates in the singing and ululating, making comments or urging the dancers on. As such, one expresses a view in response to the content of the dance, even as a member of the audience.

Third, Tanzanian indigenous dance is quite flexible and allows for much improvisation, especially of content. Songs can be composed impromptu and new stanzas added to songs by whoever feels inspired to do so. The compositions and the performance are looked on as a collective responsibility. A good dancer is not the one who dominates the show but the one who elicits participation and response from the rest. Such an atmosphere encourages everybody to participate.

Fourth, dance as an art form appeals to the emotions of the participants. And because dance in these Theatre for Development workshops was used to communicate problems about which the women felt very strongly, the women used dance to pour out their hearts. They sang of issues for which they had a lot to say, issues that touched on the core of their existence, and thus issues they wanted to communicate about.

Reinforcing Indigenous Communication

The experience with dance in the examples given here indicates that there is a lot of potential for using some indigenous communication media in communication for development with women. The strength of indigenous media lies in the fact that such media already exist and are already in use at the grassroots level. This means that the women already have the required skills for such media. It cuts down on the need to impart skills for new media imposed from outside.

The challenge that remains is for the communication agents to explore how to discard attitudes prevailing among communication professionals who see traditional media as backward and having nothing to contribute to development. Also, there is a need to explore which types of indigenous media are best suited for use in contemporary society. Not all indigenous media will automatically provide an effective means of communication for development today. Possibilities could also be explored in combining Western mass media with indigenous media to exploit the positive characteristics of both. But the most difficult challenge is how to avoid the mistakes committed with previous media and effect a genuine active participation of women in communication for development.

Notes

1. Indigenous media include song, dance, poetry, mime, story telling, talking drums, and other oral and visual form of communication that exist in a particular society.

2. For a detailed analysis of the functions of dance in Tanzania see Mlama (1973) and Lihamba (1985).

3. *Mdundiko* is a celebratory dance by people of the coastal area. It is performed at weddings; coming-out ceremonies; and in recent years, at any event calling for celebration.

4. This discussion draws briefly on the reports on the use of dance for each of the five workshops. For further details see Chambulikazi (1983), Lihamba and Mlama (1986), and Mlama (1989, 1990, 1991).

4

Cultural Distinctions in Communication Patterns of African-American Women: A Sampler

SUSAN Y. DYER-BENNEM

Discrimination and oppression are downward, vertical forces that, for the purpose of survival, are responded to with horizontal, collateral communication; networking; and resistance. On a very intimate scale, images of hands held, a choir of voices, or a blanket spread across a family may be seen as individual protests, but when an entire community or race of people share values, maintain oral traditions, and collectively participate in the "uplifting of the race," (Neverdon-Morton, 1978) an effective infrastructure and a continuity of history are recognized. African-American women have been, and continue to be, oppressed sexually, racially, and economically. A close examination of their history within the United States—from 1650 to the present—reveals extensive involvement within their communities on a multitude of levels as communicative subjects and cultural bearers, preserving an iconography and a history, rejected by the dominant culture. Documentation, including African-American quilts, church ledgers, meeting notes, and oral history projects, confirms that African-American women effected social change within their communities and cities and throughout the entire United States.

The intent of this chapter is to present a historical overview and analysis of African-American women's grassroots communication activities within the United States.[1] Emphasis will be placed on a handful of black women's

AUTHOR'S NOTE: Thanks to my husband, Christopher, and son, Ian, for their support; to Cassundra Cooper who openly shared with me her experiences as a southern African-American woman; to Mary Ellen Brown for her confidence in me; and to Pilar Riaño for her patience.

overt communication patterns and activities practiced within their homes and communities. Issues of race,[2] gender, and feminist ideologies will be focal points of this analysis. Defining the common denominators within African-American women's quilts, music, and oral traditions was primary to understanding a continuum of traditional experience within the African-American community. What was also clear was the need to recognize these commonalities as historical and contemporary sites of representation of African-American women. A key methodological question asked and responded to, although not inclusively, within this chapter is, "What are the historical and cultural artifacts/evidences that have provided a foundation for contemporary communication patterns and practices of African-American women?"

It needs to be noted that a majority of the information referenced in this chapter pertains to southern black women and is largely the result of the antebellum South's purchasing of African slaves between 1650 and 1850 and the aftermath of the Civil War, specifically the development of African-American communities within the southeastern United States. While slaves were held in other parts of the United States, specific information on cultural communication practices—the field holler, story telling, and verbal gaming—among African-American women seems centered on the South.

African-American Women's Quilts

Quilts, simply stated, are both objects and a means of warmth and comfort. Whereas Euro-Americans generally make a distinction between art and craft and between display and use, African-American art is often a functional part of everyday life (Mainardi, 1982). African-American quilts possess a multiplicity of value even further in their illustrative significance of sociopolitical communication systems identified within a visual vocabulary of patterns chosen by the quilter herself.

While Kente textiles (cloth made in West Africa) are produced chiefly by the men, African-American women are the primary quilters within their community in the United States (Ferris, 1983). Part of this production was enforced during the antebellum period in the U.S. South by slave owners who demanded that their black female slaves create quilts for their homes. As a means of preserving their individual and collective identity as Africans, and now African-Americans, the slave women altered Euro-American quilts with features of West African textile arts, incorporating patterns that were not simply decorative but symbolic of ritual and initiation, birth and death (Wahlman & Scully, 1983).

The Euro-American quilter frequently signed her quilts by stitching her name and the date the piece was completed into the top corner of the quilt. The signature of an African-American slave woman, who under slavery was denied her birth name along with any other public expression of her individuality, was expressed through an assemblage of color and pattern encoded with ritual, ancestry, and individual creativity. The Euro-American quilt, therefore, was transformed by African-American slave women into a site of historical and autobiographical representation. Ironically, the Southern plantation owners slept beneath the slaves' testament of personal and familial identity, and as these quilts were passed down through generations of Euro-Americans, they carried the cultural artifacts of African-American ancestry into the future.[3]

Like Euro-American, African-American quilting is a threefold layering of materials: the quilt top with its pattern, a backing of under cloth, and padding between the two. The layers are sewn together with tight, even stitches, generally done by hand, although African-American women have been quilting on sewing machines since the mid-1800s; the sewing creates small pouches of padding. African-American women used miscellaneous scraps, old clothes, and discarded materials from which they cut pieces for the quilt top pattern. They unraveled burlap grain sacks for thread, rolling the strands into tight balls, and they used bits of cotton, which they collected while working the fields on the Southern plantations, for padding. Early African-American women had experience in working with cotton in West Africa where it is harvested and used for cloth. The backing for the quilt was made from boiled and bleached burlap or any large piece of material (old sheets or blankets) that was available to them.

There are two specific techniques used by African-American quilters in the design of the quilt top: piecing and appliqué. Wahlman (1983) has stated that these basic styles were also used by West Africans. West Africans for centuries used small portable looms to weave long narrow strips of cloth that were sewn together to make large pieces that were used as clothing or hung as banners. This piecing together of strips is perhaps the most common practice used by African-American women quilters. This continuum of variables between West Africans and African-Americans can be traced to the 200-year period between 1650 and 1850 when Africans were brought to the United States from areas that are now known as Senegal, Mali, Ivory Coast, Ghana, Republic of Benin, Nigeria, Cameroon, Zaire, and Angola and sold into slavery.

"Hitting Each Other":
Quilts and Jazz

African-American piecework quilts have been called the "visual equivalent of jazz" (Wahlman, 1983) and are frequently defined within musical terminology attributed to jazz. Such terms include *off-beat, arhythmic, polyrhythmic, cross-rhythmic, multimetric,* and *improvisational* as well as phrases like *hitting each other* and *disruption or suspension of flow.* In African-American quilts off-beat patterns are created when strips of contrasting bright colors are juxtaposed in asymmetrical patterns, causing the colors to clash visually, or hit each other.

According to Wahlman and Scully (1982, p. 89), "black quilters seem to master a pattern and then attempt to break it with an irregular choice of color combination. They feel free to improvise." Multiple rhythms in African-American quilts can be defined as the multiplication of off-beat patterns with the design, increasing the complexity of the pattern, and the aesthetic solutions needed to complete the quilt. These solutions can be found within the structural strips, which are generally the width of a hand, that serve as borders along the quilt's edge or in suspension or disruption of flow in the entire quilt. A disruption of flow occurs when patterns and colors are doubled and tripled, creating multiple accents within the entire quilt design, which are then resolved through the fading or fragmenting of one or more of the patterns. African-American women use phrases such as the "building of a quilt" and "playing the fabric" when discussing the act of quilt making (Robert Farris Thompson in Lippard 1991/1992, p. 10).

To recognize fully the value in the comparison between jazz and African-American quilting, a clarification of similarities is needed (Robert Farris Thompson in Lippard 1991/1992). First, it needs to be made clear that jazz is not a direct musical descendant of African music. Collier (1978, p. 6) explained that "many of the most important jazz pioneers were not members of the black subculture but were the half-caste black Creoles who came from a subculture that was more European than black." Jazz is a fusion of African-American spirituals, blues, and work songs and has evolved—like multiple rhythms in African-American quilts—into increasingly complex musical styles. Because of the flexibility of the pitch in jazz, "certain notes are invariably and deliberately played out of tune by European standards" (Collier, 1978, p. 6), momentarily suspending the musical flow. Hidden cross-rhythms, like the cross-stitch in sewing in which one thread crosses over another, are intrinsic to the collaborative interplay of music lines in jazz. Here, the influence of African music on jazz is easily identified. Weaving a pattern of notes that both harmonizes and clashes, hitting each other, African music lines run in and out, intersecting and overlapping. An additional parallel links the hidden cross-rhythms in African-American quilting to "shading the count" in jazz dance, repersenting alternative articulations of ancient traditions.

Barkley-Brown (1990, pp. 9-18) identifies "African-American quilting as a framework for conceptualizing and teaching African-American women's history." She affirms a nonlinear, polyrhythmic historiography of African-American women, which is apparent within their quilting and their educational practices. Barkley-Brown defines the dualistic opposition of center and margin indoctrinated in Euro-American, patriarchal academics as oppressive and disempowering to African-American women's history. Instead, she refers to Apetheker's (in Barkley-Brown, 1990, p. 10) "pivot(ing of) the center." As in the element of multiple rhythms in quilting and in jazz, here she refers to numerous centers: each participates in their own and all others, simultaneously reinforcing a noncompetitive relationship between individual and community. Jazz has been called by Penn (in Barkley-Brown, 1990, p. 14), a "true expression of democracy" because of the community relationship among the musicians. Collectively, they work in concert while simultaneously encouraging the solo talent. If we look at the African-American quilt as a community, with each piece functioning individually while simultaneously being part of the whole, we can see that the quilt, like jazz, is a democratic ensemble.

A popular style of African-American quilting uses appliqué, a technique of stitching patterned figures onto the quilt top design; these figures include fish, people, and houses. African-American women's appliqué quilting has been compared to various techniques used in Old Dahomey, by the Fon of Bennin and the Ewe, Fanti, and Ashanti of Ghana. Bible and slave stories, important events—political, personal, and in the case of Harriet Powers, celestial—and fictional tales have all been recorded in quilt narratives. The Smithsonian Institute and the Boston Museum of Fine Arts, in the United States, both, own a quilt by Harriet Powers, a Georgian sharecropper and ex-slave who sold quilts in about 1890. In each, Powers used appliqué to depict biblical scenes. In the quilt at the Boston Museum, Powers's biblical scenes are accompanied by patterns that illustrate meteorological events that occurred during and before her lifetime. A note pinned on her quilt when purchased (written by its first owner) recorded Powers's interpretations, who did not read or write standard English. Powers's quilts are visual testimonies, each carrying a message to those of her own era and of the generations following that speaks of community support, personal strength, and religious belief.

Quilting by African-American women was/is not always a singular occupation, both formal and informal social gatherings have been held for the participatory event called a quilting bee. Informally, one woman would bring her unfinished quilt to a friend for assistance in piecing her patterns together. African-American women sat (and continue to) around the stretched quilt, exchanging stories and struggles, rocking in the sewing motion while crying, laughing, or singing. Recognized African-American quilter Pecolia Warner recalls that when she was a child she accompanied her mother to the home of a friend, where she sat beneath the body of the quilt, which was pulled across a frame and hung from four ropes in the house, listening to the women talk and learning about women's ways. Soon she began pulling a needle through the patterned cloth of her own quilt, her mother checking the tightness and evenness of each of her stitches. If the stitches were not right, her mother pulled them out and Warner did them again (Ferris, 1983). Along with teaching her quilting, Warner's mother passed on to her various mannerisms and gestures through "vibration" learning, identified by Joseph and Lewis (1981) as a means of absorbing skills, mannerisms, and information without formal lessons or even conscious awareness of their transmission. These physical gestures collectively manifest themselves in the transmission and generation of identity, in this case, between mother and daughter.

Various African-American women's clubs have collectively produced quilts as a means of documenting specific historical events or of celebrating personal or community achievement. A contemporary example is the African-American Heritage Bicentennial Quilt made by the Commemorative Quilt Committee in 1976.[4] Each of the squares is a testimony to a specific individual within African-American history in the United States. The individuals represented include Martin Luther King, Jr., Harriet Tubman, and Frederick Douglass. African-American women, including the famous Powers, have also used quilting as a means of financial support when needed—which, in the case of most African-American women's lives, has been a constant. Recognizing that an African-American quilter can produce between 20 and 100 quilts a year, the Freedom Quilting Bee Cooperative, now operating in Rehobeth, Alabama, employs local quilters to create Euro-American-style pillows and quilts to be sold to the public (Williams College Museum of Art, 1991). The cooperative provides precut pieces for their specific designs, but when working their own quilts, the women quilters often alter the patterns, cutting and piecing them into a style that promotes their individualistic artistic judgments.

Femmage Art:
Quilts as Modes of Expression

The distinction between art/craft and display/use in regard to African-American quilts has been changing over the last 20 years. Ongoing debates over the distinctions drawn between art (high) and craft (low) as well as between abstraction and decoration within the art world have contributed to the change. In 1973, Schapiro and Meyer, contemporary feminist artists and critics, coined the term *femmage* as an alternative to the white male high term *art collage.* It defines centuries of hand work done by women—sewing, piecing, quilting, and so on—as their artistic mode of expression. Masters of art have always used costly, canonized materials in the creation of their artifacts. The folk art and crafts of women have frequently been constructed with cheap materials, remainders, or discards. Schapiro and Meyers dislodge this marginalization of quality, asserting that leftovers are essential to women's experience (Aubin, 1992).

Outlining what constitutes femmage, they describe an assortment of possibilities hinged on the primary factor that it be made by a woman. Options include the use of recycled materials, drawings, or handwriting sewn in; the incorporation of photographic or printed materials; and the inclusion of themes that are relevant to women's lives along with the possibility of the femmage serving as both utility and artifact. Recognizing the lives of African-American women as being in a constant state of denial by the governing mass, the concept of "leftovers," or "discards," seems to be indicative of their experiences on a multitude of levels.

Contemporary gallery exhibitions of African-American quilts have continued to stimulate discussion and historical and artistic appreciation. "Stitching Memories: African-American Story Quilts," a traveling exhibition organized by Williams College Museum of Art, distributed a flyer to patrons that distinguished six types of story quilts that were made with the technique of appliqué: (a) "Wrapping Home Around Me" quilts refer to someone's home; (b) "Articles of Faith" quilts, like Powers's, depict biblical stories; (c) "Histories" quilts tell stories of both United States and African-American history; (d) "Family Stories" quilts recall after-dinner family gatherings; (e) "Fabrications" quilts show fictional narratives written by the quilters; and (f) "Womanist" quilts tell the stories of personal achievement. Patterned quilts that have a uniform motif repeated across the surface of the quilt and that bear traditional names like Log Cabin, Basket of Flowers, and Wild Goose were also included.

A quilt of particular interest in the "Stitching Memories" exhibition was *The Dinner Party,* a story quilt by Faith Ringgold. Ringgold used a tie-dyed design that was inspired by Nigerian fabrics to border the quilt. Ringgold has been a powerful leader of African-Americans, affirming a rich African heritage while simultaneously promoting the strength of the African-American community within the United States. During the 1960s, Ringgold joined with other contemporary women artists like Betye Saar, Elizabeth Catlett, and May Stevens in defining within their work and activism a correlation between patriarchy, racism, and imperialism (Chadwick, 1990).

Saar, in her startling box piece *The Liberation of Aunt Jemina* (made in 1972), displayed the stereotypical image of the black mammie holding the white child along with the traditional, white, patriarchal phallic symbol of the gun, which was placed beside her. From 1969 into the early 1970s, protests began in the United States against the exclusionary institutions of the art world, which had themselves promoted freedom of expression for all as an international propaganda message after World War II. In 1969, Ringgold organized a highly effective protest against an exhibition attacking the policies of the United States on war, repression, and sexism at the School of Visual Arts in New York City, but it simultaneously promoted gender discrimination by not including a single woman artist in the show (Chadwick, 1990). She is also responsible for organizing Women Students and Artists for Black Liberation (WSABAL) and Where We At, an organization of African-American women artists.

After years of working as a painter, in the 1970s Ringgold changed media and began using fabrics to create soft sculptures, collages, and later, story quilts. Ringgold's story quilts, which incorporate paint, canvas, and cloth (femmages), are sites of convergence, where "storytelling, performance and visual art coalesce" (Koppman, 1991, p. 23). Ringgold's great-grandmother Betsy Bingham passed quilting on to her daughter and granddaughter after witnessing her own mother, Susie Shannon, a slave in antebellum Florida, make quilts (Ringgold, 1992). Ringgold, whose quilts give voice to personal growth and social and political concern as well as recognition to a history denied, first experienced quilting with her mother, Willi Posey, a dressmaker. In her story quilt *The French Collection,* she derails the formal lineage of modern art, dethroning the white male demigods of modernity. Ringgold rewrites the cast, stitching herself and the African-American community into sites previously ordained as those of the Great Masters (here too, Ringgold shifts language with the pun of the "Great Masters" of art and the "Master" who owned slaves). One panel depicts Van Gogh being asked to a sunflower quilting bee at Arles. In her *Woman to a Bridge* series, Ringgold identifies black women (and girls) as the "bearers of faith and celebration" (Brown, 1991). For Ringgold, bridges signify a crossing over and serve as a link between the present reality and the hope for future. She has extended this hope to future generations, translating her story quilt *Tar Beach,* which hangs in the Guggenheim Museum, into a children's book of the same name. In the book, the character Cassie Louise Lightfoot spends the summer on the tar-covered roof of her tenement house, imagining her willed flight over New York City, a folk-tale motif in African-American tradition, creating a bridge between her grounded reality and her envisioned future.

Quilts represent a living tradition that carries the voice of African-American women of the past, the present, and the future. There is a rhythm to sewing, the machine hums or the needle pushes in and out, and the quilter rocks back and forth as the patterns are pieced together and made part of the whole. Dindga McCannon, of Where We At, has been making quilted wall hangings on a sewing machine she calls Bessie Smith, after the famous singer known as the Empress of the Blues, for the past 26 years. In African-American poet Lucille Clifton's collection of poems—titled *Quilting* (1991)—the names of traditional quilt designs serve as section titles. The stanzas are filled with fragments of her own personal history in which a rhythm is established and then broken, as the form changes. Each one of these women: Ringgold, McCannon, and Clifton, use quilting, its physical construction or symbolic meaning, as a site of individual and/or collective representation just as their predecessors did before them. These women maintain the role as communicative subjects within the African-American community and within the United States.

> *My mother, religious-negro, proud of*
> *having waded through a storm, is very obviously,*
> *a sturdy Black bridge that I*
> *crossed over, on.*
>
> Rodgers (1969/1975, p. 11)

Folklore Narratives and Oral Histories
of African-American Women

The art of story telling and the significance of oral histories is intrinsic to both West African and African-American culture. History can be traced back to an event, whether in scrolls, textiles, oral histories, or textbooks. From epic myths to children's fairy tales, these stories are central to the belief systems as well as to behavioral responses of communities and of nations. The history of West Africa, of slavery in the southern United States, of personal struggle, and of the religious and moral beliefs of a people are preserved and maintained within folklore narratives and oral histories of African-American women. It is African-American women, like other Third World women—Latina, Native American, and Asian— who have "traditionally been the keepers of stories, the holders of history" (Lippard, 1991/1992).

The education of black slaves brought to the United States was prohibited by law. The illiterate slave was a less threatening slave. Contemporary African-American writer, activist, and Professor Angela Y. Davis (1990) states: "During the slave era Black people were victims of a conscious strategy of cultural genocide" (p. 201). Their lack of command of the English language was used by slave owners to create and reinforce negative stereotyping of African-Americans. A people who were already displaced outside their homelands and barred from access to the language of the country in which they were forced to reside were labeled uneducated, illiterate, and even uncivilized by a system that conflicted with their own historical communication and education patterns and practices.

African-Americans sustained culturally distinctive communication systems based on polyrhythmic, oral patterns within the hostile country, which regulated linear, literate patterns. A primary function in maintaining oral communication systems within the African-American community, both in past and in present, is its use as a coping strategy for survival: an individual or group adaptive behavior to ensure physical and mental health (Haskin & Butts, 1973). Due to prevailing laws within the U.S. South, however, African-American slaves were prohibited from accompanying this sound with drums or with loud horns in the continual attempt to silence an entire people.

Four of the cultural sounds of African-American heritage are the field holler, the work song, the ring shout, and the spiritual. The field holler was used by African-American slaves in Southern plantations fields while harvesting crops, usually cotton. When this holler, or call, was given by one slave among others, a reply collectively followed. This call sent a message of fellowship among the slaves and gave warning that an overlord or other white people were in the vicinity. The field holler was at times also used by a lone slave who did not receive a reply, at least not one heard by others (Collier, 1978). Antiphony, or call and response, has been maintained as the audience style of African-Americans, which is identical to the participatory audience style of African-Americans, which is identical to the participatory audience style of West Africans (Smith, 1974). Other elements of the field holler include indeterminate pitch and free rhythms, variables also found in African-American quilts and music.

Slaves were permitted to sing while working because most overlords believed that a singing slave was a contented worker. In actuality, African-American slaves sung while working because it simply made the work easier. It was the work song, based on West African chants and sung by black fieldworkers until the early part of the 20th century, which is most responsible for maintaining the musical traditions of West Africa within the United States, Taking on the rhythms of the actual work being done, the work song, like the flexible pitch in jazz, varied in function, style, and content (Collier, 1978). Later, the work song split into two musical lines: devout and temporal, or spiritual and blues. The blues tonality, based on a 10-note scale, is a product of the work song and is a primary feature of jazz (Wilson, 1958).

The ring shout was a form of dance used at social gatherings. Here, a group of singers and tired callers sang the body of the song while clapping their hands and knees, African-American audience participation referred to as "basing," and a lone dancer called out a shout. At times, the leader would break off or suspend his song, leaving the others to guess his words and the basers to begin or end as they pleased (Spellam, 1968). An example of basing—the alternative call and response between audience and caller/singer—was cited by Smith (1974, p. 96) as follows: "The lead singer calls, 'Oh, Mary!' . . . the basers will respond, 'Oh Mary, don't you weep,' the call, 'tell Martha' . . . response, 'Tell Martha not to moan.' "

Around the beginning of the 19th century, separate African-American churches began to spring up as a segregation between blacks and whites took hold of the South. Perhaps the most common form of singing within the African-American community is the spiritual. Spirituals are often sung in a call-and-response fashion like the ring shout: An individual may rise up from his or her church pew and call out a part of a spiritual, while others respond with short affirmations such as "Glory be to God" or "Praise Jesus, Jesus is Lord." Prayers for the Promised Land and other religious themes, though, have a twofold meaning. Meeting God in afterlife where "the milk and honey flows" is one element of the spiritual. But the Promised Land also symbolizes freedom hoped for during physical life on earth. "African-Americans used religious themes to symbolize their own concrete predicament and their worldly desire to be free" (Davis, 1990, p. 201). Singing along with each other in the field or on the battleground of the Civil War, the spiritual signified strength, hope, endurance, and love. Spirituals were also used in various labor and peace movements such as the labor movement of the 1930s and the civil rights movement during the 1960s in the United States; the words changed slightly to convey the participants' struggles and demands. The spiritual remains a powerful voice in the African-American community.

Identifying the written word as the "tangible medium" used in a "literate culture" and "the message itself [as] the medium in oral culture," Taylor (1976, p. 212) drew a distinction between the two cultures on the basis of the media used by each. Johnson-Reagon (1990, p. 206) extended this definition to include a use of the physical space by a storyteller or caller that goes "beyond content and data; it deals directly with the power to establish the tone and tenor of the environment." In the African-American community, the power is in Nommo, which is the giver of life to all things and which is evoked through the rhythm of the spoken word (Taylor, 1976). As with vibration learning, the experience of witnessing and partaking in an oral testimony is one of identity transmission and collective empowerment. The participatory event of repetitious recitation, the telling over and over (Lippard, 1991/1992) of historical, religious, and personal knowledge reinforces a continuity of experience. Whether in a church service or through the intimate whispers shared between a mother (aunt, sisters) and her children, "you know who you are before you remember that you don't know who you are. And you know that from the women" (Johnson-Reagon, 1990, p. 207).

Sojourner Truth (1797-1893), born into slavery in Hurley, New York, was labeled uneducated by Euro-American standards while simultaneously gaining national recognition as a great orator who "sustained the most essential values of her people" (Gilbert/Gubar, 1985, p. 252). Denied the right to marry her chosen partner by her master and after being publicly flogged into obedience, she married her owner's selected partner. She gave birth to 13 children and bore the pain of watching her master sell most of them into slavery. In 1827, when New York State outlawed slavery, she took a position doing domestic work and became involved in spiritual revivalism. Leaving behind her birth name of Isabella and renaming herself Sojourner Truth, she began traveling across the country testifying to abolitionist goals and a religious morality. In 1850, while giving speeches and singing the gospel throughout Ohio, Missouri, Indiana, and Kansas, she sold copies of an autobiographical account of her life, which was transcribed by Olive Gilbert (Gilbert & Gubar, 1985).

A speaker for the oppressed, reaching out to all, Truth's most famous line, spoken in 1851, is "Ain't I a Woman?" She declared these words at a women's rights convention in Akron, Ohio. Presiding chair Dana Gage introduced Truth to a jeering and restless crowd, overlooking the concerns of other white suffrage movement women leaders that a black woman would draw attention away from the issue of the vote to abolitionist concerns (Flexner, 1975). Truth's powerful cry for dignity and respect gained admiration and support from the moved audience. As public orator, Truth's personal testimony transcended the boundaries of racism and sexism, extending a decree of human rights and equality to people of all color. Later, Truth found increased resistance to her views as she drew out a more comprehensive plan to eliminate racism and establish African-Americans on a sociopolitical level equal to that of Euro-Americans and suggested a Negro state. Still, she used her role as an orator to bear witness to the African-American experience, articulating while claiming a continual advancement toward achievement.

The day Fanny Lou Hammer decided to register to vote she lost her job of 18 years and was thrown off the plantation on which she and her family had resided for decades. Born in Montgomery County, Mississippi, in 1917, Hammer, youngest of 20 children, began picking cotton when she was 6 years old. Too poor to buy shoes, her mother wrapped her feet in rags tied with bits of string (Johnson-Reagon, 1990). When Hammer was 12 years old, her mother was blinded in an accident and Hammer was forced to leave school, carrying with her basic reading and writing skills. Hearing a speech that called African-Americans to register to vote and gain the voting power to change their lives, Hammer began an unrelenting commitment to voter registration. She used her great oratory skills to outline a mission, a purpose that she believed could eventually "free her people" (Johnson-Reagon, 1990, p. 216).

She was arrested, beaten, shot at, and continually threatened; nevertheless, she overtly challenged discrimination, poverty, and injustice. Having initially failed the literacy exam for voter registration, Hammer persisted until she finally gained the legal right to vote. Her cause wasn't limited to one people or one color, "You know I work for the liberation of all people, because when I liberate myself I am liberating other people" (Johnson-Reagon, 1990, p. 212).

Hammer was a leader, an activist, a storyteller, and an orator. She served as a field secretary for the Student Nonviolent Coordinating Committee in the 1960s. Her work with the civil rights movement led to the passage of the Voting Rights Act of 1965. Along with the establishment of the Mississippi Freedom Democratic Party, Hammer founded the National

Women's Political Caucus and worked to establish the Freedom Farm Cooperative, which serves as a day-care and a garment cooperative.

Adapting to the demands of change within the Untied States, Robbie McCauley expressed the African-American storyteller tradition, so familiar to her youth in Georgia, through contemporary performance art and play writing. Focusing on her family history, McCauley (Champagne, 1990) validated the contributions of African-Americans to their country, the United States, believing the textbooks' accounts to be significantly lacking in the portrayal of these citizens. Resisting classification of "other" or "mythic" and coming from a position outside Western history's chronological lineage, McCauley utilized a hybrid narrative drawn from tradition and experience to articulate a thematic account of slavery, oppression, and denial. Having participated in experimental and black theater in New York City during the 1960s while working as a social worker, McCauley developed her skills as a playwright. In 1992, she received a Tony award for her play *Sally's Rape* (Champagne, 1990), which traces the abuse and domination of blacks by whites in the United States back to her great-great-grandmother and grandmother's children. In the performance piece *Teeneytown*, McCauley performs a segment called "Sharks," during which she wears a tuxedo and performs ballet movements:

> *There is a place in the mid-Atlantic*
> *where the sharks go, after all*
> *these years. They still remember the blood,*
> *where millions of us got pushed overboard*
> *midpassage, to rip us apart from ourselves.*
> *They make sure our culture is forgotten.*

> *[Reprinted by permission.*
> *© Theatre Communications Corporation.]*

Performance art has consistently been used by women as a site of political and personal representation. With its roots in art, not theater, performance art is an act of public dissent (Champagne, 1990). McCuley uses the space to release her rage and actively to challenge the authoritative discourses that have censored a people's voice.

Oral Testimonies, Verbal Gaming, and Rap

Many forms of African-American verbal gaming revolve around call-and-response insults (dissed—disrespected, insulted, and putdown), braggadocio, exaggeration, and at times, lying. Popularized in the 1970s by popular culture in the United States, although noted by African-American writer and folklorist Zora Neale Hurston in 1942, rap or hiphop, with musical background, is an extension of African-American verbal gaming, folklore, and oral testimony. It is a tradition of African culture to slide into song when speaking of something that is of great significance or passion (Collier, 1978). Essential to both African and African-American folklore and oral traditions is dealing with issues that are central to daily life. Recent rap music has confronted issues of social injustice, economic disempowerment, racism, sexism, and political nonrepresentation. It has been referred to as "black cable news," "citizen band radio," and "computer bulletin boards" (Cocks, 1991). A lot of rap music comes out of the ghettos or inner-city projects where creative alternatives were needed to substitute for costly instruments and technical equipment. Like African-American women working with scraps to create quilts, rap musicians often use old turntables as a site of musical experimentation and expression, "changing the passive act of playing records into the active creation of a song" (Parles, 1992, p. 24).

Contemporary male rap music has been repeatedly criticized for its degrading and sexually exploitive representation of women. White viewers have felt threatened by a young black man on a stage yelling into a microphone about Euro-American, patriarchal oppression, resulting in both censorship of lyrics and broadcast bans on musical networks and radio air waves, in the most extreme cases. In the summer of 1982, Grandmaster Flash and Furious Five produced "The Message," a sound bite of inner-city realities that opened a passageway for the protest music of the 1990s in the United States (Parles, 1992). Raptivists began using their calls and dissing as communicative tools for education, political representation, and collective empowerment of the African-American community.

Female rappers, not including perhaps Sista Souljah, have received a more hospitable acceptance by a mixed audience while maintaining a feminist agenda within their lyrics. The current most influential of these women is Queen Latifah, who recites a proclamation that declares no to racism and no to sexism. She is a member of Native Tongues, a coalition of Afrocentric rappers, and began her musical career singing in a Baptist church. In her song "Nuff of the Ruff Stuff," on the album *Nature of a Sista,* she raps: "Na fear a black planet. Na fear a black country. Belief one tribe, one God, one destiny" (Waltrous, 1991, p. 4). Queen Latifah, or Dana Owens, is an orator of the African-American tradition, rapping her calls like the lone dancer in the ring shout, with her band and audience basing. She recites a declaration of independence from position as Other, as something less than, liberating the audience from despair with her statement "Nuff positivity erases negativity." She is a spokeswoman for "a neglected constituency, young black woman" (Waltrous, 1991, p. 4). Other female rappers include Harmony and Yo Yo. Harmony's lyrics consistently evoke an image of the intelligent black woman who is respected by the community at large. Yo Yo has a style that is assertive and has a feminist perspective; her first solo album was titled *Make Way for the Motherlode*. She recently formed the Intelligent Black Women's Coalition.[5]

The worst racial riots in the history of the United States occurred in 1992, after jurors found California policemen innocent on charges of police brutality against African-American Rodney King. Post-riot interviews were laced with hip hop messages and hand signals of gang members. One Los Angeles rapper compared today's prisons with yesterday's plantations. Male rapper Ice T and his band Body Count had a controversial record in which lyrics suggested that police officers be killed; the record was boycotted by state officials, ironically increasing sales. At a Rainbow Coalition Conference organized by the Reverend Jesse Jackson, Democratic leader of the African-American community, white presidential candidate Bill Clinton harshly criticized the young black rapper Sista Souljah. She had been earlier quoted as saying blacks kill blacks everyday, why not take a week and kill white people. In the following weeks, she was on national news programs and the covers of popular magazines; her rap was quoted in the headlines. Its significance in relation to this chapter is in recognizing the maintenance of oral traditions within the public arena by African-American women, whether Queen Latifah, Sista Souljah, Robbie McCauley, or Laurie Carlos, Nommo is their power.

Oral Histories and African-American
Traditions

In February 1927, a young, inexperienced Zora Neale Hurston returned to her hometown of Eatonville, Florida—the first incorporated, self-governing, all-black town in the United States (Hurston's father served three terms as mayor)—to collect folklore.[6] This would be the first of many expeditions made by Hurston between 1927 and 1931. Financing was initially provided by a grant from the Association for the Study of Negro Life and History, established in 1915 at Columbia University, where she was a student. Later, she gained funding from a wealthy Euro-American patron, Mrs. Rufus Osgood Mason. Hurston collected significant data that would give academic and popular audiences insight into the highly complex structure of African-American traditional experiences. Using the participant-observer method of documentation, Hurston frequently in-volved herself in the events she was recording. She held lying contests, participated in voodoo ceremonies and joined in various dances and verbal gaming (Hemmenway, 1980). She collected oral testimonies from several members of the African-American community, including two who remembered living in Africa before being brought to the United States as slaves.

Still, Hurston had difficulties in recording her data, at times changing some of the words or the sentence structure stating "for I want to leave no loop- holes for the scientific crowds to rend and tear us." Her vast records reval a rich religious and cultural heritage of African-Americans (Hemmenway, 1980). Hurston's information on African-American folk-lore and religion was frequently published in scientific journals and influnced the literary world to recognize the metaphorical quality of African-American verbal discourse. Hurston herself has been referred to as the most accomplished folklorist of her time, creating her own folklore (Taylor, 1976). Hurston died in a welfare home, poverty striken after years of unemployment, her last job being that of a maid. Like Truth, she too lost support as her thinking grew more toward the welfare of African-Americans within the United States.

During the past few decades within the United States, several oral projects have been produced by community and academic organizations. Oral histories and testimonies differ from folklore in that they are personal accounts of an individual's life experiences compared with traditional cultural events and practices maintained by a community or an individual. They also greatly differ in relationship to scientific data in that oral history projects focus on the personal and the present rather than the clinical and data-projected future. Drawn to the foreground in Hurston's writing is the concept of the intrusive I. In African-American literary traditions and oral histories, the "narrator has the opportunity to be the heroine" (Hill, 1991, p. xiii). African-American women are the recorders of their own history. They document the evidence so as to eradicate the fallacies perpetrated by the history of the ruling class (Johnson-Reagon, 1990).

The Black Women's Oral History Project, started in 1976, used a diverse and individualistic approach to data collection among its large population of interviewees. Each of the 79 women recorded was at least 70 years old, some were in their 90s, and each had been involved on a volunteer basis in efforts to better the lives of African-Americans in the United States. The only other guideline was a wide distribution of interviewees in regard to location and economic status within the United States. The interviewers were primarily African-American women with a wide range of ages. Documents used included family letters, letters of correspondence, diaries, newspaper clippings, and photographs.

The Black Women's Oral History Project saw their interviewees as "living informants" whose stories and testimonies filled in "gaps and correct[ed] distortions and corruptions in written history" (Hill, 1991, p. xiii). The project acknowledged that the tape-recorded testimony would be created by both the interviewer and the interviewee, explaining that the biases of the interviewer toward her own interests would direct the line of questioning to some degree. The interviewees were asked to explore both their intellectual and emotional experiences of a given event. The project documented that stories of historical events varied from one interviewee to another, defining memory as fallible, inaccurate, irrational, having its own order, and protective; women did not want to examine closely old wounds (Hill, 1991).

Some of the experiences recorded included being raised by a grandmother who was 18 years old when Lincoln freed the slaves in 1863; experiencing racism and sexism while working in Texas for women's suffrage; recalling Marion Anderson, an African-American woman denied the use of Constitution Hall by the Daughters of the American Revolution; singing at an outdoor concert on the steps of the Lincoln Memorial in Washington, D.C., the capital of the United States; and watching representative Shirley Chisolm, an African-American woman, announce her candidacy for the president of the United States in 1972. The Black Women's Oral History Project revealed the struggle and endurance of an entire people who were able to accomplish enormous change within their own lives and the lives of those around them.

Conclusion

Bay (1974), an African-American professor at Emery College in Georgia, in a paper on the heart-shaped motif in African art, states that historians have perpetuated a myth of discontinuity, emphasizing diversity and variety rather than commonality. Reviewing the history of African-Americans in the United States, it is obvious that the concept of an active, participating African-American community that has been maintaining continuity in its traditions, culture, and communication systems is consistent in many of the artifacts and cultural/communication practices of the African-American community, and it is important to recognize African-American women as the practitioners of rituals for this cultural preservation (Smitherman, 1977). Through the identification of specific individuals, a history of African-Americans in the United States is documented and expressed through their experiences and testimonies.

Notes

1. Unfortunately, it is impossible to cite an inclusive history on this subject within the framework of this text. For instance, information about communication networks such as those used by African-American women (and men) operating the Underground Railroad for black slaves escaping to the North will not be included.

2. This chapter's use of the term *race* is best defined by Gilroy (1992): "Race must be retained as an analytical category not because it corresponds to any biological or epistemological absolutes, but because it refers investigation to the power that collective identities acquire by means of their roots in tradition."

3. Many examples of these quilts are now housed at the Old Slave Mart in Charleston, South Carolina.

4. See Williams College Museum of Art (1991), which is the activity guide for the traveling quilt exhibition.

5. Rap Packs are popular sets of rap cards that are sold in the United States like baseball cards and are collected. The cards give historical and biographical information on rap and rappers (Daze, 1991). Manufactured by Premier Cards, text written by C. Daze, 1991.

6. During the 1920s, anthropologists collected data on south-eastern African-American folklore: songs, customs, tales, superstitions, lies, jokes, and verbal gaming (Hemmenway, 1980). Unfortunately, Euro-American anthropologists overgeneralized and inaccurately summarized, incurring an academic blind spot about the belief systems of African-Americans. The ramifications of these misinterpretations were widespread in the maintaining of stereotypes that labeled African-Americans inferior to Euro-Americans.

5

Notes for Reflection:
Popular Women and Uses of Mass Media

SONIA MUÑOZ

The following discussion is a series of reflections and questions, rather than an identification of "safe routes," and it makes explicit the precariousness of our ways of understanding society and its actors and conflicts. This chapter points out what has been missed when thinking about the relationship between mass media and popular women in Colombia. I write and discuss this as a reasonable person, but with a certain perplexity. The excessive emphasis put by critical research traditions on explicitly ideological factors has disregarded the complex changes occurring in society and the ways mass media have related to those changes.

One cannot think of women and men as if their forms of communication were ruled by a unified and coherent worldview that could be understood rationally. I am sensitive to the idea of a social subject that is increasingly fragmented, multiple, and in permanent reconstitution. This idea of a complicated subject challenges our ways of thinking about society and our pretensions about research's exhaustive understanding of the actions of social actors. Perhaps for this reason I feel it necessary to rid ourselves of certain habits of thinking, which generally follow the logic of one discipline, and to attempt to point out a more difficult path, which is perhaps slow and precarious but surely more comprehensive. This chapter takes this challenge, looking at the relation between popular women and mass media from a multidisciplinary perspective. It first introduces the dimensions of my analysis, discussing the historical and local changes that have had an impact on the ways women use mass media. Second, it develops an analysis of the notion of subject and its various understandings from critical research traditions. Last, it looks at the ways popular women, as cultural subjects, use mass media. This reflection is based on ethnographic research carried out on women from the poor neighborhoods of the city of Cali, Colombia.

The Dimensions of Analysis

In considering some of the analytical avenues from the social sciences for studying the relationship between popular women and mass communication, I will suggest new directions for action and research. From the outset, I make explicit that this discussion is relatively new—it casts light on a problem that has traditionally been studied in Latin America almost exclusively from the analytical background and notion of alienation, privileging the messages of mass media for objects of analysis.[1]

Currently in Colombia, studies and research about popular women and mass communication from a different perspective are relatively scarce. My discomfort with this is not that the messages of mass media are privileged objects of analysis[2] but, rather, that this analysis has not taken into account the transformations occurring in society, the mass media and, consequently, in the relations between the mass media and women.

I will highlight the two major questions that were generally disregarded in the majority of studies that examined the connections between popular women and media before the mid-1970s.

Which Type of Society
Do the Research Questions Address?

Can we permit ourselves invariably to pose the same questions, as if there had been no change in the society in which diverse communication texts circulate and are consumed? As part of this analysis, is it not necessary to examine how these texts have themselves filtered societal change? Can we afford to overlook the profound transformations through which Colombia has gone in recent years, as if they had no impact on the relationship between mass media and women? Has the situation of women not changed or have the forms of subordination not been transformed? Do the conceptions women have of themselves continue without variation? Is the particular nature of their struggle unchanged? Are the relations between women and the media and the role the media play in the lives of women immutable?

Yes, subordination and inequality persist, but this commonsense affirmation will not enlighten us if we do not attempt to understand the ways women carry out the struggles and negotiations that permit their survival.

And here, we need to learn from Foucault's analysis of power, which he imagined in the forms of capillaries, as a net, rather than as lines of power from above. In the daily exercise of power, dissimilar and changing relations are woven; constant tensions that reveal explicit or surreptitious forms of response, challenge our resistance (Foucault, 1988). Outlined here are some of the key changes in Colombian society that have occurred since the 1950s:[3] the evolution from a predominantly rural country to an urban one; the explosive growth of the cities; the changes in the configuration of class structure and in the nature of social struggle; the diverse ways and degrees of integration with the urban world by individuals, groups, and classes; the modernizing role of schools among the popular urban sector; the appearance of multiple forms of solidarity and survival in the urban popular sectors; their relations with the state; the modification of traditional family structures and social roles; and the expansion of the mass media.

The consequences of these social, economic, cultural, and political transformations for the popular sectors and for popular women sketch a portrait of a conflicting, dynamic, and heterogeneous society.

1. The urban migration characteristic of the country between the 1950s and 1970s created a meeting point for the poor population, which came from different regions of the country and from strong agrarian backgrounds. The city became the scene of encounters between diverse regional and ethnic cultures (indigenous, black) with varying degrees of familiarity with the urban world.

2. These groups landed in many urban areas that were still in the complicated and slow process of becoming citylike. At the same time as the popular sectors learned provisional and precarious ways of being urban, they imprinted ways of being popular on the city. These circumstances made possible the development of an urban culture deeply rooted in cultural mixing, or *mestizaje*. The rural and the traditional became important components of the everyday life of the city.[4]

3. The 1970s are considered by many as a fundamental turning point in the development of Colombia's largest cities (Rueda, 1989). These cultures, that had only recently adapted to the urban world, also had to accommodate rapidly to such modernizing processes as productive work, modernization of the schools, the industrial culture, and the re-creation of popular culture.

Productive Work. Since the 1970s, the majority of Colombian cities have experienced an increase in informal work[5] and more variety in the kinds of work available. At the same time, there was a decisive entrance of women into the world of the market and an increase in the number of women working outside home. This new relationship with productive work contributed to the modification of the traditional family structures and to the configuration of new forms of family (predominantly the modern nuclear family) affecting traditional generational and sexual and socialization roles and the familial and cultural conditions for the transmission of popular culture.[6]

Modernization and the Schools. If adult members of families of rural origin saw education an ultimate good, the younger generations, who began to enter school at progressively earlier ages, saw education as the space for socialization. It also contributed to the formation of modern notions of citizenship, culture, politics, and history, and because of this, it simultaneously acted as the apparatus that systematically suppressed popular culture. Although the dissemination of this "other" modern rationality is not always successful, the lettered world, that of the school, tends to become the only legitimate way of knowing, putting into doubt traditional knowledge via oral transmission.

The Industrial Culture. As we know, industrial culture and its messages, especially those of radio and television, are becoming the cultural experience of the majority. Lifestyles, customs, fashions, and information are received daily through the media by the popular sectors; sectors that have few possibilities of access to alternative institutions of cultural diffusion.[7] Industrial culture contributes to the creation of a syncratic collective imaginative universe that mixes traditional and modern notions, scraps of disappeared worldviews, and popular memories that still resist. While industrial culture reinforces the heteronymous character of popular culture (a culture that is determined in part by an exterior force), it activates the existence of cultural matrices that allow its continuity. In his discussion about the ways the popular appeals to us from the mass, Martín-Barbero (1987a) points out ways to understand how the popular is identified in mass culture:

> How much of what constitutes part of the life of the popular classes and is rejected from the discourse of culture, education and politics, ends up as an expression of the mass culture of industrial culture? This kind of expression

may be deformed and recast as a functional support of the social system, but nevertheless, it is still capable of activating [popular] memory complicit with the imaginary universe of the masses. What activates this memory has nothing to do with content or even the codes. It is a question of cultural matrices. (p. 250)

Spaces of Re-Creation of Popular Culture. The effectiveness of the media cannot be studied without considering how work, new conditions of life, and the urban environment of fear (violence and security) tend to erode the spaces in which popular culture has traditionally been transmitted and re-created: in the street, neighborhood, and fiestas. Community life and strong social bonds are progressively displaced by the home, the privileged site of the reception of mass media. With this comes a modification of the character of stories (in which the language and imaginary constructs of the media are increasingly present), of the function of storytellers (who among us have always been the old and women), and of the spaces that permitted a kind of experience that ensured the transmission of tradition (Benjamin, 1991).

These ways of popular existence should lead us to suspect that the role of mass media, in its expression of the popular urban world with its actors and demands, has also been transformed. The mass media in Latin America contributed to the creation of the city and its culture; they have played a preponderant role in the transmission of ideas of modernity as well as in the continuing existence of anachronisms. At times, the media have had more sensitivity to the complexity of women's lives than some academic and institutional approaches. A complexity that recognizes women as subjects defined not only by biology but by their history, their social and cultural origin, their age, their work, and their ways of integrating with the city. The dominant academic analysis used by some feminist groups, nongovernment organizations, and government organizations has placed little attention on the selves and situation of women. Instead, they look at women as demographic categories or as components of the productive apparatus, as workers or as consumers.[8]

We can conclude then that the media have specific ways of articulating themselves in people's everyday lives, daily lives with different structures and rhythms among individuals, groups, genders, and classes. It is for this reason that research on how media shape daily life is needed: How do the media organize time, leisure, and work habits; how do they become means of expressing rage and passion; how do the media contribute to the expansion of orality and the perpetuation of silence (Muñoz, 1992b)?

It is time to examine the encounter between what the mass media propose—their ways of representing women and their surroundings and conflicts—and what in fact popular women perceive. And from this perception that can be emotional, distant, serious, or full of laughter, we should look at how women use media (Muñoz, 1992a). This last question relates particularly to popular women who have been the guardians of stories, customs, and popular practices. They are privileged owners of a memory unrecorded in books and are the most tenacious transmitters (as the focal point of the family) of popular culture. They are also among the most dynamic actors in popular organizations.[9]

If the active creation and capacity of popular women to make positive uses of media are not recognized in the area of symbolic exchange, how can we resolve some of the paradoxical conceptions held in Colombia about these women? On one hand, women are considered capable of creating new strategies of survival, of expressing solidarity, and of inventing effective and horizontal methods of struggles. But, curiously, on the other hand, these same women are not considered capable of defending themselves against the "harmful" seduction of the media.

How to Think About the Relations
Between the Reader and the Text

In this section, I look at the notions of text and reader to further explore the relations between media and women. The majority of the studies I review have a poor (for lack of a better term) conception of what constitutes a text. Literary studies propose a notion of the text that focuses on the relation between the reader and the text and helps redefine the perspectives of content analysis and even some of the purely semiological analyses of texts (Iser, 1989; Warning, 1989). I mention here some of the issues central to the reformulation of notions of the text.

1. Readings are plural. Interpretation is the process by which the expert or analyst uncovers what the text is "hiding." But this cultivated form is not necessarily the only or the best way of approaching a text. Because, as Iser (1989) said so well, interpretation does not explain the way that texts can incite the reader; "if the text possesses only those meanings obtained through interpretation nothing would be left for the reader. It would only be possible to accept it or reject it" (p. 133).

2. Meaning is constructed in the relation between the text and reader, in the process of reading. To know the possible meanings of a text one must study the particularities of that text (structures, genre, relations with

tradition, forms of reproduction and circulation, etc.) as well as how it is read and who its readers are.

3. Last, a key point: Any text, regardless of its process of production (industrial or artisanal) or of its form of consumption (cultivated or mass), takes form only when it is read. The text possesses a certain degree of indetermination, it is a type of "skeleton of schematized aspects that must be actualized or concretized by the reader" (Holub, 1984, p. 84).

This quality of the text, its indetermination, suggests to us that the reader is invited to participate through different kinds of play. In the reading there exists expressions of freedom that are not circumscribed or openly determined by the text. Texts can contain "empty spaces" as Iser would say, spaces that invite creative appropriation. Readings are, therefore, indeterminate, modifying themselves according to the time, the reader, and the value that both imprint on the text.

Looking at the Social Subjects

Perhaps one of the notions that has undergone the most profound transformation is that of the subject. Whatever perspective the researcher chooses to privilege, it is necessary to question the presence of the subject, who while leaving his or her footprints in the text (that is to say, who works the text) is also a subject with a certain propensity for change. In their patterns of consumption of certain media, in their taste, and in their readings of media, women manifest the force of their daily habitus.[10] Yet, simultaneously, they assume different positions in changing situations, dependent on the time and the vicissitudes imposed by their present condition and future plans.

In the following sections, I mention some of the changes affecting the notion of the social subject in studies of communication.[11]

The Subject of Necessity

Many of the studies that have been influenced by the North American school of uses and gratifications describe the relationship between the media and women as receiver guided by necessity. The subject is portrayed as needing affection and entertainment, as being guided by strong desires for evasion, and as receiving gratification through encounters with the media and their messages. Thanks to the influence of psychology, the subject is evaluated according to his or her individual background, highlighting some aspects such as class origin, age, sex, education, work, and membership in organized groups. A more or less direct relationship is suggested between the needs that originate from it and the satisfactions that the subject encounters in the media. Although this vision uses psychology to examine the motivations guiding the individual's consumption of media, in the end it is only necessity that is used to explain consumption.

The determinist psychology of these approaches neither addresses the complexities of the individual nor conceives of a subject constructed by the history of her time, the dynamics of the society she lives in, the requirements of her culture, or the freedoms permitted within that culture. Here is the paradox: If this perspective emphasizes subjectivity, it is almost always to censure its force. Feelings, affection, and passion are not seen as constitutive of socialization processes or viewed as the basis of a "critical" vision or attitude that could go contrary to what the media propose. On the contrary, the profound expression of being, which does not always arise from reason, is seen as a remnant, a weight that inhibits the will and thought or an obstacle blocking action and correct perception.

A powerful example of this is provided by the Argentinian group Mothers of the Plaza de Mayo who organized to march weekly to demand information about their sons and daughters who have disappeared. Their organizational process and public demonstration speak of their force for participation, struggle, and justice and for overcoming the fear that the feelings provoked in a mother whose son or daughter has been killed, lost, or disappeared. Less well known, but equally important, we must consider the role that feelings and affections play in women's life projects for an egalitarian society. We lose sight of these projects if we only see their value in terms of rationality—the efficiency of the productive work or their social cost-effectiveness.

Feelings, passions, and affections are, as we know, attributes that common sense grants to women. We should not forget that they have always been considered weaker than reason. But as Heller (1977) said so well, the thought of human beings existing without feelings is simply nonsense. This denies the feelings of humanity and neutralizes the force of feeling. As a consequence those media messages, such as the so-called sentimental or romantic narratives that are often seen, read, or listened to with pleasure by popular women are understood only as the vicarious substitutes for necessities not attended to by other sources in one's surroundings. Women are seen as subjects moved only by the weakness of feeling. I believe that the close and passionate relationship that women establish with some mass media television dramas or radio programs is related in part to the identification in these programs with an aspect of their subjectivity. It is the force of their feelings that is so often silenced or denied in other contexts.

The Subject of Action

The rich production of research from the critical period in Latin America originates from the framework inherited from dependency theory[12] and from those influenced by the Frankfurt school on industrial cultures. These two perspectives generated a critical view of society that denounced the social functioning of media, industrialization, and the homogenization of media cultural products. In both of these frameworks there is an implicit subject who receives the effects of what occurs from "above" in the sphere of production. The subject is dominated, alienated, passive, and defenseless against media power but has the potential to become a political subject, critical of media and of society.

This perspective views the subject as capable of articulating a critique of any one of the different spheres of public life in society. The importance given to the political produces two profound disjunctions: the public space (which produces material goods, class struggles, political parties, and artistic and scientific production that are marked as male activities) is split from the private space (which reproduces the family, women, domestic work, private leisure and are the "natural" space of appropriation of mass media). On the other hand, historical time is separated from the time of living[13] and its fragmented and diverse ways of existence. The intensities and discontinuities of living time empirically are forgotten and, consequently, so is the structuring of daily routine of individuals, groups, and classes.

Ultimately, then, this is a subject moved only by external forces such as the economic and political ones: fundamentally, those that should be fought in order to transform society. And, consequently, only certain groups of social actors are taken into account: working class, proletarian, peasants, and political activists. However, this view disregards how and by whom the political is built into everyday life, for example, in neighborhood organizations; in informal meetings of women, and in indigenous ways of transmission of knowledge, values, and traditions. Needless to say, this particularly affects popular women who, according to national statistics, are the most politically passive, although they are active participants in networks of neighborhood support, community work, and mobilization to solve community problems. Activities happen *despite* the intense relationship with mass media that these women have.

The Subject of Cultures

The awareness of the singular ways in which our cultures have become modern has shaped a stream of thought in Latin America that focuses on the study of communication from a cultural perspective. This stream of thought emerged in the 1980s and attempts to construct objects of study sensitive to the ways of living, reproducing, and communicating in our cultures.[14]

To approach the popular and feminine ways of symbolic appropriation and perception (Bourdieu, 1991) requires a consideration of the cultural origin of its members, their accumulated and transmitted memories, the cultural capital they possess, and the practices that activate their expression. These practices, from the most visible and typical (such as fiestas and religious rituals) to the most routinized in daily life (such as ways of domestic transmission of popular culture or the appropriation of mass media) reveal a subject in a continuous and ambiguous struggle.

From this new perspective emerges another view of the subject that has up to now been denied by political analysis, because its presence was visible in spaces alien to those interested only in public action. I refer here to regional and ethnic groups, popular women and youth, marginalized urban groups, and cultural producers outside of the commercial or enlightened circle.

Some of the studies from this perspective that explore the relation between the cultural industry and popular groups have pointed to the conflicting ways in which women experience modernity (Alfaro, 1988a, 1988b; García-Canclini 1989; Muñoz, 1990). Women are the keepers, transmitters, and re-creators of popular cultural traditions. Their conflicting ways of experiencing modernity are expressed in the way rural and urban women practice indigenous medicine while accepting the scientific logic of the official medicine. Another example is in the secular-modern position they assume in organizing savings and provisions: They use rational organizations of domestic economy while at the same time maintaining a magic-religious worldview (using herbs, viewing some natural phenomena as enchanted, not trusting explanations based on a cause-and-effect relationship). These women keep a very close relationship with mass media, using the information acquired there to activate their oral forms of transmission and to strengthen their solidarity networks. Ignoring the repulsion that high culture elites have of radio, commercial songs, or some television programs, women enjoy them and obtain a pleasure that seems to be reserved only for the elected spirit: a poetic pleasure.[15]

Social Uses of Mass Communication

Another of the notions that is as difficult to define as consumption is the social uses of communication. *Uses* can initially refer more to a conceptual category than to a descriptive notion of an empirical fact: the diverse ways in which groups, classes, generations, genders, ethnicities, and institutions socially use communication. In other words, *uses* refers to the ways media are integrated into the culture and daily lives of people, how they circulate and re-create the meaning of messages, and how at the same time cultures and subjects help themselves to what the media offers.[16]

It is worthwhile to keep in mind the key aspects of this notion: Like other material goods, symbolic ones are also used. The uses that groups and classes make of communication do not always fulfill a function or dysfunction, are not always guided by necessity, and cannot be determinable or quantifiable. It is helpful to remember that uses of media reveal paradoxical and ambiguous ways of expressing freedom: Subjects watching or reading messages and genres that deny or parody them adopt tactics ranging from perverse readings to laughter and ridicule to criticism and complete rejection.[17]

The environments, actors, and processes implied in the uses popular women make of the media are multiple and complex. I would like to attempt a synthesis, to suggest some theoretical and practical clues for research.

Specialized Culture and Everyday Culture

In speaking of social uses of communication by popular women, I am specifically referring to the dimension of everyday culture. Brunner (1987) described it as "this infinitely opaque and persistent intercommunication of highly routinized meanings that make up the small world of each individual and his or her daily world and its daily reproduction" (pp. 12-13). However, one cannot lose sight of the complex interactions that everyday culture weaves with the dimension of specialized culture. Specialized culture, according to Brunner (1987), "does not signify superior, high or elite culture; certainly, it includes that, but much more, comprising all the products and processes of generation of the so called mass or industrial culture" (pp. 12-13). Because of this, no perceptible changes in the use that individuals, genders, groups, or classes make of symbolic goods can be explained only by examining the transformations that occur in the dimension of everyday culture.

Spaces, Discourses, and Actors in Everyday Culture

It is important here to look at where, how, and by whom this infinite and dense network of exchanges of meaning is unraveled: What are the spaces that privilege these exchanges (the house, street, neighborhood, church, other public meeting sites, schools, etc.) and who are the most active actors in these exchanges of meaning? In the case of women, for example, what are the identities they display: mother, young woman, student, inhabitant of a popular neighborhood, or member of a party? How, through communication, do they articulate and mix public and private roles? How do they produce discourses and re-create world visions that intersect diverse worlds: the intimate (that of family, domestic economy, love, and sexuality), the transcendent (that of life, death, religion, and destiny), the industrial culture (that of television programs seen and fashion), and the political (local organization, responses to the state, and ideas about one's own identity)?

In an enquiry of this type, we must look at the ways women make new meaning of media messages and how these messages either activate or neutralize a mode of socialization that in popular sectors still defies the impersonality that modern rationality imprints on all spaces. Popular socialization is expressed in noninterested solidarity, in potlatch-like celebration, or in tactics that ridicule—for better or worse—the imperative of hard work and maximum production. This mode of socialization articulates the struggle of some to maintain and explain themselves, giving continuity to their culture and adaptation to the new requirements of the surroundings.

Routines and Times

How time is used by individuals, genders, groups, and classes can at first seem a question unrelated to our discussion. On the contrary, I think it is relevant because it helps us to understand how the daily life of women as subjects is structured: How much time do they dedicate to work and to leisure (sports, media exposure, products of erudite culture, etc.)? How is time distributed between the multiple functions of daily life (public and private spaces and their different dimensions of socialization); how are temporal habits of women lived, transformed, or reaffirmed in their relations with the media? And, most important, who fights and how for the appropriation of time? Among popular women, the struggle is constant: They fight to take time to watch *telenovelas*, to converse with neighbors, to attend a training course in the neighborhood, and to be alone to think about their things. These struggles reveal not only the misfortunes of material and cultural dispossession but also a tenacious desire to carry out a project, to change a life.

Cultural Competencies

Cultural competency is understood here as a system of knowledge that derives from different sources and is constantly being reconstituted. Cultural competency is this unconscious knowledge, not rationalized as such but that is continuously used in the execution of different practices of everyday life. In relation to media, this knowledge not only is present in the moment of consumption but also contributes to the configuration of the expectations that subjects have of the media. It becomes active even in the moments of waiting, in those empty spaces of which Iser (1989) spoke. Cultural competencies often integrate aspects of the so-called indigenous, or everyday, knowledge that is generally of oral transmission and carried out by women, with aspects related to the world of specialized knowledge. One of the sources of activation of these knowledges is, obviously, industrial culture. For example, urban popular women who in general have listened to radio *telenovelas* for many years and know how the genre functions activate this knowledge in the expectations that they hold of *telenovelas*.[18] Although cultural competencies unite a variety of knowledges, they distinguish between groups, genders, and classes by the type of knowledges integrated and by the way they are pieced together.

Ways of Seeing

The discussion here is illuminated by some of the findings of an exploratory case study that proposed to understand how adult women in a popular neighborhood (barrio) in the city of Cali perceive and use the television *telenovelas*. The women are older, with little schooling and are mainly rural immigrants. They have an average of 12 years of residency in the city. All of them are mothers and none of them works outside the home. Sporadically, they perform paid activities in their homes (washing clothes, selling food, etc.). They listen to radio in the morning and part of the afternoon seeking music, advice, and news. Television is watched with less frequency and is almost exclusively limited to *telenovelas*. (For a detailed description, see Muñoz, 1992a.)

There are three interrelated aspects at the base of the readings that these women make of the *telenovelas*: It is a reading mediated by a certain poetic sensibility (a particular kind of aesthetic enjoyment), by a way of conceiving time (live), and by a way of piecing together and articulating knowledge. These aspects model a sensibility among women that seems essentially anachronic; that is, it is expressed from a time and a logic that is not contemporary with those in the center of modernity.

Radio is the medium that has always accompanied the popular family and that has been present in all the stages of life of adult women. Women listened to radio before putting their hands on a newspaper, going to the cinema, or watching television. This long familiarity with the medium has constructed a competency, a taste, a way of listening, and expectations with respect to other media, especially television, the medium encountered in the city. Thanks to radio, rural women have contact with urban life, and when they arrive in the city, this makes possible a continued connection to their place of origin. In the barrio, women establish an even stronger relationship with the medium by communicating to radio stations by mail or telephone. If in the country radio attended to the desires of women through song requests, birthday or mother's day wishes, or more sporadically, messages or announcements of employment opportunities for *campesinos*, in the city, it constitutes the medium that will follow the life of the barrio from its beginnings. Women who are always limited to the space in the home or barrio learned through radio about the life of the city, constructing a particular way of understanding the urban world. Through radio, women understand that perhaps their city is the city of the poor, a perception put into doubt everyday by television.

In regard to *telenovelas*, it is important to emphasize that the first, and most intense, relationship of women with melodrama happened through radio in their daily listening of soap operas, dramatizations of adventures and terror, and romantic song. Popular women formed a competency and a knowledge of melodrama that became an effective bridge between radio and television soap operas. This knowledge was key for their first reading of the television soap opera, which they saw as more glamorous; that is, they saw it as a genre they recognized and as being enriched by visual images and movement. For the adult women, the *telenovela* is a genre with a history, whose relative permanence is a guarantee of recognition as well as being the fruition of melodrama as grand discourse. It is exemplified fiction: poetic fruition, testimony of life, an example to follow, a drama that comes—like life—to repeat itself.

Television, when popular women began to watch it, had no history for them and was the basis of a completely new experience. Situated for the first time in front of the screen, their naive eye could imbibe a fascination, which other groups with longer urban tradition did not enjoy, for the contemplation of an incessant flow of mobile images, produced in the house, coming from diverse and changing universes. It was perhaps a view from an abstract space that still had no television genre as a reference, with the exception of soap operas. It was a contemplation based on simple pleasure in the changing succession of images. Once they acquired the habit of watching images, women resituated themselves with their own classificatory system and temporal routines and were able to integrate the stories of television: advertisements, news, and soap operas.

Television, thanks to its audiovisual language, also signifies for women a return to a world of transmitted knowledge (preliterate) that does not need to be formally taught or learned. In the written or graphic text, the visual image functions as an aid, a continual and necessary referent in the development of the reading. Let us remember that the newspaper, the photonovella, and the illustrated novel were produced following the ways of seeing and reading of literate culture. The placement of visual images (drawings, photographs, boxes, verbal balloons, and headlines) and, obviously, of text is molded around the way our culture reads and writes: from left to right, top to bottom. With this logic, the story becomes intelligible.

Notwithstanding the above, women often invert or mix the order in which one "should" understand each one of the verbal or iconic components of these publications. They construct their own syntax based on the articulation of other texts and the call of extratextual elements: Women will often leave the page, question or discuss what they have read, and then return to the text, integrating this new information. At times they will supplement their lack of instruction by skipping paragraphs or phrases they do not understand and will fill the vacuum of their incomprehension by referring back to the memory that has molded other practices of message consumption.

Telenovelas, made in a "total language," continue to be deconstructed by women who call on other analogical-referential operations. An established knowledge of the genre permits them creatively and continuously to refer to other melodramatic texts. This implies a permanent activation and reconstitution of a competency: Women perceive and hope that the *telenovela* develops in a certain manner with a foreseen end. The competency gets put to work, synthesizing and expressing itself in attitudes, morals, feelings, personalities, actions, and conflicts that continuously mirror life. "I like *telenovelas* because of the problems one sees there. You see a lot of real life," women affirm. In this reading, the soap opera remains a fiction; the story is like life. Not being life but being able to refer to it is what permits recognition and pleasure.

This dramatization appeals to women and even today in television resembles the anachronic language of certain baroque literature or what is tacky in love songs. Those endings that are unbelievable for the cultured viewer are enjoyed in a kind of ambiguous halfway point between reality and fiction. The life of women, then, highlights, blends, and pacifies and, therefore, transforms the plot. And although it may seem contradictory, we can say that women derive examples, models of behavior (of a country, modern, regional, urban, or violent realm), and information that they may put into practice in their daily lives. It is legitimate information that can be reclaimed, even though it comes from fiction, from a *telenovela*. For women, truth or informative, practical value does not rest in the narrative form but in the degree of closeness that they feel it has to their lives. While they think it can be legitimately believed, used, or put into practice, it is strongly tied to sentiment and experience. This manner of conceiving information puts into question the truth of journalistic discourse, whose objectivity is constructed with a narration without a subject and is spoken in the third person, simulating a world that is totally understood and in order, composed of sections (front page or economic, international, and social sections). For women, the reading, the repetition of other texts in this reading, and the aesthetic pleasure are all intimately connected. It is the pleasure of seeing and re-seeing and reknowing—again and again—illusion, poetic illusion, that which has been lived and known. This is the pleasure of a vision of the world seen from continual return, the pleasure of foreseeing and guessing. This poetry is anchored in a worldview (premodern and mythic) ruled by destiny and the immutability of an order made from the repetition of cycles (for women, to be born, to grow up, have children, to die, of a poverty that remains unchanged) much like—a paradox?—the cyclical repetition of television and the *telenovela*. The pleasure of repetition is in the certain verification of the existence of immutability and permanence. Conservatism? Alienation? Or, rather, a resistance to recognize change? As women can testify, history has not modified the painful order of life.

Looking at *telenovelas* from another perspective, some are positive expressions of norms, of ways to be, and of utopias for women, representations of struggles for justice or for the achievement of values (equality, filial affection, and popular or gender identity). They relate struggles and generally have a woman protagonist who has the values, patience, and kindness to carry out a heroic project.

What can we conclude from all of this? Perhaps only two things: First, our cultures and their subjects are opaque and complex. Because of this, we must doubt the true efficiency of the concepts and methods employed to study them. Second, we must look into the gaps and margins in those spaces, where as we have been taught, we cannot find the great themes such as ideology, politics, culture, or history. Yet aren't these apparently small and innocuous spaces where women and men daily create and re-create culture, establish equilibrium, and respond to disorder?

Notes

1. Since the 1970s there has been a growing concern in Colombia to study the ways in which mass media represent women, in television, advertising, cartoons, radio soaps, and photonovelas. As Anzola and Cooper (1985) indicate, although these studies were undoubtedly of great value, they were strongly influenced by the then-dominant critical school that viewed the mass media as having an incontestable power of homogenization. Research carried out under this framework did not use tools of analysis that could allow for richer comprehension of the media texts, nor did it develop methodological innovations that could overcome content analysis.

2. An innovative perspective was developed by Chilean Sunkel (1985) in his research on the ways of representing the popular universe in various newspapers (mass and popular). Sunkel showed how, in the narrative forms employed by the mass popularized newspapers, there is a coexistence of symbolic-dramatic (i.e., the melodramatic) and rational-enlightened (i.e., the Western news format) matrices. This methodology is being applied in a research project with university students in Cali and Bogota that is looking at the ways of representing women and childhood in the information field.

3. These phenomena were clearly evident by the end of the 1950s in the Colombian national civil war between the two dominant parties, known as La Violencia.

4. Romero's (1979) study on Latin American cities and the development of ideas reveals the various ways in which the mob in these years transformed the cities.

5. In Latin America, the *informal sector* refers to productive work that is realized outside of the industrial sector. This work is in family and small-scale production, informally distributed through interpersonal and family relations.

6. In this chapter, I do not use the terms *popular sectors, popular women,* or *popular culture* to describe only a situation of economic deprivation or authentic cultural characteristics. I refer to a more complex and dynamic situation: to cultures that are the result of the unequal economic and cultural reproduction of society and to the unequal appropriation of economic and cultural goods by different classes and ethnic and social groups. The term *popular* refers as well to cultural appropriations, including the various ways in which diverse social groups satisfy their needs, organize their conditions of life, and interact. For this reason, "the popular cannot be defined by its origin or its traditions, but by its position of being constructed in front of the hegemonic" (García-Canclini, 1982, p. 9).

7. This idea is confirmed by research carried out in the city of Cali on the ways and types of access to cultural goods by different classes, genders, and generations (see Muñoz, 1992b).

8. It is relevant to ask how feminist groups, nongovernmental organizations, and government institutions in Colombia, which design plans of action and development for

popular women, conceive and attempt to resolve the situation of women by only taking into account their economic position or their subordinate position to men.

9. For a detailed analysis of women's leadership in popular organizations see, for example, Lobo (1984), Valdes (1988), Alfaro (1988b), and Jansen (1984).

10. Habitus, according to Bourdieu (1991), produces ways of perception and symbolic production.

11. A serious effort to understand the dynamics of subjects (what they like and how they live, struggle, and communicate) in the relation between media and reader, viewer, or receiver is fairly new. This analysis, however, can only have been made from a nonspecialized approach that overcomes the disciplinary boundaries imposed by dominant studies on mass media.

12. Dependency theory explains the presence of social inequalities as the product of international economic relations sustaining an imperialistic power, socioeconomic dependency, and unequal economic distribution. A basic stance of this theory is that underdevelopment is the opposite consequence of development. In Latin America, political scientists and researchers such as Quijano and Laclau applied these principles to stress how the entire history of Latin America, since the Conquest, has been part of a dependent process.

13. Historical time is a lineal, chronological time that explains social conflict by the methods and relations of production. Living time is that of daily life, of repetition and routine.

14. This stream of thought, concerned with the study of cultural phenomena, is neither a school nor a shared approach. However, in Latin America, it represents a new disciplinary specialization, at least in sociology (despite the fact that its practitioners come from the sociology, anthropology, philosophy, or communication). The articulation of this stream of thought is not provided by one theory but rather by a set of common elaborations that rejects the savage intellectual process of incorporation of foreign models and that, in practice, converges in a common terrain of intellectual operations (see Brunner, 1987).

15. This sensibility of women that encounters poetry in some of the mass media programs recalls the postmodern aesthetic.

16. Generally, studies made on the social uses of symbolic goods privilege a quantitative vision of the phenomena. This is a necessary approach, but it can account for only a limited aspect of the process of appropriation and use of media (that of the type of programs, preference, and hours of consumption).

17. In my own research, I found that older and younger women from Cali expressed their rejection of traditional politics by changing channels or turning the television off while political advertising was broadcast or during speeches made by the president.

18. The *telenovela* is an industrial narrative genre, articulating television's way of telling and the melodramatic vision of the world that is a long-standing popular tradition.

6

Understanding Women's Grassroots Experiences in Producing and Manipulating Media

MARIA PROTZ

The development of communication discourse, as Riaño pointed out in the Preface, has provided little critical analysis of how the complex variables of race, gender, culture, class, history, and power "intersect and shape women's communication experiences."

This chapter provides a theoretical starting point for analyzing these factors as they relate to women's grassroots experiences in producing and manipulating media. It does so by using Schutz's (1962) phenomenological theory of commonsense knowledge as a tool for first mapping out these variables and then naming the relationships among them. This framework can help us later understand some of the tensions that arise in the course of women's grassroots communication experiences. These tensions have to do with the challenges posed to women's concept of self and gender identity and with the challenges in family relationships and in relationships among women of different classes and races who are involved together in group development. At the core of all these tensions within the participatory communication experience, as will be shown, is the process of negotiating and renegotiating an appropriate balance between the experience and revelation of our unique selves and our common experience as women in the development process.

Commonsense Knowledge and Meaningful Communication

Schutz was an early-20th-century sociologist who developed a theoretical framework of how daily life experience shapes and constructs the knowledge used in human communication. According to Schutz, human communication is possible only because partners in communication take it for granted that a certain knowledge of the world is shared among them and understood as being common sense. Two main assumptions operate at this subconscious commonsense level:

1. The reciprocity of perspectives or the idealization of interchangeability of standpoints: I take it for granted and assume the other does the same that if we change places with each other, I shall be at the same distance from things, or experience them the same way, as does the other and, therefore, with the same relevance.
2. The idealization of the congruency of the system of relevances: I take it for granted and assume the other does the same that the differences in perspective originating from our unique situations are irrelevant for the purpose at hand (Schutz, 1962, pp. 11-12).

When both of these assumptions hold true, usually with others of our own culture, social class, and sex, and when the purpose of the communication effort is clearly identified by all parties involved, then meaningful communication is possible. Communication does not occur, or misunderstanding results, whenever one or the other assumptions is not actually valid but is still thought to be so by one or both parties.

There are several factors that may influence the validity of these two assumptions. I will thus examine these factors here as they are defined by Schutz, because they will later prove instrumental to understanding some of the dynamics underlying women's participatory communication experiences.

Commonsense Knowledge and Typifications

The reason that the commonsense world is taken for granted and understood as familiar to us, according to Schutz, is that our thoughts of it are largely constructed of "typifications," or simplifications of reality. As children, we experience daily life events and objects as "types": We learn general categories for persons, foods, and animals and begin to anticipate typical conformity of new objects and experiences with what we already know to be typical and usual. The process of typification, therefore, is actually quite complex and consists of ignoring what makes a particular object, experience, or person unique and instead categorizing it in the same class with other objects, experiences, or persons that share the same traits or qualities (Heeren, 1970). Thus the process of taking common sense for granted occurs in part because it is developed on a subconscious level.

The In-Group and the Social Distribution of Knowledge

The extent to which we can actually ignore uniqueness and can apply typifications, however, also varies, depending on a number of factors. The typifications we use in our daily life are socially constructed and distributed or rooted in the particular sociocultural milieu within which we live. Our typifications, therefore, include not only types for objects but also for rational behavior and the accepted mores of conduct as decided by the particular "in-group" to which we belong.

Schutz distinguished between two main social groupings: (a) existential groups, or those into which we are born, and (b) voluntary groups, or those to which we choose to belong. Members of a particular in-group share the same body of typifications as common sense, the same system of relevances, and learn to orient their behavior to coincide with the standards established by the in-group and understood as being "right," "rational," "good," and "common sense" (Schutz, 1962, p. 348). This shared common sense of the world allows us to anticipate or predict how others within our own in-group will act or behave.

The Unique Biographical Situation

Another factor that affects the degree to which typification is possible is our unique individual biographical experience. Despite the pervasiveness of the commonsense world and the role of typifications in determining behavior, the way in which these forms are translated by each person depends on the totality of experience a person builds up in the course of his or her own personal existence (Schutz, 1962). Thus the process of learning also involves the testing of typifications based on our own unique biographical experience. It is the accumulation, therefore, of tested typifications that determines our commonsense "stock of knowledge at hand" (Schutz, 1962, p. 9).

Pragmatic Interest

The final deciding factor that influences the extent to which stereotypes or typicality (common sense) can be applied is our pragmatic interest, or our purpose at hand. Types are always formed in relation to some interest of the moment, determined by our individual biography, and it is this immediate interest that defines our situation for us and that determines which traits of a new object, person, or experience will be equalized and hence to what extent individuality will be ignored (Heeren, 1970).

Thus in our daily life, we are content with what is ordinary and typical to us and, therefore, economize our time and energy on what is extraordinary and important to us at specific times. Schutz (1962) called this economical thought process of seeking out the unusual the "natural attitude of daily life" that is necessary for surviving in the "world of work" (pp. 208-209).

Cross-Cultural Communication

The complex interaction among commonsense typifications, biography, and pragmatic interest are more obvious when applied to studies of cross-cultural communication. Fuglesang (1982), a practitioner in the field of development communications, recounted several cultural differences in the commonsense construction of knowledge as exhibited in language forms. In different societies in which people's daily life work situation and pragmatic interest necessitate a different mode of production and survival, different thought constructs develop and so do different language and prescribed values or meaning for words. Here's an African example:

> Mama Muhambuwatu of Tongaland . . . knew the names of several hundred plants, roots and shrubs in the bush. It is significant that she knew the names of plants for which she had a use. Those for which she had no use, she had no name. . . . People develop the language they need for processing information about their reality in a thought-economic way. (Fuglesang, 1982, p. 36)

Human Relationships in Communication

The existence of a unique biographical situation belonging to each person implies that in human communication we can never fully grasp the individual uniqueness of the other. Commonsense knowledge, however, allows us to perceive the other as at least a "partial self" and gives us the chance to understand the other at least sufficiently well for our pragmatic interest of the moment (Schutz, 1962). For many purposes in daily life, it is not necessary to understand others in their entire uniqueness. For example, it is sufficient to know the person who delivers the mail as the "mail carrier." For these purposes we know people as types (and maybe even as stereotypes: doctors, police officers, store clerks, and so on).

For other purposes, however, we may require more precise understanding of the individual uniqueness of the other. Schutz (1962) called these people "consociates." They are more intimately involved with us because the purpose at hand requires this intimacy. Thus, while most of our knowledge of the world and of other people is typical, in one kind of relationship—the "face-to-face we-relation"—we more closely experience and come to know the uniqueness of the other. Using the analogy of a continuum, the closer and dearer relationships to us are those that are characterized as relationships of consociates instead of types and are closer to the face-to-face we-relationship at one end of the scale. Those relationships that mean less to us and in which we reveal less of our own uniqueness and perceive less uniqueness of the other are those that are more typified or stereotyped.

The assumption of the reciprocity of perspectives, therefore, often does not hold true when the differences in individual biographies are too pronounced for the purpose at hand, or when culture and class differences are too pronounced. In these instances, more explicit and conscious knowledge of the differences in common sense is necessary before meaningful communication is possible.

A venture into human communication, therefore, presupposes that a system of relevances is shared that is sufficiently homogeneous in structure, scope, and content for the practical purpose involved. Thus four main dynamics are at work in the process of meaningful human communication:

1. The personal biographical situation that acknowledges gender differences, personality differences, and unique life experiences of those who enter into a communication process.
2. The commonsense world and its typifications within our working world and within our own particular in-group (class, race, and culture).
3. The existence of multiple realities (other classes, races, and cultures).
4. Sufficient knowledge of one's own pragmatic interest and the purpose at hand as it relates to the other so the corresponding necessary relationship, of either types or consociates, is developed.

The Commonsense Difference Between Traditional and Participatory Communication Approaches in Development

The reality of commonsense differences is evident in many of the traditional attempts at cross-cultural communication in development. In many instances, the four key factors necessary for meaningful communication have not been properly recognized, and as a result, communication efforts have relied on relationships among "types" when, in fact, the purpose at hand has really necessitated a relationship of consociates.

The problem of the commonsense dynamic is particularly evident when one reviews early diffusionist efforts at development communication from a feminist perspective. While culture, class, and race are very real dimensions in the communication disjuncture, gender is another. In many instances, communication has been attempted while maintaining the assumption that there is a reciprocity of perspectives when it simply could not hold true because of relevances specifically related to gender.

Some particularly striking examples from agricultural extension show the neglect of women's indigenous knowledge by diffusionist approaches to development. In many instances, it is still male extension personnel and farming systems researchers who locate, interview, select trial cooperants, and target disseminators. A consequence of this staff imbalance is that women farmers are frequently overlooked because most male extension agents find it easier to deal with men than with women, and vice versa, wherever their particular sociocultural conditioning demands it. These gender differences, therefore, influence the results of development research:

> The researcher is concerned with the measurement of time, but the woman is concerned with the measurement of "readiness" and there is no reason why the measurement process should not begin with "readiness" (what does it look like? Is it hard or stiff or does it run?). . . . Researchers and extensionists alike are trained in the concepts of scientific agriculture and these concepts may have no equivalent in the knowledge system of the woman while the woman is trained in the concepts of her indigenous knowledge system and may have no way of knowing the significance of the concepts used by the researcher and extensionist. (Jiggins, 1988, p. 53)

The difference between traditional approaches to rural communications and a participatory communication methodology is that it does not assume a relationship of types or stereotypes (peasants, poor women, researchers, and so on) but of consociates in true we-relationship, wherein the commonsense relevances of each party are not taken for granted as being common sense but are instead uncovered through a problem-posing methodology and perceived in their uniqueness. Freire (1983) explained:

> That which had existed objectively but had not been perceived in its deeper implications (if indeed it was perceived at all) begins to "stand out," assuming the character of a problem and therefore of challenge. Thus people begin to single out elements from their background awareness and to reflect upon them. (p. 70)

Women's Experiences in Producing and Manipulating Participatory Media

Stage 1: Seeing Ourselves:
Experiencing a Unique Self

I now wish to explore in more detail the manifestation of these dynamics in women's grassroots experiences of producing and manipulating media. Specifically, I will look at

How the unique biographical situation presented through concepts of self and gender identity, as well as family relationships, are challenged in participatory communication processes.

How women create new in-groups and, therefore, a new common sense in their formation of grassroots communication organizations.

How competing goals are negotiated and renegotiated, thereby affecting the communication experience of women's organizations.

How fiction or tension along the lines of race and class may arise among women participants when there is a change in priorities and the assumption of reciprocity of perspectives is no longer possible.

To do so, I will draw on experiences from the Caribbean, Latin America, and Asia.

The power of the participatory communication process, especially in its first stages, is its potential to provoke an experience of deeper personal uniqueness among the participants. However, because the process really does involve a provocation whereby what was perceived as being typical is now seen in its uniqueness, tension is also experienced. In the instances in which a woman's self-concept and gender identity are challenged, the tension may be acute.

In one communication experience from Lima, Peru, a social researcher used participatory photography as a research tool for interviewing urban working-class women about the adjustments they "had made in order to survive within an underdeveloped, dependent, capitalist structure" (Bunster, 1977, p. 278). The researcher developed a photo album portraying many scenes from the daily life situation of similar women in another community. These photographs were used as codifications in the process of asking informants whether or not they felt the scenes accurately illustrated the everyday life of women workers like themselves or if other photographs should be added to capture their existence (Bunster, 1977).

Through the process of interviewing more than 200 women this way, patterned statements about the women's lives and their priorities were realized. Of the pictures shown, all the women identified the same one as their favorite: a scene portraying a working woman at home, sitting at the table with her husband and five daughters. The recurrent evaluation of the family scene by all of the informants was, "It is a beautiful photograph because the family is together." Most of the working mothers interviewed rarely have the chance or the time to enjoy being with their families and this photograph triggered this desire (Bunster, 1977).

Other photographs elicited responses indicating the women's aspirations, desires, and perceptions of their own realities. The most revealing photographs, however, for all the working-class women, were the ones illustrating the most significant events in a woman's reproductive life cycle: pregnancy, childbirth, and motherhood. Photographs portraying pregnant women generated the most detailed accounts of the way in which these women viewed themselves as women. In fact, a photograph of a woman factory worker breast feeding her baby was rated the most beautiful of all and stirred the women's hidden emotions.

The photo album technique also had a cathartic effect on the women in the sample. Through the interviewing process, women were often moved to tears and strong outbursts of emotion at the recognition of the significant experiences in their lives. The researcher repeatedly heard statements such as, "I have seen my life before my eyes and I cry for my sorrows and for the hard life of the working mothers like myself" (Bunster, 1977, p. 290). Through this process, the women's own unique and intimate experiences as mothers were affirmed.

It is interesting that many participatory communication experiences begin with this fundamental part of women's lives, because it is what is unique to us as women. Sistren's experience, for instance, began with the play *Bellywoman Bangarang* and was devoted to single working-class women's experiences of pregnancy. According to Ford-Smith (1986), the play

> exposed and confronted society with the autobiographies of four women. . . . It dealt with the way in which they had experienced motherhood and the experience of being girl children. It raised questions of rape, domestic violence and domestic work. It showed connections between these things and un-employment and urban poverty. (p. 124)

The potential that participatory communication offers either to affirm or to challenge the unique self-identity of women is also evident in a participatory video experience from Nepal. In this case, Worldview International

Foundation was involved in training rural women in the basics of video production skills and using video as a way of allowing the women to see themselves as the other women in the group viewed them:

> In the first video that the group produced, each woman spoke directly to the camera. . . . One of the producers, a woman with a harsh voice, was shocked to see herself sounding angry when she meant to be giving thanks. The woman softened her voice and her attitudes, and as a consequence, the whole group grew more cohesive. (Burkert, 1989b, p. 13)

Another experience from CENDIT in India shows how participatory communication may improve the self-confidence of individual women as well as bringing isolated women together around a common issue or concern. In the case of video, because it is perceived as a high-status medium, the communication tool itself may influence the level of confidence that is generated. The empowerment that comes from seeing oneself portrayed on this high-tech medium and manipulating video can have tremendous impact. CENDIT's experience revealed:

> At a very simple level, merely to see themselves on a video screen, in a laudatory manner was in itself a great incentive to the women who featured in the program . . . to know that their achievement and effort will be visually retold in their own words to others and that they may well be instrumental in helping people, gives the participating women a sense of self-confidence and achievement. Furthermore, even to make the effort to break away from their habitual self-effacement, to face the camera, to know that their men would also hear them, even if it be through a medium, was a satisfaction that added to self-confidence. (Ghosh, 1986, p. 35)

The Face-to-Face We-Relation
and the Family

Another reason why tension or friction is often experienced, particularly by women at the beginning of participatory communication experiences, is because in addition to challenging their own self-identity, the process also challenges the perceptions other family members and community members have of them. To understand why conflict and even violence sometimes result in this type of family crisis, it is necessary to examine how the face-to-face we-relationship is manifested in the family. This analysis will also help us later understand the tension that sometimes arises in the growth and development of women's grassroots organizations.

In the everyday working world that is necessary for survival, individuals use their stock of knowledge given by society, but in the family, individuals experience themselves constructing a social reality and generating their own stock of knowledge required to be a competent member of the family. As a private in-group, the family has its own knowledge and consistent logic of knowing and acting that applies only within the family. This family-owned common sense includes family rituals, family traditions, and family norms for behavior. These rituals may be compatible with, but may also contradict, the everyday world of work, creating tension (Blasi, da Silva, & Weigert, 1978).

In the ideal family, therefore, all members are involved in a face-to-face we-relationship of intimate consociates, who are mutually involved in constructing and maintaining the private family world of common sense (Blasi et al., 1978). Compared with the experience of self in the everyday working world, wherein actors experience themselves as typified by others, the family self is experienced as uniquely private, spontaneous, least typified, and "thus as uniquely authentic." The typified self that we present to the public in the everyday world is "counteracted" when we return to our family's private and unique arena of meaning. The family is the focus of our primary we-relations and the grounds for our self's outside identities (Blasi et al., 1978).

Thus the basic feature of the family is its uniqueness that is experienced by all family members. Because family members ideally have direct access to each other, the we-relationship experienced in family is characterized by a unique intimacy and intensity as well as unique mutual knowing. It is this experience of and preservation of uniqueness that creates the intimacy in family. And it is this intimacy that is eroded or challenged when family members typify each other or negate their respective individual uniqueness. Because of the potential to be typified within our own most intimate relationships of family, the family is also an inherently fragile arena, wherein all family members risk vulnerability (Blasi et al., 1978).

Some examples from participatory communication experiences show this negotiation and renegotiation of the family relationship and reveal the tension that commonly occurs when some family members insist on typifying others. In many women's experiences, conflict arises when the participatory communication experience challenges the typified way in which their menfolk often view them, their marriages, and their family relationships in general. When the participatory experience reveals the uniqueness of women, men who may have been relating to women as types rather than as unique individuals, are forced to reconcile this new revelation with their previous experience. The depth of these stereotypes is shown in men's concerns about a communication project with CENDIT in India, "They are like a herd of cattle. What do you want to do, going about asking them questions? They don't know anything" (Ghosh, 1986, p. 33). In another CENDIT participatory video experience with rural women, a fight actually broke out among the men, some of whom were angry that other men from the community had broken cultural taboos by allowing their wives to be videotaped. In other instances, men have been known to beat their wives and even to kill them.

Participatory video has sometimes been used to focus directly on the problem of power imbalances within the family household. Women who are often reluctant to confront their menfolk directly with their problems sometimes feel more comfortable doing so indirectly through the medium of videotape. This type of video experience provides witnesses to the women's testimony and has occasionally been helpful in improving family relationships by validating women's work and women's perspectives through the use of this high-status medium.

Stage II: Showing Ourselves:—
Tension Between the Unique and the Typical

> One way of becoming the creators of our own images—images which correspond to our true identity and not to a model of women which does not represent us—is to begin by defining ourselves from the inside. We cannot diminish the importance of women's image. An image is a means of knowing and we can use it as an instrument to help change ourselves. (Jelincic, 1986, p. 23)

While the first stage of the participatory process involves the revelation of things hidden and thus a reanalysis of the balance between what is unique to us as women and what is common or typical in our experience, the second stage of the participatory process usually involves women's production or manipulation of media in the way we wish to show ourselves to others. At this point, the goal or purpose at hand of the participatory process may change, and with it, the measure of uniqueness and typicality to be shown through the communication product may be renegotiated. This means that women may shift from presenting their concrete realities to expressing their ideal selves or the selves they aspire to become.

The following examples show how although the reality of women's hidden unique reality is exposed and affirmed through the initial step of a participatory experience, when other goals are identified, women may choose to present a more typified self. For instance, an experience from Peru involved women in the production of print materials through a participatory action research process with health workers. The aim of the effort was to paint pictures of a healthier lifestyle of people in urban marginal areas. The health workers spent weeks observing the health habits and lifestyles of 350 children and their parents. They then developed drawings portraying how the same community would look in an ideal world and invited 120 women from the area to critique the pictures when they were done.

Because women are the key agents of change in the family, their opinions were crucial. However, their general opinion in this case was that the pictures were not idealized enough. Over a period of several months, the women made the changes necessary for the pictures to be acceptable to their community:

> The women insisted that babies should be shown sleeping on soft beds with dazzling white sheets in rooms with elegant curtains. The mothers themselves opted for genteel dresses with spotless aprons. Their loose hair was tied back and their expressions softened. Toilets consisting of a hole in the ground, which is all any family has in the real Canto Grande, were upgraded to gleaming toilet bowls. (Robson, 1991, p. 10)

This enhanced vision suggests how different women's aspirations or ideal selves may be from their true reality. By using pictures showing an enhanced reality that most of the people in the community admired and identified with, the health workers hoped to inspire healthier habits among all the parents.

An example from St. Lucia shows how a production's purpose influences the balance between what is typified and what is expressed as unique. A total of 12 rural women were involved in a participatory photography experience to develop literacy materials for use in their own community. The women were trained in the basics of black-and-white photography, design, and layout techniques for developing simple print materials and subsequently chose to produce a literacy booklet on the work they did in their daily life. Photographs were taken of several activities: walking to the fields in the morning, doing agricultural work before breakfast, preparing the morning meal, getting children ready for school, washing clothes, and so on.

However, one of the key pictures that the group of women wanted to include was a photograph of one of the young women breast feeding her baby. She was also a member of the participatory group and, at the time, seemed to have no problem being photographed by the other members as she fed her child. However, when it was necessary to make the final selection of photographs to be included in the booklet, she removed the pictures, while no one was watching, that showed her breast feeding.

As the facilitator in this group, I concluded that this intimate portrayal of herself was something she did not want to have reduced or typified in her own community. Because the materials were meant to be used in the local adult literacy program, her intimate experience would have been typified by the very people with whom she lives and works, in fact the most significant and personal relationships in her life. Although the rest of the group had been pressuring her, she obviously felt these relationships would be threatened.

In the same St. Lucia community, a popular theater experience with youth revealed the importance of self-aspirations among young women. These young people's lives were characterized by low educational levels and limited economic opportunities. Formal education was over for most by the time they were 12 or 13, because limited spaces were available in secondary institutions. Virtually no local employment opportunities existed, nor did any organized youth activities. Not surprisingly, teenage pregnancy was a rampant problem. By the age of 17 or 18, most of these young people were parents with little hope of being able to provide for their new children.

In this case, the drama facilitator was a middle-class woman from a completely different island. She would come to the community dressed in silk crepe pant suits, with coiffed hair and lacquered fingernails. However, she was a Caribbean woman and thus a compelling role model for the young women. A self-composed, independent, and attractive person, she was able to command incredible respect and response from both the young women and young men in the group.

As an observer, I found this discounting of class quite interesting. Research in the community had shown that these same young women did not identify with any of the middle-class Caribbean women portrayed in professionally produced print materials dealing with the subject of teenage pregnancy (Protz, 1987). When asked who the message was for in these professional materials, the overwhelming response by these same young women was generally, "Not for anyone in this community, certainly not for me. Perhaps for ladies in the town or for ladies from another island, but they don't look anything like us, their hair is different and their clothes are different, too. This message is not for us" (Protz, 1987, p. 267). These young women were completely detached from the message presented in the professionally produced materials, which they experienced as talking *at* them.

Yet, apparently, these young women did aspire to the middle-class portrayal of being independent and well-educated, because they jumped at the chance to work with the drama facilitator. Through the entire theater experience, there was a distinct desire to be like her, and a personal relationship of consociates developed, which inspired a new self-identity among the young women. Interestingly, the play they created was also about teenage pregnancy and their own rural reality as unemployed youth, but through collective discussion, analysis, and reanalysis, they found a dramatic solution to some of their problems in becoming economically independent.

Tension Between the Unique and
the Typical in the Long Term

As in the family, in many ways the creation of a grassroots women's communication group involves the creation of a new, voluntary in-group. In participatory communication, members have experienced the face-to-face we-relationship of consociates and wish to continue this unique experience in a more formalized way. For women who have not experienced being part of a unique we-relationship in their own families, the bond formed through the development of a grassroots women's group may be particularly strong. Ford-Smith (1989) described how important this feeling of belonging has been to Sistren's members:

> According to the majority of the working-class founding members themselves, the major achievement of the organization in their view lies not in its impact on the position of women in Jamaican society as a whole, but rather in what the organization has been able to provide for its members. In the early days, the majority of the members of the group regarded our work as an exercise in self-help. (p. 32)

In the early stages of a participatory group's development, the purpose or aim of keeping the commonsense revelation, "jolt," or "ah-ha" experience fresh and sharing it with other women in the same situation becomes the dominant goal of the group. All members are committed to this goal at this stage in the group's evolutionary process. But over time, whether the group recognizes it consciously or not, this goal must be renegotiated as it comes in conflict with other competing interests.

This same process of renegotiation and repriorization of goals also occurs in the family. Each time goals are renegotiated, family members must also renegotiate a new reciprocity of perspectives on the matter and must determine whether or not unique individual biographical differences are going to interfere with this reciprocity. In this process, there is also a shift in the balance between their own experience of uniqueness and typicality. We see this in marriage, where, "as the honeymoon ends, as children grow older, as routinization wins out, family is lived in increasing typification. The defining of intentionality changes and family is constituted in a different manner" (Blasi et al., 1978, p. 290).

This same process also occurs in grassroots participatory organizations that try to achieve we-relationships, such as women's groups. As in marriage and family, the rules of behavior, norms, and purpose of the new in-group are created by the members themselves. Moreover, all the members within the organization assume that the differences in their biographical experiences (including race, class, and educational differences) are inconsequential to the purpose at hand or are at least not so pronounced as to hinder the achievement of their overall goal.

As the group develops and even gains recognition, however, these assumptions may prove invalid and the group's priorities may be harder to maintain. Some satisfaction within their new we-relations will have been achieved, and the members of the group may then begin to reconsider themselves as individuals and as distinct from the group. Unless conscious effort is made to keep the unique experience fresh, members' personal individual needs for growth and development become their primary interests and compete with the overall goals of the organization.

In Sistren's experience, as documented by Ford-Smith (1989), the commitment to a common goal was lost at one point, as the group struggled for funds and experienced extenuating outside social and political pressures. In the process, the group's practical priority was forced to shift from one of development through conscientization to one of group survival. But because the assumption was mistakenly made that all members viewed this new priority with the same relevance, in fact there was a great deal of dissension at a commonsense level with respect to goal priorization. The biographical differences among the members became pronounced, particularly along the lines of race and class. Ford-Smith (1989) described how overwhelming the tension became within the group at this point: "Our struggles with each other are often as real to us as those with our society" (p. 15).

According to Litwin (1984), all community development practices are eventually subject to the same dilemmas. In a participatory experience, groups pursue goals that often compete for priority:

> The first is the integrative goal, whereby groups use participatory media to improve group cohesiveness and integration.
>
> The second goal is the sociotherapeutic goal, whereby a media process is used as a consciousness-raising tool among similar groups.
>
> Finally, there are environmental change goals, whereby media are used by organizations to communicate with groups outside themselves (Litwin, 1984).

Community development implies that a mixing of goals must be expected and that the group must be aware that the goals are mixed. According to Litwin (1984), a failure to realize this "may doom the entire project" (p. 137). All communication efforts within a given situation need to be based on a clear concept of desired goals as well as a consensus (or as close as one can get to a general agreement) among the participants concerning goal primacy. In Schutzian terms, obtaining a consensus involves achieving both a reciprocity of perspectives and a shared agreement of the priority purpose at hand.

Ford-Smith (1989) wrote extensively about the dilemmas that have arisen in Sistren's experience when these competing goals were not recognized. She described the confusion over goals and goal priorization that occurred in an effort to keep a democratic structure to the organization:

> Related to the problem of organizational structure is a deep confusion about organizational priorities. For example, there is a lack of clarity about what kind and degree of emphasis should be given to the development of individual members as against the delivery of services to women. The present structure [of Sistren] does not allow the two goals to co-exist in one group. (p. 35)

The failure to recognize these competing goals and needs precipitated tension in the unique-typical dynamic along the lines of race and class. Sistren's experience was unique in this sense, because it specifically brought together, middle-class women (largely as resource people) and working-class women to work on a supposedly equal basis. . . . The working relationship between the middle-class and working-class women in Sistren was one of the most creative features of the group. It was also one of the most problematic. (p. 73)

Ford-Smith (1989) also explained that the real major difference had to do with education, but the educational differences were deflected along the lines of race and class. The educational qualifications of middle-class women were high, and they concentrated

> many of the skills needed by the collective to manage its affairs and to deliver a service which would be of a "high" enough standard to be taken seriously. . . . More importantly, their qualifications were recognized outside of the collective in the wider society. (p. 73)

The working-class women, on the other hand, were trying to upgrade basic education skills, but it was they who through the richness of their experience contributed the material and life knowledge that forms the foundation of Sistren's work. Ford-Smith (1989) explained that in the early days the collective achieved balance because the knowledge all members contributed was understood as having equal status. Over time, however, as the group struggled for economic independence,

> the way the members came to define "knowledge" shifted. The particular areas which working-class women had knowledge of no longer seemed to count as "skills" or knowledge. . . . A central ingredient of the early work got lost: the focus on working-class women reflecting a "hidden" aspect of working-class culture and communicating that to a broader audience. (p. 75)

As a result, over time, all of Sistren's members experienced a reduction in their own sense of uniqueness as it contributed to the common goal of group development and instead experienced an increasing sense of being typified by the other members. This mutual stereotyping resulted in the typifying not only of the working-class women involved but also of the middle-class resource people along race and class, as French (quoted in Ford-Smith 1989) testified,

> The failure to fully conceptualize the role, function and needs of the resource people, led to their skills being seen as something which was tied fixedly to

their class and colour, rather than as skills which could be acquired if studied in a conducive situation. (p. 76)

Many group experiences working with participatory video have paralleled Sistren's experience. In India, a number of groups using video have found that there is a tendency for a "video fetish" to develop, whereby one or two people or a small cadre of video people form to coordinate video productions for the entire group or organization (Protz, 1991). Because of the attraction to the high-tech medium and its perceived higher worth, a video fetish often develops so that the skills of the video facilitator come to be valued more highly than the skills of the other members, and issues of control then come to develop around the medium itself. Unless care is taken in each instance to reassess the appropriateness of video as a means for the groups's expression, the medium itself can become a stumbling block to group development (Protz, 1991).

A central concern of all participatory communication processes is what will take priority, the process or the communication product? Which takes precedence, and when, and how is the loss of one reconciled with the other? The product versus process dilemma is present in all community development initiatives, but when certain media such as video are involved, the strain may be magnified (Litwin, 1984) as will the extent to which underlying assumptions are or are not valid.

Conclusion

This chapter has offered a theoretical tool for naming some of the dynamics occurring through women's grassroots communication processes. We have tried to show how the combination of commonsense differences due to race, class, culture, gender, and experience with media, in conjunction with a lack of goal clarity or consensus about the purpose at hand, may contribute to miscommunication or to tension in group development.

Part of the intense frustration and confusion that is often felt when this type of shift occurs in our experience is because the real dynamic happens at the subconscious commonsense level, at the level of assumptions, and is, therefore, not recognized, except in hindsight, on reflection, and after much emotional tension has been generated. The tension is also the result of disappointment at the feeling of being typified within our closest and most meaningful relationships.

By using Schutz's theory of commonsense knowledge to name some of these relationships here and by showing how they may be experienced through some actual examples, it is hoped that their inevitable occurrence in women's grassroots communication experiences will be more easily recognized as such and will, therefore, be more easily modified or handled as they arise. Finding an appropriate balance between our experience of our unique selves, our common experience as women, and our common experience as human beings and renegotiating this balance through the pursuit of various development goals are the challenges that face us in development communication.

PART III

Women as Media Producers: Developing Media Competencies

A group of Mexican feminists commented that any expansion of women's consciousness seems to almost inevitably bring a "need to break the silence, an urgency to take over the microphones, the cameras, or the pens: indigenous women participating in local radios, the lesbians producing audiovisuals, the telephone operators, the urban popular women, and the domestic workers producing newsletters and publications of long tradition, the young creating comic magazines" (Otro modo de ser, 1991, p. 62). It is this connection between the desire to communicate and the decision to use media that we address in Part III.

This part looks at the skills, dynamics, and processes that are developed when women engage in participatory processes using communication media. We start with the argument presented in Part II regarding the cultural and communication resources that women bring to participatory communication activities. These are resources shaped at the level of everyday life in the execution of women's community, family, and individual tasks. Women's communication and cultural background necessarily affects their ways of communication and representation and the skills of the participants in media production.

Media have been used by women in a variety of frameworks (cooperative, community, and commercial) and formats (small format and mass media). According to the context, the goals, and methods of the initiative, different means of communication are chosen and different processes and results are promoted.[1] Our inquiry into participatory processes of media production in a group context is from various angles: from the individual and group dynamic generated in the process of production, from the competencies women acquire through media production, from the representations and images collectively produced, and from processes of meaning generation and reception.

The chapters in this part address key questions regarding the sociopolitical impact of individual and group communication practices and the potential of participatory media to provoke or have impact on social change. More specifically, we inquire about the potential of women's media productions to address key issues of class, race, and gender, to mobilize for action, and to have an impact on public opinion and policy making. In this regard, the part gives particular attention to the critical issues emerging from the evaluation of these processes.

Individual and Group Process

In this part the authors emphasize the capacity of participatory processes of media production to foster a range of individual and group explorations of issues of identity and representation. This potential of media to go beyond their function as instruments to inquiry into issues of social and political concern (demands, problems, and policies) or social consciousness constitutes an area explored by the authors of these chapters.

In the discussion presented in Part I on gender and communication, I argued that the excessive emphasis placed on issues of access and equity of representation has silenced a more central structural question regarding the absence of voice of subordinated groups in the media. Participatory practices of media production have placed this issue at the center, defining themselves as spaces for grassroots communication, for the building of representations that foster communication of the others (of women, ethnic immigrants, minorities, and homosexuals). These practices, therefore, challenge dominant representations and forms of communication. This association is explored in this part by first looking at what happens at the individual, group, and community levels when a process of media participation is developed.

In Chapter 8, Rodríguez explores the practices of video production with women in Latin America. Her analysis provides the starting point for identifying what happens at the individual level when women join together in a process of media production: Generally for the first time, women have the opportunity to look at themselves and others (through seeing themselves on the screen or through the viewfinder). The operation is one of taking a distance to look back at oneself, the surroundings, and the others. The process is also one of relocating the experience within themselves. In Chapter 7, Kawaja writes about video production with minority women in Canada and expresses how the production of a process video relocates the experience within the individual and group, allowing people to investigate their own reality. This idea can be followed in the analysis presented in Chapter 6 by Protz, regarding the power that participatory communication processes, especially in their first stages, have "to provoke an experience of deeper personal uniqueness among the participants."

Although they might have a diversity of social goals, experiences, and media literacy, individuals using media in a participatory format find themselves becoming part of a collective experience of deconstructing images and identities. This experience may challenge their self-concepts and self-definitions and, therefore, create, as Protz noted, a continuum of tensions and challenges.

This process of collective exploration and encounter has been named by Fugglesang and Chandler (1986) community or group "selfhood," the developing of a cultural identity and self-confidence and the identification of a collective selfhood that maintains participation. Ultimately then, practices of media production are relevant not only because of their introspective and inquiring potential at the individual level or because they constitute sites of creative exploration of identities and definitions of a collective self but also because they provide a site for social struggle and resistance. It is at this site that alternative images are created as well as the development of a communication proposal that addresses the group, the community, or the audience, through the identification of common goals (struggles, needs, entertainment, and pleasure).

At the individual level this process is part of a self-exploration and discovering of voice, of the valuation of the individual and her words. This discovery is analyzed by Mata (Chapter 11) as fundamental to empowering feminine experience as the territory of a new speech, the territory for renaming. In the group context, because of their characteristic of a collective project and their social change goals, participatory processes operate as bridges for the construction of collective histories (see Chapters 7 and 15). Highlighted here is the process whereby the production of a collective history implies the bringing together of a multiplicity of individual perspectives and experiences. It is a bringing together that, as Protz emphasized, requires a process of negotiation and, as Kawaja explains, the building of a common sense through difference and commonality.

The goals of transformation and social change motivate individuals and groups to engage in participatory uses of media rather than to rely on the traditional or mainstream media. Overall, the decision to engage in producing media of their own is a political decision that tends to privilege resistance over negotiation and the construction of the group's own messages and perspectives outside the constraints of the commercial format or of political censorship. However, many groups and organizations are successfully using commercial and mainstream media to explore a variety of formats and ways to impact larger audiences.

In the chapters of this book, we repeatedly read the outcomes of the participatory process at the individual and group level: women winning a voice; assuming ownership of their voices and representations (see Chapter 11); losing the fear to speak; discovering their potential as transmitters of knowledge (see Chapters 8 and 9); naming collective experiences and struggles; linking needs to action (see Chapter 10); recuperating dignity; constructing their present, past, and future (see Chapter 7); and creating spaces, texts, and images for encoding their history. In other words, results that impact and strengthen the self-expression, -recognition, and -esteem of women.

The mediation of the media technology and the acquired control of media language and its genres are fundamental in breaking the fear of speaking and deconstructing myths of women's silence, while making evident the outcomes at the individual and group levels. But it is important to keep in mind that these outcomes or achievements do not imply that women only acquire a voice or speech within the participatory process. We are not referring to a women's lack of voice, but to the absence of women's words in the public space and how through participatory practices a presence can be established. Mata concludes in her review of popular radio in Latin America that to be a woman in this field is still a difficult task. It requires the breaking of barriers that identify the public and the private as belonging to one or other gender. Once those barriers are broken, radio practice will fully recognize the feminine and masculine experiences and voices.

The potential of participatory media in this light is far reaching. However, Mata reminds us that this outcome of coming to voice does not necessarily imply the presence of feminine speech or women's words. Participatory experiences (whether popular or community based) have tended to emphasize speech that privileges rational and moderated forms of communication as the ways to address class, race, or gender issues, while they have denied other forms that privilege the affectionate or the intimate. This disregard contributes to the silencing of a feminine expressiveness and speech based on these elements.

Media Competency

Through the process of collectively producing a performance, a video, or a radio program, individuals enhance their dramatic and visual skills. When this production is made for the promotion of a social or community goal, dramatic and visual skills become tools that assist individuals and groups in expressing their needs, interests, and perceptions of reality. In India, the experience of the Centre for Development of Instructional Technology (CENDIT) shows that media production develops special skills for participants in identifying what they want to say and how they want to represent it visually. Process skills also develop, not as a simple, direct outcome of becoming media producers but because of the context and framework in which individuals engage. The dramatic, visual, or broadcasting skills developed become tools for inquiring into daily reality and for identifying and assessing needs. In this regard, media production is seen as potentially reaching beyond the immediate outcomes of reflecting realities to become tools for researching the community's needs, issues, and social contradictions (see Chapter 3). Participation in broadcasting, visualizing, dramatizing, and defining narrative contents are ways of discovering and developing participants' creative skills. Furthermore, this kind of participation sharpens their perception of specific issues (e.g., their understanding of the causes of specific problems) and the commonality of a problem with others like them. Associated with this is the development of skills for problem solving (see Chapter 13). To communicate effectively, the individual or group needs to internalize the message it wants to convey. Through dialogue, individuals validate data and establish their intended message, achieving a deeper understanding of the reality. Dialogue and collective production reinforce individual perceptions and analytical skills and enhance a process of developing a collective message (Deza, 1989).

The use of media in a participatory format also promotes the individual's critical engagement in message receptivity and the development of skills for sharing information. Nair and White (1987b) and White and Patel (1988) tested a model of participatory message development in the village of Sonori, India, and in Washington County, New York, and emphasized this point. Proposing video as an effective way of disseminating information at the grassroots level, they described the potential of participatory media as an instrument of change. The participation of the receiver in message development cultivates perception and enhances the individual's capacity to analyze and evaluate what he or she is dealing with. Video is seen as particularly suited to this. Its immediacy and flexibility allow the active involvement of the audience. By seeing themselves or because of the immediacy of seeing others like them, video acquires more credibility, and subjects develop the ability to look at themselves and others critically (Protz, 1991; Rodríguez, 1989; Stuart, 1989b).

Some of the chapters in this part describe how the process of becoming media producers necessarily involves the assuming of a critical view of mass media. Accompanying the process of acquiring media production skills is the process of developing the elements for a critical reading of the mass media, their messages, and their narrative forms. In this way, individuals develop a capacity for decodification and a critical eye to evaluate the narrative, audio, or visual forms; the content of the messages; and the potential uses of the technology.

The strength of participatory processes in demystifying technology is particularly significant for women, because technology operation has been identified as a male domain. By using the technology, women realize the simplicity of the technological operation. Once the technology is demystified, women's shyness in the production process disappears. Women then are able to explore their communicative potential and creativity. Alfaro (1988b) explained how a group of women producing radiosoaps in Peru evolved from a functionalistic and inhibited use of language to a polychromatic use of voices (tones and effects), improvisations, and total expressiveness. Furthermore, the stereotyped idea of women's lack of confidence to express their ideas in front of men and their silence disappeared: "It is in the process of learning to use communication media and in the action of communicating, that shame disappears and trust emerges" (Alfaro, 1988b, p. 28). However, as with any other technology, communication media are not neutral techniques. The machine itself responds to specific cultural codes, reinforces a particular language, and has specific connotations. The decision to use a particular technology has wider implications: The same content delivered orally might change if delivered in a written or electronic form.[2] In this regard, one of the chief risks involved in the introduction of a technology into a community or group is their possible "colonizer bias."

Representation, Validation, and Evaluation

A critical moment in media production is deciding how to represent themes, arguments, and characters. This dynamic involves the group or individuals looking at how they want to convey their messages and images to the others. Thus, for example, many Third World women writers have chosen the testimonial as their mode of representation and story building, as a way to represent people as the subjects of struggle. These narratives make possible the moving of the reader and the writer beyond the text to social action. This movement from the act of reading, writing, or telling to the possibility of action is what has been described as empowerment (Mishler, 1986).

Stories are a preferred motif of representation and dramatization as they document women's expressiveness, ways of communication, and their modes of resistance in their daily lives (Sistren & Ford-Smith, 1987). Writing, dramatizing, and performing represent ways to erase invisibility and to create identity through words, images, and voices. Mohanty (1991) noted that at the center of the writings of many women of Color and Third World women is a need for the construction of "a collective self and consciousness" which defies Western-based views of the individual subject as producer, artist, or writer.

The chapters in Part III pose a number of questions to the dominant modes of representation in participatory practices. Furthermore, they inquire about the ways these images are going to be received and consumed by others. Ruíz, in Chapter 9, discusses the training of native urban Aymara women in Bolivia and poses an urgent question about the distance that exists in most of the projects between the formation of a strong group of participants who produce radio and video and the audience, the people. She asks how the goal of social circulation of ideas and their impact can be measured and achieved in participatory processes.

There is a tendency in communication processes guided by objectives of social change to privilege representations that focus on images of women in struggle, as members of subordinate classes, as activists, or as housewives. However, representations in which women recognize themselves as *women* in all personal and collective dimensions or from which they can derive pleasure and entertainment are often not considered in these projects. This discussion is developed by Mata in her chapter on popular radio.

It is in this light that questions regarding the lack of evaluation mechanisms, the fragmentation of the universe of representations in participatory processes, and the lack of attention put on distribution and reception are posed by the chapters in this part. Kidd's (Chapter 10) exploration of 20 years of video practice in Canada poses a number of questions regarding the tendency to evaluate success by the numbers or by equating the democratization of expression with access to media. These questions link with those formulated in Part II in terms of how we might evaluate the contribution of these initiatives: What do we know about the nature of the transformations taking place (see Chapter 10)? What are their relations to changes in the public and private sphere (see Chapter 10)? What level of impact are we choosing to have (see Chapter 9)? Do we want control of a small audience or the power to influence a larger audience? Evaluation is further problematized by the mediation placed by dependence on external funding in most of these initiatives. Donor agencies, policy makers, and government institutions rely on using measures of cost-effectiveness in their evaluations. Because of this financial dependency, groups very often have to struggle to adapt to a preset evaluation agenda and to the funding priorities and methods (short-term projects, tangible outcomes, progressive linear evolution).

This review of participatory media production with women shows that there are no unique or settled ways to encourage participation, to measure success, and to affect the audiences. There are no success formulas. There are, however, some basic social and cultural conditions that seem to be fundamental. Protz (1991) stressed the importance of dealing with the multiple social barriers to using media languages and understanding communities as complex organizations of class, caste, gender, and competing interests. The identification of local needs and of influential local institutions helps to establish grassroots processes on a practical basis. The emphasis on the process rather than on its product addresses the importance of communication as part of a more general process of individual and collective emancipation and change. Dialogue and cooperation, respect and social accountability are the guiding principles for real democracy in grassroots participatory processes.

The first chapter in this part, by Kawaja, looks at the use of process video in Canada with groups of immigrant and refugee women and teenagers and with women growing up in families of alcoholics. Kawaja outlines a step-by-step approach to how each of these projects developed from inception to completion. She also discusses key issues regarding the participants as agents of change, their links with the community, and issues of ethnicity and identity. The next chapter is by Rodríguez, who reviews process video experiences in Latin America. She analyzes how video production at the grassroots level has generated a qualitative shift: Latin Americans have gone from being audiovisual *consumers* to audiovisual *producers.* This shift has many implications, stirring up a number of psychologi-cal, political, and existential processes. Ruíz (Chapter 9) looks at the work of a women's communication center in Bolivia in radio and video training and produc-tion with native urban Aymara women. She explains the potential uses of com-munication media as tools against women's discrimination, for the defense of women's rights, and as spaces to affect larger audiences. Ruíz addresses the tension (generally present in participatory processes) between the expectation and goals of the facilitators and those of the participating women. Kidd (Chapter 10) reviews the use of video in Canada as a means to express the perspectives of different social movements and, therefore, as a tool to provoke change. Kidd follows her own personal practices of video production, situating them in a national context, in particular in how women in the diaspora of North America have been reclaim-ing their memories, histories, and experiences. The last chapter in this part is by Mata, who looks at popular radio in Latin America, outlining the problems of building a feminine identity. The first section of the chapter provides a provoca-tive discussion about issues of language and particularly of women's speech. Mata stresses the potential of **popular** radio to create new identities but also notes the tendency to deny the entertainment and pleasure dimensions of the communica-tive relation.

Notes

1. Several possibilities exist in using audiovisual, dramatized, printed, and small-format media. Since the 1960s, radio has been the mass media used most for educational and developmental purposes. Radio's potential to suit rural audiences and to adapt easily to oral forms of transmission have made it a popular medium. Radio is used in a variety of forms: radio schools; noncommercial popular radio; popular programs in commercial radio stations; and new uses of radio means such as peasant and clandestine radio stations, loudspeakers, and cassette forum (see Burke, 1987; Kaplún, 1984; Mata, 1989, 1990; O'Connor, 1989). Video is at the moment inviting the interest of almost every institutional and organizational level in development programs and processes. In many parts of the Third World, video is used for community and development purposes, just as it is by community media groups in Western countries (see Belbase, 1988; Calvelo, 1989a, 1989b; Gómez, 1990; Jumani & Jumani, 1991, 1993; Ogan, 1989; Stuart, 1987, 1989a, 1989b; Tomaselli, 1989).

Among the performing arts, theater is most commonly used in development. The capacity of theater to involve audiences (dramatically, physically, and emotionally) is a powerful tool in encouraging critical skills and action. The special potential of theater lies in its continuity with oral and performative traditions and its combination of festival, leisure, celebration, and dreaming that make drama a powerful communicative and experiential means of communica-tion. Theater, it is argued, incorporates and understands the cultural process that leads up to a desire to celebrate, criticize, and reflect. Performance, furthermore, acts on the cultural history of the community while opening the audience's emotional and analytical senses (see "Communication Research Trends," 1988; Kidd, 1982, 1983; Kidd & Coletta, 1980).

2. Innis (1951, 1952) stressed how every machine has "ideas of its own." He traces through history the evolution of the various technologies and their radical impact on society—changing

habits and minds and creating new concepts of time, space (the written word), scale (the printing press), knowledge, and ways of organizing ideas (narratives, genres, abstract, direct, etc.). Communication media privileging the oral such as human speech have a time bias and favor "relative close communities, metaphysical speculation, and traditional authority" (Carey, 1989, p. 134). Media privileging the written word have a space bias. For example, space-binding technologies such as print and electricity "were connected with expansion and control over territory" (Carey, 1989, p. 134).

7

Process Video:
Self-Reference and Social Change

JENNIFER KAWAJA

It's 12 o'clock on St. Christopher, better known as St. Kitts, a former British colony in the Leeward Islands in the eastern Caribbean. At lunchtime everything is closed down. It's too hot. Besides, the news punctuates that part of the day, it tells us where we are. Or aren't.

The image of people with their heads pressed up against portable radios, or crouched down by stationary ones is marked in my memory. Where I grew up, we were taught to believe the things that were important happened somewhere else. There were, of course, cricket match scores and calypso king finals. But nothing else really. Except when the *Christina* sank and 250 people were killed. Dismembered bodies were floating around the channel because the sharks had a feast on the frenzied drowning people. I remember, because my grandmother just kept running from her store to the wharf with blankets to wrap up the dead bodies that had been brought to shore by local fishing boats. "We mek 'de news'," my grandmother said. We knew the foreigners would come to examine the remains, we were on the news. That's what made the event real, valid.

It wasn't long after the sinking of the *Christina* that a girl in my class asked me over to her house after school. It was a special occasion she said. When I arrived other friends were there. Their living room had been rearranged with all of the chairs facing in one direction. It was just 4 o'clock and Sally's mother was sitting down to watch *Another World* on their new television. They had a TV before when they lived in England. I think we were supposed to feel lucky that we had been invited to come and see what it was like. When the program began everyone stopped talking. It seemed an eternity until it ended. I think I was 10 then.

A few months later, another friend had a TV delivered. After *Another World,* the TV played *I Love Lucy* and then *Gunsmoke.* During and in between the programs there were advertisements for products we could only hope someone would bring back for us when they went away to America, or Canada, or England. Slowly, over the next several years other families got televisions, in general the order in which they arrived related to existing racial hierarchies—white, ethnic, black. The introduction of television further served to cement the effects of the educational system that, existing as it did within the social realities of a segregated colonial and postcolonial society, had already made it its business to deposit alien knowledge and information in us on a daily basis. As with many countries in the South today who continue to face the effects of imperialism, the production and dissemination of information about ourselves continued to be owned and controlled by those outside of our own communities and country.

As a member of the "middle category" of people in that society, television replaced the image of the colonial master. In this context "here" becomes transitory, because the goal is always to go somewhere real, somewhere important where you could buy the things that were advertised on TV. The role of all the media with which we came into contact, or should I say came into contact with us (print, television, film, and radio) contributed to locating the center outside of ourselves, our experiences, and our communities. Television complimented, in particular, the social and political construction of colonized desire—to be elsewhere, to be other (white), to be able to buy products only available in Britain or America.

The practice of participatory, or "process," video I am involved in attempts to name and deconstruct this desire and redress this balance between the viewer/consumer and the world in which he or she lives.[1] It tries to relocate the center of experience and power within individuals and their community by allowing people to investigate their own lives and then describe and (re)present this experience in a manner that is authentic to the context of production. My aim here is to raise a series of questions around the politics and possibilities offered by process video. In order to do this the process itself needs to be specified.

Each process video is an intimate, transient social relationship. Each project has its own set of historical and cultural circumstances and, therefore, outcomes. Each requires a new openness and flexibility in planning and facilitation, and each responds to my own investigation into myself and this medium in different ways. As the term implies, this type of production is part of a continuum that does not have an easily defined beginning, middle, and end. If there is a conclusion or resolution, it is fleeting and occurs in the intersection between individual life experiences and the life of the group and not in the final product: Meaning resides in the social and political context of each individual; the social and political reality that is created or constructed from their coming together; the individual's and the group's ongoing relationships with the final product; and finally, the relationship between the viewer, the material product, and the presenters/ participants.

The intention of process video projects is to create a site of struggle where there is, depending on the specifics of the project, a daily or weekly practice of defining one's own past, present, and future history. The influence of media in my own life, in the Caribbean and in Canada, has led me to investigate a practice that is motivated by the belief that traditional film and video production does not have a direct causal role in this type of struggle. No matter how progressive or challenging the content/form of a completed video or film—whether it is video art, experimental, educational, or commercial film and television—the process of production and distribution itself has been and continues to be embedded in a culture and politics of privilege and exclusion.

Mass media is a way of constructing reality and knowledge about the world in which we live. And like other institutions, the mass media has perpetuated the image that women lack the capacity to produce knowledge for their own problem solving. Most women still face economic, social, and cultural constraints that make it difficult if not impossible to communicate in the public sphere. Increasing access or representation of marginalized and excluded groups within the mainstream media does not challenge the cultural hegemonies but disguises them in favor of cosmetic pluralism. Ideas about representation and freedom of speech have perhaps obscured the essential structural questions of how power manifests itself in the way we are allowed or not allowed to take part in communicating about our lives and experiences to one another.

This reality, that a small group of people control communication in any society, is not particular to Eurocentric societies. Michaels proposed after living with the Warlpiri at Yuendumu in Northern Australia that information in that society is owned, inherited, and regulated in complex ways. From this perspective, cultures are viewed as systems of communication regulated through a social system (Ruby, 1990). His research challenges the idea that information ever flows freely in any direction, in any society, and suggests that it is always a select few who really hold power and that it is those who hold power who determine how and when communication will take place. Within this context, silencing does and can take place within communities; however, when this control and power is held by one selected group external to the group of people or community being silenced, its effects are quite different and often more critical to their survival.

Process video, in a Canadian context, attempts to resist the effects of this external control and mainstreaming by the communications hierarchy and its partner, corporate culture—effects that serve to oppress by denying the real-life experiences of women, the naming of their relative lack of power, and their experiences of racism, sexism, and so on by using the technology to discover similarities, differences, and relevance within *local* realities. As a proxis to reveal to its participants the marketed illusion of a mass culture that is founded on anything but the uniting of different constituencies in their desire for similar products. For a period of time during a process video the individual participant is no longer a single consumer on which a seemingly monolithic society can impress its agenda.

Primary influences on my own practice of process video in Canada are the popular education and popular theater movements of the South and particularly the resistance-based media efforts of many African and Latin American educators. Their work has been adapted for use in many contexts here in Canada, though mostly in the area of community-based theater and not in process video.

In the last decade, many countries in the South have been preoccupied with challenging the prevailing order of communications. In general, they are now working with video in three ways: the development of popularly produced video (process video), education for critical reception, and reclaiming the mainstream airwaves for more populist representations. To this end, they have adapted production and distribution methods that provide alternative visions for communication (Thede & Ambrosi, 1990). My process video practice draws on the work of these Southern partners as well as on the work of feminists theorists in North America who have problematized the relationships between artist and audience, identity and community, as well as traditional notions of authorship and the hidden assumptions behind the helping professions.

The Community Context

During the last six years, I have worked on a variety of community-based collaborative video projects some of which have been process videos. There are three examples used in this chapter. The Immigrant

Women's Video Workshop Presents: *Beneath the Mosaic* involved women discussing their lives in Canada as immigrant women, *Video Stories* involved immigrant and refugee teenagers telling stories about leaving their homes and coming to Canada, and most recently, *Through Our Eyes* brought together teenage girls who shared their experiences of growing up in homes where there was alcoholism and substance abuse.

There are various levels of consultation and participation involved in many film and video projects. I make a distinction between community-based collaborative productions and process video productions. Only those projects whose message, production, final editorial control and distribution rests with the participants is considered a process video project. Those projects that include the community and end users for research and feedback purposes but do not relinquish final decision making to the community are not identified as process videos but rather as projects that exist within the framework of traditional media practice. Naturally, the distinction is not clear-cut; there are many ways in which control and power are mediated, whether through funders, the individuals in a group, a community organization's agenda, or the facilitators/media producers themselves.

The point of initiation for a process video usually comes from a particular community. Although the original idea for *Beneath the Mosaic* was personal, a community-based immigrant service organization became involved in the project while we were still in the fund-raising phase. They, in turn, worked with us to reorganize and redefine the project. *Video Stories* and *Through Our Eyes* as well as other projects presently under discussion were initiated by the relevant community organizations.

A group or organization identifies programming or service needs within its constituency and tries to develop programs to meet those needs. The participatory paradigm creates a possibility for social workers, for example, not only to reach an underserved segment of people but to put them in a position where they define their own needs around programing, point out the existing inadequacies in the systems meant to serve them, and in turn, participate in creating messages that are more responsive to their communities needs. Most important, the participants practice the skills required to negotiate with the services and systems with which they come into contact and eventually increase their control over the distribution phase of their work.

Once a community-based organization commits itself to the process and acknowledgment for the funding is received (not an easy or quick phase in the development of this type of project), there is often already a strong sense of involvement and political empowerment. The community perceives that some action is being taken around a particular issue. The fact that the tool being used is video does not go without inference to its potential power. The process creates a new point of departure and becomes a visible milestone in the history of the community.[2]

A network of groups, organizations, and individuals are then contacted to assist in identifying participants who may be interested or who may find the project helpful. This process of identifying and selecting participants is a complex one. To begin, it is facilitated by the powerful lure of the media, which, significantly, is one of the first topics for the participants' investigation. In general, the reasons people may be hesitant to commit to the process may include fear of political reprisal, being worried that they will not be able to master the equipment, not wanting to talk about themselves, thinking they have nothing important to say, and worrying they will not get home in time to cook dinner for their families.

Challenges to the selection process lie also with organizations who may want to promote multiple agendas, for example, the learning of English-language skills in the *Video Stories* process. In the case of both *Beneath the Mosaic* and *Through Our Eyes,* the intention was to try to alleviate the barriers of isolation some women experience and help them make connections to other support groups for women.

In all cases, the process is seen to be risky and unmeasurable by social service workers using more traditional approaches to their work. During the development of *Beneath the Mosaic,* a community worker from a local immigrant service organization insisted that the process would fail because there were going to be women of different ethnic and racial origins in the same room together, "These people," he suggested, "will not get along." If I had agreed to change my mind and limit the group to women from only one cultural/racial group, he would support the project and assist in making sure that as many women as possible heard about the project and participated. This type of gatekeeping is typical of the reactions to the process both in the planning and the production stages. Two addictions counselors visiting during the *Through Our Eyes* process to give us a workshop were convinced that this group of young women were not being controlled enough by me and would consequently not accomplish the difficult task of completing a video production.

Further challenges are rooted in the degree to which the process is inextricably tied to institutional demands and traditional production structures. For instance, funders can apply certain restrictions that may have a

bearing on scheduling, for instance, thereby limiting the scope of participants or how much participants are remunerated for their involvement and
work. In *Beneath the Mosaic,* for which all participants were women with
children, the concerns and realities of women's lives were a basic consideration in the process from arranging on-location child care and coor-
dinated meal times to details relating to both the workshop and production
schedules.

In some cases, such as in *Through Our Eyes,* the timeline had been
established before contact with potential participants. In the cases of *Video
Stories* and *Beneath the Mosaic,* the participants who wanted to be involved
suggested the type of schedule and time span that would be best for them.
Once the participants are named they begin to talk to their friends and
families about the project and the communities involved often become
more interested in the project. In all three projects, several participants
brought friends to the second session who ended up staying in the
workshop.

Media Analysis

When the participants have made a commitment, the process proceeds
in a layered way, with media deconstruction, self-investigation, group building, media construction, and production taking place simultaneously. The
first part of the process is designed to encourage analysis of the media as
it pertains to the producing groups' particular realities. This work is done
through popular theater exercises that analyze actual programs watched
at home by the individuals in the group along with discussions about their
watching habits and the viewing of a selection of programs relating to the
common issue the group will be exploring.

In *Beneath the Mosaic,* the women discussed how they initially watched
TV as a way to learn more about Canadian culture and how they as parents
relate to their children differently. This led to discussions about the power
and contradictory influences of the images to exacerbate feelings of
inadequacy and difference while at the same time provide an accessible
source for information. In *Video Stories,* much of the exploration around
the media was expressed through popular theater exercises and through
individual drawings depicting the way TV made participants feel and think
about themselves. In an effort to subvert these messages, small group
collaborative drawings depicting a society in which the values portrayed

on TV were taken to their logical extremes were completed, presented, and discussed. In both projects, issues around race, representation, and class were central. In *Video Stories* some of these discussions about media found their way into the final tape.

In *Through Our Eyes,* a large wall was created on which, over a period of 4 weeks, participants pasted up images of women from the print media. Images directed specifically at women and those targeted toward wider audiences were used. Ongoing formal and informal discussions were held as the image bank grew and the women's view of themselves and the society that produces the images changed and developed. During the 4th week, a video artist from the community worked with the group for 2 days to reconstruct, reinterpret, and reclaim the images by making puppet videos with voice over, dialogue, narration, and music.

While the portrayal of women in the media was not directly addressed in the final video, the form that was chosen by the group, a fairy tale, was intended to subvert the notion of the perfect woman and the perfect family that is often presented on television and to explore the way in which women's real-life experiences are denied, invalidated, and homogenized.

Although the "media literacy" exercises are carried out differently in each context, in my experiences, there are similarities in the dynamics that occur among groups. The workshops often provide a forum for participants to express feelings of isolation and alienation from personal/collective histories. These feelings of alienation often serve as a commonality for the group—a shared experience of oppression: the experience of being made marginal.

At the same time there existed an illusory sense that each member knew the other precisely because the identity of otherness that seemed so familiar was one constructed in and through television. And the participants in the group knew television. In both groups the fallacy of sameness was exposed while the experience of otherness was at once validated and problematized.

Script Development

The next phase in the process is to develop a video that allows individuals in the group to reflect their major concerns, experiences, beliefs, or imperatives around a particular issue. This phase is accomplished through a variety of popular education methods. Brainstorming from words to building group stories and scenes, writing of poems, short stories, and plays are some methods. As well, an ongoing series of informal discussions by individuals as well as small- and large-group story telling take place. The script development phase for the final video production often grows organically out of this process. It uses and builds on scenes developed during this period.

It is important to note that each group brings together individuals across class, race and cultural boundaries who have at least one significant common experience. The process then uses this commonality to build a sense of community and collectivity that tries to unify without homogenizing. The goal is to acknowledge sameness while educating one another to differences. The divide and conquer politics of the mainstream is directly opposed to this type of heterogeneity. As such, the process tries to challenge social and political agendas that segregate and separate.

The process of developing a script builds on the earlier exploration of the media by acknowledging personal/collective history as a point of identification or, more specifically, as different points of identification for different individuals and groups of people. The emphasis here is on memory, on the importance of memory within the shared context of the group's reality. Through the process, histories are named, and another is created—the history of the group. It results in a combined history which is composed of a multiplicity of experiences and perspectives on different issues—immigration, racism, abuse and so on.

While all process videos set out with a primary focus, the process always becomes subject to a complex set of social forces. For example, in mixed groups where there might be white people involved, the facilitator must ensure that difference is not treated as a deviation from the norm, the norm being white as is reflected in mainstream media. Related to this problem in terms of process is inequality and silencing based on race and the fact that even in a supposedly egalitarian setting, racism is often "managed" (i.e., by white people) in an effort to exercise control. In other words, there are no neutral spaces, and the process does not try to pretend that the context of a process video provides that space.

If the group is mixed along gender lines, the degree to which women are denied access to communication within the context of the process also becomes a critical issue. The *Video Stories* process involved both men and women and dealt primarily with their experiences as refugees. Much commonality was discussed, yet its expression in this phase was initially dominated by the male participants. Naming this problem and changing the balance of expression became underlying preoccupations during our work together. This power imbalance manifested in our work with the equipment as well, and the group had to discuss and address this inequality directly. For example, during one period of training and production work, none of the men was permitted to use the equipment or "assist the women." In general, women are immediately comfortable with this process. The personal nature of the conversations that have to take place as part of the process to promote a nonhierarchical relationship, in which experts or heroes do not have a long life span and no one person has or can have all the information all of the time, appears to be more comfortable for women than for men. In all three projects, women reported feeling both stronger from the process of talking about their experiences and a high degree of comfort with conversation, which was aimed at making connections through the sharing of personal stories.

Production

The third layer of the process is to create a production that tries to go beyond the conventions of representation found in mainstream media production. Production training often shatters some hard-held myths about the media and reveals the fact that the invisibility of its form is the result of calculated manipulation by a series of professionals.

Production training takes place throughout the process based on the assumption that we learn best by doing, especially when the reason to learn is relevant and empowering. There is usually a movement back and forth between the personal to more generalized projects, but within this is a linear movement from short, simple productions to longer more complicated ones. The different kinds of struggles that each individual goes through in this process is acknowledged and discussed by the group on an ongoing basis.

This phase of project often challenges and balances notions of the supremacy of the individual over the collective as we move back and forth between individual, small-group, and large-group work. Production training takes place parallel to script writing and the intersecting discussion between these two layers of the process is often a contentious, difficult period during which the group is deciding whether they will make individual videos, one video together that is unified in its message and presentation, or one video using individual stories more or less tied together.

With *Video Stories,* the group decided to weave together individual stories to reveal their diverse experiences. At the same time, commonality was expressed by selecting single icons and stylized settings to use as backdrops for the individual stories. With *Beneath the Mosaic,* the women first discussed and agreed on the messages they felt were most important to convey. They then decided, as a group, which stories could be used or adapted to this end. As a group, their priority was first to speak to other immigrant women and second to speak to social service agencies about what they felt were the greatest frustrations they faced.

The women in *Through Our Eyes* decided that despite their different backgrounds and experiences they shared an overriding desire to portray the emotions that children of alcoholics go through by developing a short drama with a single narrative line presented through the eyes of one composite character. They wanted to avoid creating a production that would be seen as "representative" of any one class or racial group. It shows characters who are alcoholics, swear profusely, and who are sexually and physically abusive. Finally, the fairy tale in the end is presented as a dream. This attempt to subvert notions of the normal family, particularly those presented on television, provides fertile ground to continue the challenge to mainstream production conventions during discussions with their peers in distribution presentations.

Up until this point in the process, the facilitator experiences a constant struggle to find a balance between being directive and letting participants take initiative, between structuring and planning and letting things evolve spontaneously, and between authoritarianism and nondirective dialogical approaches. The challenge is to create a space to construct multiple perspectives that do not marginalize and fragment experience and that encourage different ways of seeing within the context of individual and collective empowerment. In this context, the ongoing task is to explore notions of the other as expressed in the retelling and discovery of our own stories and as expressed in the mainstream media—a key site in the production and constitution of otherness. Generally, at this point in the process I, as a facilitator, take on the role of a production consultant more than an overall facilitator of the group.

Voluntary teams are created to complete the preproduction work of scouting a location; gathering sets, props, and costumes as necessary; and casting. Participants have to go into the community at large to find and/or purchase what is needed for the production. The group has a budget for the production and has to organize how it will be spent. During the production phase of both *Video Stories* and *Beneath the Mosaic,* members said that finding what was needed for the productions was an important experience in that there was negotiation with the larger public of the city (having to speak English, being unfamiliar with the city, etc.) but there was, at the same time, the support of other members in the group.

In *Through Our Eyes,* the group members said that seeing scenes they had written, scenes they had experienced being acted out by someone else had the most significant impact in reflecting their experiences back to them. Because this production was a drama, there was the additional task of casting. A group of four participants was selected by the group to cast and each audition was taped. After watching all of the tapes the whole group voted on who should be cast.

In *Beneath the Mosaic* and *Video Stories,* all of the roles and responsibilities during production were done on a rotating basis, while the logging was done by everyone and the final editing completed by one team. In *Through Our Eyes,* a production team was chosen; everyone was responsible for one aspect of the production throughout shooting. In all stages of postproduction, there was a system of rotating pairs put into place to complete the production. In all three groups, these decisions were negotiated after lengthy discussions about what individual preferences were, how to balance opportunities, and so on.

Distribution

As social intervention, process video is biased toward reflexivity rather than toward direct political action or intervention. However, by taking control in the distribution phase as well, participants become active producers not only by creating images of themselves but by determining some of the overall political effects of their work.

In the distribution strategy for process video, women can become even more empowered to become communicative agents within their communities. "Women's communication talents and capabilities can be discovered and recovered by participatory methods. Participatory communication techniques provide ways to break women's self-marginalization from the public word; reinforce women's communicative functions in the private world and within the family, community, and workplace; and integrate women's forms of communication (emotive, personal, and familiar) in public communication" (Riaño, 1990, p. 41).

At the end of production, agreement is always reached within the group as to how the tape will be distributed and who will do it. The *Video Stories* group and the *Through Our Eyes* group agreed they wanted the tape distributed to schools and groups beyond their city. In both cases, text material was written to accompany the videos in a manner that situated the program within the context in which it was created. In the first case, the focus was discussed by the group but the text was written and designed with the group having no final editorial control. This was a condition of one of the funders and was made clear to the participants from the beginning. As an aside, the same funder was extremely displeased with the outcome of the video, describing it as too hardlined against racism (it was in fact extremely mild). The second group wrote, illustrated, and designed their own text and maintained final control.

With all three projects, members of the group continue to present the tape and lead discussions in schools and communities on an informal basis. The first two groups have continued these efforts through the work of individuals. The *Through Our Eyes* group has developed a more formal strategy for distribution. They initiate and respond to requests for screenings and accompany the tape in alternating groups of three to talk with their peers about childhood sexual abuse, substance abuse, and growing up as a child of alcoholic parents. Two years after the production of the video, the group still meets and is connected to the community health center that initiated the project. I am invited from time to time for discussion around certain issues that may arise through distribution, such as the one described below.

The follow-up support of the community organization has been instrumental in assisting the group in carrying out this distribution activity. For *Through Our Eyes,* money was raised and put aside so that presenters and discussion leaders could be paid an honorarium during the distribution phase as well. Because direct presentation by the initial project participants continued for 2 years when funding was no longer possible, groups requesting the presentation were asked to contribute a small donation to help cover costs.

Approximately 100 screenings have taken place to date and all the questions asked and responses to them at each screening have been documented. An evaluation is now being completed by the group related to their own experiences within the process and related to the evaluations they have received, both written and oral, from viewers.

As with each stage of a process video, distribution denies the notion of a mainstream person or mass audience. Instead it targets small groups with both similar and vastly differing realities. By concentrating on narrowcasting and target-specific presentations that address the needs of particular groups, process video distribution implies different unifying points of identification for each specific community of viewers.

In much the same way that video art becomes self-referential and the audiences become other video artists, process videos are often appreciated most by the peer groups of the video-producing group. Just as video artists gain entry into their own self-referential group, participatory video tapes gain credibility within specific audiences. This is not to say that groups outside of that specific audience cannot find meaning in the tapes as well. But one of the important aspects of these tapes is that they play a role in a process rather than standing on their own as "products." In this way they present a resistance to commodity culture. The end product in and of itself does not confer meaning, it is the end product in the context of reception—the process of viewing and the collective authority this engenders—which produces a dynamic source of communication.

In each project, my sociopolitical assumptions about the process and my knowledge about the medium in which I work are called into question and challenged. As a film/video producer, these projects permit continued investigation into the possibilities of breaking down the boundaries and barriers between subject and observer; eliminating the power and privilege of the observer (film/video maker); and collapsing the subject, producer, and viewer into an integrated continuum in a way that empowers people in their interactions with other people, the media, and other mainstream institutions. This provides a place to experience and investigate the complex relationship between context and form.

In the distribution phase of both *Video Stories* and *Through Our Eyes,* my role and responsibility was called into question. I was faced with two questions: How do I, as a facilitator, deal with issues around the creation of images that I find irresponsible in a context in which I relinquish final control? How can a process, a seemingly politically conscious one, guarantee the creation of images that are not stereotypical, racist, sexist, classist, and so on?

For example, in *Video Stories* one of the funders as well as a teacher in British Columbia, Canada, argued that I had been irresponsible in allowing the group to portray the countries they had fled as dangerous places to live. The argument was that it supported the already held belief that countries in the South were governed by right-wing dictators. Although I did not agree that the group should not have been allowed to represent their experiences the way they felt was best, it raised a number of concerns about my role in the process.

During the distribution of *Through Our Eyes,* the group was invited to present the tape to various community groups and their constituencies in a nearby city. The tape was then sent to other community groups to determine whether they were interested in hosting a similar event while the group was in their city. One organization felt the video was racist. The only person of Color in the tape was a friend of the main character, who played a doll and a real person intermittently. At the end of the video, she was symbolically killed by the real character. This relationship had been developed by the group to reveal a part of the psychology of children of alcoholics and the way in which both anger and love can be displaced on people with whom they had the most positive meaningful relationships.

Although numerous discussions had taken place around issues of race and representation, and we had color blind casting calls, this did not prevent the tape from being racist. A positive result of this concern being raised, however, was that it continued discussion around the issue of race and representation, one that led to the further politicization of white women and women of Color in the group. There was a decision to do some more work around these issues.

The production of this tape and the ensuing exchanges have caused me to reflect on my position in relation to this work in a different way than I had previously done. How can/should I stop the production of a tape which I know is problematic without betraying the process? How am I responsible for and "present in" this work? And related to that, in what ways does the work belong to me as a producer/facilitator and as a participant? And finally, can those contradictory positions be reconciled?

The final issue facing the facilitator, regardless of the amount of power she has relinquished during the process, is the reintegration of herself and group members into the community. With the *Beneath the Mosaic* and *Video Stories* groups, the transition was smooth, particularly with the women involved in *Beneath the Mosaic* because the process was part-time and because many of them continued to see one another through the multicultural women's center that had provided us with our work space during the project. However, this transition was extremely difficult in *Through Our Eyes.* Even though the women cited many similar qualitative outcomes such as a stronger sense of identity, greater self-reliance, and so on, the group was left with a sense of confusion concerning their next step. This may have been a result of the fact that all the group members decided that they wanted to continue working together but were faced with the decision of what they would do together, whether they would just form a support group or whether they would try to plan another project together. If this is something the group desires, it becomes crucial that the supporting community organization plan for this transition from the beginning of the project, especially when teenagers are involved. In sum, within the realm of a mainstream image production, the deconstruction and location of the center, the subsequent self-investigation, reconstruction, and, finally, creation of images becomes an important social and political act. The final video may be of broadcast quality, but it is not important to receive recognition by the mainstream, nor does the final product need to be integrated into the structures of mainstream communication. The intent is to provide new narrative threads that will weave themselves throughout and underneath the dominant narratives being presented by systems and structures presently in place. With this comes the challenge to accepted relations of communication.

If the feedback to date is in any way accurate, the process helps women remember and realize that they have the capacity and not just the right to express themselves in personal, artistic, social, and political realms. Marginalization often negates this capacity. As Stuart (1989) suggested, the power of this type of videotape rests with its capacity to extend people's responsibility over their own lives by giving them direct access to the experiences of others like themselves.[3] This in turn can facilitate political mobilization.

It would, at best, be suspicious if I did not return to the introduction of this chapter and acknowledge that, in many ways, my practice and investigation into the nature and function of process video relates to my own desire to reclaim and use the technology to name certain realities and to examine my own questions about the constitution of the other as it is represented and reflected both in mainstream media and in the process of uncovering or accessing my own history.

From this perspective, the writing of a chapter such as this one is problematic on a number of levels. It can be likened to someone writing a review of her own film or video and describing its meaning or giving an interpretation to the work. In many ways, my description of the process, its goals, and its potential results probably has more to do with what ideally should take place and with what I experience than with what transpires for the other players involved from the inception to distribution of one of these projects. As the questions about my participation highlighted above indicate, reflection of the way in which I facilitate and participate in this process needs to be analyzed at this point.

There are a variety of other important questions raised in practicing this process that I have barely touched on or points that I have not argued substantively for or against, such as the following:

- What is the potential and the limits of process video in the process of social change?
- Does it act as a catharsis in the community and prevent action toward more lasting social change?
- What are the contradictions in using a media that is inherently centralizing to explore concepts of locality?
- What, if any, is the impact of process video on the institutions of mainstream media?
- Are alternative production experiences transferable from one context to another?
- What are the problems and ironies inherent in using a mainstream technology to empower and validate people's experiences and realities on the margins?
- How do you measure intervention, because no participatory experience is pure?

Alternative media practitioners and theorists are beginning to look at these questions more carefully, and I believe more and more literature will be written in the near future exploring some of these questions and many others on which I have not touched. In 1990, Vidéazimut, a coalition of media practitioners working in independent and alternative video and television from every continent, was founded specifically to discuss these questions. In addition to annual meetings, its members act to promote the democratization of communication in their respective countries on all levels of production and dissemination, using a variety of strategies and practices—one of which is process or participatory video.[4]

In context of this "New World Order," in which bodies continue to float ashore and the so-called "new communications media" promise to be accessible to only a privileged few (even with the development of interactive video, small satellite dishes, compulsory media literacy in classrooms, experimentation with virtual reality projects, and so on—all developments that add a new context to the practice of process video), alternative or alterative practices that open up the possibility of delegitamizing or contaminating mainstream communication structures have an important albeit knotty role to play in women's lives.

Notes

1. The word *participatory* to describe this video practice is used so often and so loosely that it has become a vague and meaningless reference. Participation is the catchword of the day. It has been co-opted into the bureaucratic and corporate agenda. Instead I prefer to use

process video, a term used by some alternative media practitioners in the South, particularly in Peru and Bolivia.

2. For an interesting discussion of the way the use of this technology can transform a community both negatively and positively see Turner (1991).

3. *The Independent* (1991); a publication of the Association of Independent Video and Filmmakers.

4. For more information on Vidéazimut, contact Vidéo Tiers Monde, an organization located in Montreal that is working with alternative media practitioners in the North and South.

8

A Process of Identity Deconstruction: Latin American Women Producing Video Stories

CLEMENCIA RODRÍGUEZ

The following pages will explore in detail the processes of change that take place in the lives of those involved in a participatory video production experience. This exploration is based mainly on my own observations while being part of production crews producing participatory videos in Colombia.

Inspired by Freirean approaches to popular education, and by the new-born movement to alternative communication spreading at the time throughout Latin America, I began experimenting with participatory video production in 1986. Initially, my reasons for setting in motion this type of processes had an underlying political agenda: the belief that democratization of communication implied putting the media in the hands of the people. However, as I started witnessing how this theoretical statement took form of real production routines, I realized that the consequences of "putting the media in the hands of the people" went well beyond an abstract political ideal. Right before my eyes, drastic processes of individual and group transformation were taking place; I began recording my observations in a diary, which has become the main source for this study.

Three different video production experiences became the core of my ethnographic observations. The first one took place from June to September, 1986. For four months I worked with a group of women from Ciudad Bolivar, a poor *barrio* in the midst of Bogotá's misery belt. Our goal was to produce a video about their community day care centers. The second experience, which slowly developed along 1987, involved a group of women working in the health sector; the final result recorded their struggle trying to transform the maternity clinic where they were exploited employees, into a worker-owned institution. The third experience, also conducted in 1987, involved a youth group from Perseverancia, a *barrio* located in downtown Bogotá. The group's goal was to recreate the history of their *barrio* in a video piece. Most of the group's members were women.

Later, I started finding coinciding observations in systematic recollections of similar cases of participatory media production recorded by others. Some of these experiences have taken place among communities in places other than Latin America (eg., India, Canada, The Philippines).

Because I am aware of the cultural grounding of my observations and reflections, I would like to limit the scope of my conclusions to communities in Latin America. However, the fact that similar processes have been pointed out in different cultural communities could be perceived as a trace of a cross-cultural phenomenon.

Some Definitions

The use of video for development[1] is wide, diverse, and heterogeneous throughout Latin America. Broadcasting popular documentaries in parks, street corners, and plazas (TV Viva in Brazil); alternative news video programs (*PROCESO* in Chile), and video as a communication strategy between agencies and *campesinos* (*Centro de Servicios de Pedagogía Audiovisual para la Capacitación*, CESPAC, in Peru) are only some examples in which video is used for development and social change. All of these can be categorized as popular video, alternative video, or video for development. However, this chapter will focus on a particular use of video by development workers and poor communities: participatory video production.

Participatory video production (PVP) is understood as one in which a communicator and a community engage in video production. That is, the whole process of producing a video message (planning, script writing, shooting, viewing, editing, and showing) is shared by both, the "communication expert" and the community.

To illustrate this process, I will describe one of the projects that I was engaged in while working in Colombia for the Department of Popular Communication of CINEP.[2] In 1986, an organized group of women from a poor barrio in southern Bogota came to CINEP looking for assistance; they wanted a video about their success in developing community day-care centers in their barrio. We made a counterproposal; the video would be produced by them and us working as a team. Our proposal was accepted. Next we planned a 1-week video production workshop where the group would come in contact with the technology as well as the narrative possibilities offered by the medium. Through the workshop, the group became familiar with camera angles, camera movements, different frames, and so on. My role as a facilitator was (a) to communicate the basic notions of video production (e.g., camera functions and sound and lighting concepts), (b) to coordinate critical video review sessions, and (c) to guarantee access to all the needed resources (e.g., video cameras, editing labs, and videotapes). The following step was to plan a script and a shooting schedule. The resulting script was a combination of genres, in which documentary and drama were intertwined to express different aspects of their experience as women and mothers trying to better the lives of their children. Although the script and shooting schedules were greatly detailed, the actual shooting kept changing throughout the process, either because the team found images they wanted in the video but could not anticipate or because predetermined images were impossible to get.

After the team members decided they had enough material to illustrate the story they wanted to tell, we hired the services of an editing lab, where for 3 days the team edited a final 45-minute version of its story called *Sembrando Jardines, Cosechando Futuro* (Planting Kindergartens, Reaping a Future). Finally, several copies of the video were made and shown to others involved in the project, to funding agencies, and to other barrio groups (e.g., PTA associations, women's organizations, and youth groups) as a motivation tool to engage others in similar community day-care center projects. A simple experience. But there was much more going on during those weeks of learning, shooting, viewing, editing, and showing. At the end, the eight women involved in the video project were not the same. Something deep, definitive, and irreversible had happened to them. That "something" is what I want to explore next.

To better understand PVP, two categories have been constructed to distinguish the use of video for development: video as a product and video as a process (Gómez, 1990; Roncagliolo, 1991; Valdeavellano, 1989). The main criterion used to differentiate these two modes of video production is the intentionality of the result generated. While the quality of the final product is the main goal of video as a product, the richness of the production process itself is the priority for video as a process.

Video as a product implies a communication expert who makes contact with a community to make a video about an aspect of their life: an everyday life problem, a successful development project, a cultural aspect, and so on. The communication expert approaches the community members as potential informants, and generally this is the only way the community participates in the making of the video. Since the audience is originally thought to be wide (from television broadcasting to public showings and festivals), the technical aspect is managed as carefully as possible; similarly, the narrative is shaped according to the aesthetic standards recognized by film and video makers (in terms of duration, framing, cuts, camera movements, angles, locations, acting, etc.).

Video as a process involves a communication expert *and* community members in all phases of production. It generally implies an initial phase of knowledge exchange, during which the communicator learns about the community and the community learns about the technology and the intricacies of video narratives and genres.

Some have suggested that video as a process does not result in an edited product (Gómez, 1990; Nair & White, 1987a). However, video processes that aim to tell a story to others demonstrate that final edited products are often achieved.This is the case of the three video production processes on which I conducted ethnographic observations: *Sembrando Jardines, Cosechando Futuro,* about day care centers in southern Bogotá; *Huelga en la Sala de Partos* (Strike in the Maternity Ward), where a group of women tell their story as protagonists in the transformation of a private maternity clinic into a worker-owned institution; and *Perseverancia,* where a group of young people from a poor, but long-time extablished barrio in downtown Bogotá recreates the history of their barrio through interviews with the community elderly.

Grassroots communications activists and scholars record similar observations in other Latin American contexts: in Peru, the Video Team of Calandria documents the making of *Madres Unidas por el Vaso de Leche* (United Mothers for a Glass of Milk), where poor women from Villa María del Triunfo, a low income *barrio* in Lima, narrate their success in implementing a community project where a glass of milk is offered daily to every child in the community (Calandria, 1989); in Ecuador, Maria Augusta Calle records the production process of *Sahuari,* where the Balda Lupaxí, an indigenous community recreates their marriage ritual and its meaning (Calle, 1990). To sum up, the need to communicate a story to others rends unavoidable the editing phase. In fact, the mere idea of producing a "narrative" necessarily implies the selection of those fragments of our lived experience that, woven together, constitute a linear version with a beginning, a middle, a climax, and an end.

Although there is a final product that is thought to be shown to others, PVP "is in itself an experience of *collective* decision-making and power"

(Gómez, 1990, p. 16). From this perspective, PVP can be better understood in the frame of group media, defined by Muller as "any medium which can foster the process of group interaction through communication based on the life situation of the group members, and sharing of personal experiences that will lead to common endeavors and actions" (quoted in Tomaselli, 1989, p. 12).

The Context

Television has expanded throughout Latin America since the 1950s. Either as a commercial venture or as a tool for political legitimization, political and economic powers have made it a point to make television reception widely available. On the other hand, an intense process of migration and urbanization has brought large populations to urban centers, where television becomes one of the primordial commodities. In other words, most marginalized communities have been exposed to television for more than 2 decades. Therefore, by the time women groups become involved in a video production process, they have already had a deep televisual experience; they are not blank slates. Although they are familiar with the medium, their experience has been limited to that of a spectator. Access to this medium has been systematically denied to them. Therefore, the shift from being a televisual consumer to being a producer serves as a catalyst for multidimensional processes that range from the psychological to the political to the existential.

The Viewfinder as a Mirror

To be a poor woman in Latin America implies a situation of marginality: marginality from resources, services, and power. In addition, there is a cultural aspect of marginality generally overlooked by development workers and social researchers: marginality from cultural texts. In other words, while other social sectors can look at themselves in cultural texts that range from literature to mass media programming, poor women watching television, listening to the radio, or reading popular literature have to look at the faces, the bodies, and the lives of others. For decades, their own self and their own universe have never been focused on by the makers of cultural texts. Radio and *telenovelas* clearly illustrate this: The leading character is either a rich young woman or a poor girl whose portrait belongs more to the aseptic view of poverty shared by television producers than to a real character construction.

When involved in a PVP, a poor woman takes the camera for the first time and focuses it on one of her women friends, on her house, or on her barrio. At that moment, a qualitative shift in her self-perception occurs. The viewfinder, acting as a *mediation* between her and her world, creates an artificial distance. From this distance, women are able to look at themselves and their world in detail: from the way their faces and bodies move to the aesthetic characteristics of their environment. A metaphor of somebody looking in a mirror for the first time could illustrate this phenomenon. Fuentes (1985) beautifully described this process in *Gringo Viejo:* General Arroyo's men and women attack the Miranda's hacienda. They burned and destroyed everything, except for the ballroom's mirrored walls, where thanks to the revolution they can look at themselves for the first time: "Paralyzed by their own images, by the full-length reflection of their being, by the wholeness of their bodies. They turned slowly, as if to make sure this was not another illusion" (pp. 39-40).

By the same token, the video production team of Calandria (1989), a nongovernment organization working with poor women in Lima, observed, "We started [the workshop] with ludic exercises to make an initial contact with the medium. The body of one of them would be focused by the video camera. They looked at themselves for the first time" (p. 4). As the production process goes on, their new vision reaches their environment: "When they started shooting the barrio they said, 'this cannot be possible, this is not Pamplona, how can it be so beautiful?' " (Calandria, 1989, p. 4).

Fraser (1990), in evaluating video production experiences in rural areas of Yucatán, Mexico, observed: "It was, obviously, the first time they observed a peasant face like their own on television. Moreover, it was the first occasion in which somebody spoke Maya on the screen" (p. 80). Some have equated this phenomenon with a rational process of acquisition of knowledge (FASE, 1989; Gómez, 1990). From this perspective, a subject has to take some distance from an object to perceive it, reflect on it, and express it—three elements that integrate the process of knowledge. However, this type of explanation limits the process to the *rational dimension* of the relationship between women with themselves and with the world around them. It excludes all other nonrational dimensions, like all emotional, aesthetic, or moral aspects of this relationship. Beyond a knowledge-acquisition process, I would suggest that what takes place during a PVP is a whole and integral process of identity deconstruction.

Everyday Life:
From the Background to the Foreground

Once the production team has gone through the learning phase (generally in the form of a video production workshop), the group is ready to start constructing their story. They have all the elements: facts, characters, equipment, and training. However, the elements are disassembled and it becomes the group's mission to put them together. Like solving a jigsaw puzzle, they have to choose certain images of themselves and their communities while at the same time rejecting others. Suddenly, everyday life, generally taken for granted, becomes the focus of attention: How do we dress? How do we eat? How do we love? These are common questions women are forced to ask themselves when making their video stories:

> We began realizing the importance of gestures and faces. An interesting discussion arose when one of the women said: "But we are not pretty; how can we be television actresses?" "But when we are at home we don't wear make-up," mentioned another woman. From that moment on, their reality assumed the role of the protagonist in the project. (Calandria, 1989, p. 4)

For the women making a video on day-care centers in Bogotá, it became of vital importance to express what the city has meant in their lives. On the one hand, Bogota is the overwhelming urban monster that threatens all their cultural and social patterns as rural immigrants. On the other hand, it provides a setting for a whole new experience of being together: the barrio, with all its emotional links of family, friends, and neighbors. They traveled with the camera on a journey that began at the core of Bogota's downtown anarchy and culminated in the intimacy of a family bedroom.

The process of looking again at one's reality implies the reevaluation of certain aspects of community life. In some cases, social roles of elders become altered through PVP. Older community members are generally excluded from the workforce. Moreover, they are often not involved in community organizations. For these reasons, they can be disregarded by the younger generations. However, in some cases only the elder can provide some of the pieces needed to reconstruct a story. For a group of young Filipino fishermen from Laguna Bay, older fishermen became a crucial element in their story: "[We] started interacting with elderly fishermen, listening to their experiences with regard to fishing during their times" (Deza, 1989, p. 5).

During the making of *Perseverancia,* a participatory video developed by a youth organization about the history of their barrio, the young producers had to give up their leading role and stay behind the camera. They were too young to know the history of the barrio; the elderly had this knowledge and thus had to be heard. Their presence in the community became visible, for the first time.

The possibility of looking at one's everyday life and environment through a camera brings about a complex process of change in groups' self-perceptions. Moreover, the need to reconstruct that new perception into an image of oneself to be seen by others, by the rest of the world, makes the group members engage in a profound process of self-investigation. In other words, since groups have to create an image of their members' own selves to tell their story, they have to search for, and gather, the pieces of a fragmented reality; within this process, they encounter aspects, feelings, characters, and landscapes previously unimaginable.

Breaking the Boundaries of the "Televisable"

One of the strongest characteristics of audiences' attitude toward television is the mystification of the medium, and Latin American viewers are not an exception. From the unattainable nature of *telenovela*[3] stars to everyday routines that evolve around television schedules,[4] television is perceived as "the magic box." However, women who have participated in a video production project drastically change their relationship with the medium. They do so by becoming familiar with lenses, frames, angles, zoom-ins, and zoom-outs, which lead them to a new way of looking at television programming. Once the intricacies of televisual language are understood, the magic of the box "fades to black." This process, called by some communication scholars audiovisual literacy, is the first step in reaching a critical viewing of television.[5] Nevertheless, it would be naive to think that solely by shifting from being a television consumer to becoming an audiovisual producer all internalized patterns will break. In fact, one of the limitations frequently observed by communicators involved in this type of experience is that people tend to copy mainstream television angles, frames, and sequences in their own video productions. Prado (1985) claims that "empiricism inevitably leads to the reproduction of those known patterns, production routines and genres most frequently broadcast" (p. 57).

From this perspective, it will remain a challenge for PVP to design strategies for developing audiovisual codes, narratives, and formats truly anchored in the lives and culture of marginalized women; that is, strategies to free the imagination so this form of communication production can attain its fullest potential.

Second, as I mentioned before, cultural texts, including television texts have strongly delineated what is and what is not televisable. Not much television viewing is necessary to know that poor women, their faces, their bodies, and their lives are not included into what mainstream Latin American programing considers televisable. This has been internalized by society to the point that their absence from the screen is taken for granted. However, PVP necessarily engages women in discussions and questions about it:

> [In selecting locations] we were looking for a very poor house and one of the women said: "the neighbor doesn't want to offer her house 'cause she says: How come my poverty is going to be seen on T.V.?" This conflict made possible a discussion about how their own surroundings could enter the screen. They could not assume this at first, because normally the scenarios for television are of a different kind. The experience with Calandria contributed to changing that initial "uneasiness;" later the women would offer their houses without any embarrassment. (Calandria, 1989, p. 4)

Along the same lines, Hartmann (1990) said about the popular video movement in Latin America:

> Suddenly, on the same screen for Roquesanteiros and Porcinas [famous Brazilian *telenovela* characters], the pretty faces of Rita, Antonio, Luis and Ana appear; real faces, faces from the people. That was the first impact: to empty the glass of "gods" and return to the people their faith in themselves. (p. 72)

During the Ciudad Bolivar video production process, the barrios, with all the dirt and poverty that has made them "too ugly to be on TV" suddenly take over the television screen. This simple phenomenon breaks preconceived notions of what is considered worthy to be on television and what is not. In other words, it alters sedimented stereotypes of what is socially recognizable and what is not. For poor women, this implies a qualitative shift in their self-esteem. PVP becomes then a strong tool for the empowerment of poor women.

PVP as a Way to Reverse Power Roles

For the women workers of the maternity clinic, making a video about a strike gave them the opportunity to reconstruct their leadership and to rethink themselves as a unit. Those women who had become powerful leaders during the strike had to accept, during the video production process, that they were not always the best storytellers. As Deza (1989) pointed out in reference to the fishermen experience in the Philippines, "the process of production was itself a way of surfacing hidden talents and capabilities" (p. 18). Similarly, *Huelga en la Sala de Partos* gave unnoticed women the opportunity to develop their story-telling skills. Telling anecdotes in front of the camera, re-acting some of the scenes, and finding the right angle to express a specific atmosphere were talents never before recognized by the group. Those who had these talents were then considered new leaders, while the traditional leaders were displaced to secondary places. This way, the collectivity redefined its identity during the process, reversing power roles and creating new self-images and new relationships. In other words, PVP facilitates a creative collective dynamic that can challenge institutionalized leadership roles: "The focus of production is not, therefore, set by an individual, no matter how perceptive he or she may be, but by a group which wants to document its own situation" ("Video Animation," 1989, p. 1).

A similar challenge can confront gender power structures as well. When PVP women's groups produce a story, they often have to include men, but it is the women who direct. In these cases, gender power roles can be altered. Calandria's (1989) video team described the following:

> Ability to dramatize was different for women and men, and this created some team conflict. The gentlemen got uncomfortable when criticized or directed by the ladies. The tortilla had flipped around. We think this did not originate in their skills, but more in how participants had established a different relationship towards this dynamic of communication. The women felt they owned the story, from the selection of a main character—an organized woman—to the main conflict, which concerned all of them. So, while the males *acted,* in the professional sense of the term, the females *re-lived* the situations. (p. 7)

As a technological tool per se, participatory video will not promote changes in authoritarian structures. However, PVP as a process of story telling that implies self-investigation can challenge deeply internalized power relations.

Story Telling as a Search for
Collective Strength

Many have called it fatalist cosmovision. This concept designates a community's conviction that they are unable to change their predetermined destiny. This *fatalismo* is one of the factors that strongly constrains social change in Latin America. However, women who participate in a participatory process of video production have the opportunity to witness their ability to transform experience, facts, places, people, feelings, and ways of thinking into a story. This process serves as a catalyst for reevaluating their ability to transform. In other words, trust in one's collective capacity and strength to determine reality can reach new and unknown levels, leading to group collective strength. Ogan (1989) observed how this process took place in a group of poor women in Nepal:

> The video-making experience had empowered these women to see solutions to their problems. In spite of their lack of education and position, they were ultimately able to participate in local political meetings formerly an exclusively male right. (p. 2)

Leeland Dalania, an Indian leader of women vegetable vendors, recalls her own process:

> I did not know what video was . . . still, I learned to make programmes, to operate equipment and to do replays. I am illiterate and do not have electricity in my house but I learned to make video programmes and became a producer. (quoted in Stuart, 1989b, p. 2)

Stuart (1989b) said about the videos made by Dalania's group: "They raise spirits, inspire confidence and solidarity, and communicate effectively the importance of collective action" (p. 8). By challenging fatalismo and increasing groups' trust in their self-determination, PVP can reinforce collective strength.

Conclusion: Films of Discomfort

Participatory video productions could be categorized into what Brazilian film director Rocha called films of discomfort: "The discomfort begins with the basic material: inferior cameras and laboratories, and therefore rude images and muffled dialogue, unwanted noise on the soundtrack, editing accidents, and unclear credits and titles" (Tomaselli, 1989, p. 11).

However, it seems like the sensation of discomfort is felt more by communication experts, filmmakers, and professional video producers than by the ones actually involved in PVP.

In fact, many NGOs, including the Colombian CINEP whose experimentation with PVP made this study possible, have opted for professional video production processes, excluding community participation in their electronic story-telling projects.

Both participatory video producers and their audiences engage in a process that goes far beyond the normal production and appreciation of an audiovisual message. Gómez (1990) would agree: "Participatory video products usually do not show the complexity of the participation process involved in their development and production."

It is this complexity that I have tried to highlight and elaborate on throughout these pages. I have suggested some of the dimensions participatory video production takes: processes of identity deconstruction, personal and group empowerment, demystification of mainstream media, reversal of power roles, and increasing collective strength. Yet, I want to make clear that my efforts to conceptualize these processes are no more than intuitive attempts. Interaction between poor women and video production is so complex that any venture to reduce it using these concepts as formulas for social change, community organization, or development will inevitably be led astray. PVP is like an unknown adventure, and two adventures cannot be exactly alike.

Notes

1. Video for development refers here to the use of video production technology aimed at improving the quality of life of a targeted poor community. Video for development is distinct from many other forms of video production in that it strives for social change with its end result.

2. CINEP is the Centro de Investigación y Educación Popular, which is an NGO working with different organized groups and communities in Colombia.

3. *Telenovelas* are daily melodramatic television series. They belong to such a specific genre that they cannot simply be thought of as soap operas.

4. See Martín-Barbero (1987b) in which he noted that family eating times were adjusted to accommodate television viewing times.

5. See Valerio Fuenzalida and his works on *Recepción Crítica de Televisión,* published by Ceneca, Chile. In these works, Fuenzalida explored the mystification of television and suggested how it could be confronted.

9

Losing Fear:
Video and Radio Productions
of Native Aymara Women in Bolivia

CARMEN RUÍZ

In both urban and peasant communities in Bolivia one frequently encounters groups of residents discussing and debating their affairs. Men form the closed part of the circle, expressing opinions, suggestions, and disagreements. Women are often found in the open part of the circle, behind the center of discussion, together, as if seeking protection; present, yet at the same time absent; listening, but without a public voice. "I'm afraid," say the women, "Perhaps I won't use the right words, or maybe they'll laugh at me."

Although half the membership of most of Bolivia's worker, merchant, or neighborhood associations are women, these organizations are usually represented by men, not only in the executive but also in the public sphere. Organizations such as the guilds that represent street vendors and small businesspeople may have up to 80% female membership, and yet the majority of their leaders are men.

It is not only in grassroots organizations in which the voices of women do not appear very often or are badly represented. Social, economic, and political indicators of daily life in the country also demonstrate this absence. For example, the lack of women's representation is evident in the different expressions of formal political power, such as political parties, the government, and the parliament as well as in diverse expressions of civil society and the mass media.

According to the indigenist position that recognizes the native population as a fundamental part of the nation,[1] Bolivia is a country unfinished as a nation. The native population has been marginalized economically, politically, and culturally since colonization. According to politicians,

Bolivia is a country facing the contradictions arising from poverty and from external and internal colonialism; and according to the different expressions of the women's movement, Bolivia is a country affected by gender-based oppression.

In this country of many and diverse faces, in the relations of everyday life, and in the mass media, the voice of women is not only one more absent expression but clear testimony of how silence and oppression coexist.

This chapter summarizes a project initiated in 1984 by the Gregoria Apaza Center for the Advancement of Women (CPMGA)[2] called A Thousand and One Voices: Communication With Urban Aymara Women.[3] The project with Aymara women has three lines of action: training, production, and reception of mass media, particularly radio and video. We use mass media to help bring about a change in the discrimination and subordination of urban Aymara women.

This project developed mainly with groups of Aymara women and residents of the different neighborhoods of the city El Alto, a region of predominantly Aymara immigrants located 15 miles away from the capital La Paz.[4] Our communication experience will be retold here in chronological order, including explanations of the groups involved and of the methodological criteria developed throughout the process.[5]

The communication program of the center consists of:

A daily radio program—*La voz de las Kantutas*—which broadcasts testimonies, interviews, and dramatizations of the daily life of Aymara women who have migrated to the city.

Educational video productions for a variety of campaigns such as violence against women, cholera prevention, reforestation of the neighborhood, and so on.

The popular reporters project, which trains Aymara women in reporting techniques for radio and television.

A community short-range radio station that is a key aspect of a local development plan for the enhancement of women and the defense of their rights.

Urban Aymara Women and Communication

Our Throats Come Alive

The first time we evaluated the results of the communication project, it became clear that there were two different social actors, each with different expectations: the urban Aymara women and the group that worked at the women's center.

Aymara women were interested in the processes of media production and in the possibility of training themselves in the use of modern and urban language: "We lost the fear of speaking" was one of the most common expressions used in the self-evaluation of their participation. "Our throats came alive," said some. "We ourselves direct our words, and in this way everyone knows that we can," said others. The most succinct evaluation was given by a woman who had participated in various radioplays and in the presentation of a staged theatrical work in front of a large audience. She said, "Now I speak better, I am more sure of myself in front of people from the city [La Paz] when I enter an office. I'm losing the fear of speaking."[6]

The experience revealed a diversity of achievements. On one hand was the institutional perspective, closer to a communication strategy, in which the use of the radio as a mass medium was thought of as a way to achieve more social impact on larger numbers of listeners. On the other hand, were the expectations of the trainees who were learning to use words, as instruments of new relations and communicative exchanges with the urban, modern, and mestizo world.

To understand these two dimensions and the expectations held by each group of women, it is necessary to outline the social and cultural realities of El Alto and the history of the institution.

Impact of the National Crises on Poor Women

Bolivia is experiencing a period of intense economic crisis for which no short-term solution is foreseen. This crisis, which has placed 80% of the Bolivian population in a state of critical poverty, affects poor women in a distinct manner. Poor women are responsible for the administration of family income and are increasingly responsible for subsidizing a deteriorating household economy through diverse survival strategies.

This situation of crisis is felt in El Alto and particularly in *Villa 16 de Julio*, a barrio in the northern section of the city of El Alto. Since its creation in 1946, this barrio (with a population of 30,000 or 10% of El Alto's population) has been a focal point of Aymara migration from rural areas to the city.

The conditions of scarcity force the population of *Villa 16 de Julio* to live by a logic of subsistence, for which the key phrase is "survive day by day," and to put their energies into diverse activities that together form what has been called strategies of survival. The women of *Villa 16 de Julio* play an important role as administrators of scarce family resources. They work in the informal sector of the economy or participate in organizations seeking to increase family incomes. For example, women group together to accept donated food, to participate in educational programs, to be in service activities, and to be in labor unions. This participation of women in a diversity of organizations is combined with work in more strictly economic activities such as small-scale commerce, family enterprises, and occasionally, salaried work in small factories. More frequently, women are to be found working as house maids in the center of La Paz.

The inhabitants of *Villa 16 de Julio* form a kind of small city, a *mestiza* society that draws sustenance—and not in a harmonious manner but rather in constant tension and conflict—from what is traditional Aymara and what is modern, urban, and mestizo. Even if it seems easy to distinguish the various elements that feed it, the result of this mixture is a unique culture of conflicting codes.

The strategic proposal of the center for a plan of local development based on the perspective of gender is the result of 8 years of work in the city of El Alto. The proposal is based on the premise that there is no possibility of transformation in the situation of subordination of poor women if at the same time one does not fight against poverty. Equally, it will be impossible to eradicate poverty if simultaneously action is not taken to make substantial changes in the situation of subordination and oppression of women.

Identity: A Game of Mirrors and Reflections

One of the distinctive characteristics of the community of *Villa 16 de Julio* is the strong relations maintained between residents and their originating communities (90% of which are rural communities in the altiplano region of the department of La Paz). Links with the communities of origin are maintained through frequent travel to the countryside, participation in planting and harvesting, exchange of products, and through participation in festivals and rituals.

Consequently, the barrio of *Villa 16 de Julio* maintains a particular place in the urban world. The community's daily life evolves in a syncretic mix of two worlds that attract each other but that relate in a conflicting, sometimes antagonistic, manner: the Aymara and the Western/mestizo world.

Given its population density, El Alto has considerable importance in the spatial distribution of the altiplano region and its politics. This, however, has no correlation with the amount of attention given it in terms of necessities or urban services. As El Alto became a target for the different social and political expressions of local and central authorities, local outlets of the mass media and particularly commercial radio were established.

Daily Language and Expression

The living conditions of women in *Villa 16 de Julio* are characterized by economic and social subordination and the absence of political representation. Part of the living conditions are the "conditions of expression"; those that are latent in daily verbal or nonverbal language as well as in the codes of mass media. In this sense, the silence of women can be seen simultaneously from various perspectives. One of these is that verbal silence is com pensated by a nonverbal language expressed in the domestic environment.

The communicative expression of Aymara women is limited by their precarious mastery of the official language (Spanish), their migrant status, their use of traditional costume (skirt, shawl, and hat), their low level of education, and their condition of poverty. These factors inhibit them from establishing an efficient relationship with the public, urban mestizo, world: "When they see that we're wearing a traditional skirt they ask: 'What do you want!?' then they make us wait and leave us there for an hour. If a *señorita* [a women dressed in modern, Western clothes] comes in they attend to her first" (Centro Para la Mujer Gregoria Apaza [CPMGA], 1991). In this context, the use and control of words takes on vital importance, as vital as the satisfaction of basic needs.

Social Silence

In El Alto as in La Paz, most women work for themselves in intermediary activities (Fernández, 1988)[7]. Reinforcing a circle to meet daily necessities, women do what they know best and what also permits the continuation of daily life: domestic labor. The fulfillment of domestic responsibilities constitutes for these women a reference point for their identity, which proposals for participation and social communication cannot afford to ignore.

Poverty and scarcity goes deeper than the obvious material conditions. They affect the most intimate construction of identity for urban Aymara women. Such notions as self-esteem, the exercise of power, representation, and the carrying out of roles that give one a place in society are all profoundly marked by their contradictory position—the highly valued domestic role and function of motherhood on one hand and the discrimination and an overload of responsibility on the other.

The discourse of urban Aymara women about their own family and community roles and responsibilities is very sensitive to this contradiction. Overlaid with a profound experience of ethnic/cultural discrimination, the contradiction is expressed both in the relation between women and mass media and in women's mastery of public speech.

The Institutional Program

The communication proposal of the CPMGA arose in 1985, with the idea of designing and carrying out a project that could respond to the critical period Bolivia was facing. This was a period of deep economic and political crisis characterized by the emergence of diverse expressions of women's movements around the need to find solutions to the severe consequences of the crisis. During this period, a number of NGOs were created that were oriented to collaborating with the women's movement, while alternative communication proposals were promoted to recognize this movement. These programs saw the use of communication media as an arena to discuss the situation of women, as a motivator of participation, and as a denouncer of oppression. The communication proposal of the center was generated on the following premises:

The necessity of incorporating groups of women (their experiences, struggles, sentiments, and daily lives), as the protagonists and broadcasters of an alternative message to the traditional images transmitted by the mass media.

The need for the use of radio as social communication, and as an alternative to the traditional radio practices in the history of both Bolivia and of popular organizations.

The implementation of a methodology that would combine group and mass aspects within an educational perspective for the promotion of women.

We began with a weekly 15-minute radio program for women, called *La voz de las Kantutas,* which eventually became a twice weekly 30-minute program broadcast by three stations. Simultaneously, we worked on video programs, educational pamphlets, and articles in the press.

Radio Production: La voz de las Kantutas

The CPMGA chose radio as the mass medium to initiate the project. Radio reaches virtually the entire urban and rural population, overcoming scarcities of infrastructure and electrical power. It corresponds to a strong oral tradition in Andean cultures and has played an important role in the struggles of Bolivian popular movements, such as the miners' stations,[8] the Educational Radio of Bolivia (ERBOL), and the labor union radio.

In Bolivia, traditional radio broadcasting has privileged the use of native languages. Its programming fits the schedules and habits of people's daily life, becoming a permanent companion in domestic spaces and with work outside the home. Its traditional uses have led to the development of unique formats based on Andean culture such as messages, greetings, congratulations, and story telling. Finally, radio has lent itself to a strategic combination of group and interpersonal means articulated as a mass medium. Initially, *La voz de las Kantutas* (named after the Bolivian national flower) had a radio magazine format. It included interviews, music, and commentary by two hosts (a man and a woman), professional speakers, and sociodramas prerecorded by groups of women and later edited to follow a central theme put together by the hosts.

The sociodramas were produced in workshops. They were seen as a connection between the educational work of the center's development teams and the center's communication production. Stories were later recorded following various forms of expression: from stories to dramatizations, or more simply, the recording of testimonies, commentary, and opinion.

Radio production followed thematic cycles that were decided according to the thread of reflection in the work of the center with different groups of women. The process of production began from the moment of data collection, through discussion with the community and organizations, to field recordings of radio dramas, debates, interviews and testimonies, script writing, processing of information, broadcasting, and finally to the moment of evaluation and planning.

Our starting point was the recognition of women's reality, through testimonies, stories, dramatizations, secondhand documentation, and interviews. Following that, there was a reflection on the data or more qualitative information on the reality in which women find themselves. This debate was carried out with motivational elements such as games, paintings, sociodramas, and simple conversations. Last, there was the design of a material proposal, its editing and broadcast.

During the design and execution of these steps, we took into account criteria such as the recognition of the principles and values of urban Aymara culture, the role of radio as a mass medium in the daily life of the urban Aymara population, the relationship between urban Aymara women and their consumption of radio as a mass medium, and the self-training of women in the use of radio. In this process, women became active broadcasters of their own discourse. This last element was intended as a way to subvert the traditional relationship women had with radio by locating them as active broadcasters of their own worldview and using their own language.

However, this format did not identify the impact that our programs were having on the audience. While in producing the program there was a very close relationship with the participant women, the circle was artificially closed with the transmission of the program. In the closing of the first cycle of radio programming we identified numerous conflicts regarding the relationship between our programming goals, the methods of participation, and the relation with the audience. We referred to the goals guiding the practices of the institution, that is the promotion of women and the focus on gender, culture, and poverty.

The women participants perceived the program as an opportunity for participation, training in expression, and the possibility of broadcasting their group experiences, advances, and achievements. Their emphasis on practical gains reflects their strong feelings about the potential of becoming their own broadcasters of messages. This self-recognition means that these women value themselves as possible educators of other women. In conclusion, the perception of the program held by these women was very much related to their participation, and from that a sense of ownership developed. They recognized themselves as broadcasters and educators of other women.

For the center, the educational potential of radio broadcasting was related to the possibility of orienting the community's thoughts and attitudes about the demands of daily life and the possibility of establishing a connection between the domestic and the community's public activities. However, various difficulties hindered a more widespread continuation of the program.

A Conventional Analysis of the Program's Impact.   Our impact analysis had not gone beyond what is conventionally analyzed in mass communication (i.e., audiences, tendencies, and opinions). We did not take into account the impact of participation (as producers or audience) on the daily behavior of women, on attitudinal change, and on social relations. The focus of this alternative approach is on evaluating less measurable effects and intangible achievements, such as the increase in self-esteem, the development of creativity, and the opening of opportunities for pleasure, or in short, the evaluation of women's experience of moments that are rare in lives dominated by the need for survival. For the urban Aymara women, the project has stimulated and strengthened their self-esteem. There is no doubt that the project has achieved an improvement in the expressive capacities of the popular women involved. The project has trained them to better control resources, incorporating them in the production of materials that adequately describe their daily problems.

The Planning and Evaluation of the Objective of Influencing Public Opinion.   We identified an excessive emphasis on activities designed for strengthening individuals and groups, and a relative disregard of proposals directed at public opinion and the mass media. We can say little about achievements in terms of social circulation of ideas or of the institution itself, where the success of a project of communication must also be measured.

The emphasis of the project on the personal growth of small groups of popular women presented a number of concerns: To what extent was such production and broadcasting underutilizing a mass medium? To what extent was the absence of institutional mechanisms for following up the audience reception ignoring an important dimension of the project? Was this disjuncture a result of a flaw in the design, or a result of how the communication proposal found a place in the institutional proposal?

In part the answers to these concerns can be found in the theoretical contributions of those who underline the importance of examining social uses and consumption of mass media. They refer to the fundamental role that the use of mass media, in a strategy of development, can have in the construction of collective identities and in linking the strategic interests of various popular groups (Alfaro, 1988b, 1990; Mata, 1985, 1991).

From Magazine to Drama

One of the most important practical recommendations by the women participants in *La voz de las Kantutas* was to increase and improve the space given to radiodramas. As a consequence, we set up a drama workshop. The format of radiodramas breaks with the academic tone that dominated the magazine style and responds to the demands of the women.

The workshop focuses on the construction of collective stories that reflect the lives of the participants. The goal is to look critically at these stories with the intention of discovering the causes of problems and to propose concrete actions to resolve them. The content of the dramas presents a wide range of events from daily life; women are the protagonists, but also examined are their most intimate family relations, their desires, their expectations, and their problems. In the workshops, the following steps are incorporated: brainstorming to select a theme, a roundtable discussion to relate stories based on the selected idea, the determination of the central message, plot construction, the selection of characters, the division of the story by chapter and scene, direct lineal recording, the recording of the narration, editing, adding music and effects, and the broadcast. These radiodramas are fictitious narratives that represent the scenarios and situations of daily life in El Alto.

The principal achievement in the production of radiodramas is the method developed for plot construction. It puts emphasis on participation, on the Andean narrative, and on the expression of feelings, while at the same time it makes spaces for pleasure, reflection, and spontaneity. However, in the evaluation, participants noted that the themes are not developed enough in terms of drama. They were seen to be superficial, both in terms of content and in the format itself. Their perception was that the radiodrama is slow and linear and that it does not produce a sufficient degree of empathy with a mass audience. Another important element is that the expectation of production with a competitive quality (in commercial terms) has not been reached. The production is by amateurs and has the logic of a workshop formation or production.

The Second Stage of La voz de las Kantutas

Beginning in 1988, and as a consequence of the evaluation of *La voz de las Kantutas,* it was decided to put more emphasis on both participation and training in specific skills. This was the origin of the workshops on radiodrama production that allowed for the production of messages more relevant to the problems, interests, and forms of expression of the target audience.

In 1989, the same principle was applied to the production of *La voz de las Kantutas* through the training of a group of popular reporters. The intent was to promote a format that better responded to the language of the audience, facilitated greater participation, and met the demands of the audience, all through the creation of spaces for information, advice, and open discussion.[9]

We intensified activities in this period, moving from 2 to 4 hours of programming a week. This was accompanied by a diversification of format, by adding radiodrama to the radio magazine space. At first the recording studios, technicians, and announcers of *Radio San Gabriel* were contracted to produce the program. With the purchase and installation of a studio in El Alto, production passed into the hands of the Communication Program of the center, which allowed for popular groups' participation. From 1989, the services of an Aymara announcer and a radio operator were contracted part time. During the last 3 years, there were a total of 120 broadcasts of *La voz de las Kantutas.* A total of 89 hours were broadcast through the Aymara-language radio station *Radio San Gabriel.* The radio magazine was also broadcast through commercial radio stations such as Avaroa, Mendez, and Chusquisada, doubling the number of hours broadcast. To date, four radio soaps have been produced, with an average of 20 episodes of 15 minutes each. There have also been 12 drama series.

By the number of spontaneous visitors to the recording studio in the first half of 1990, it is clear that there is growing interest in radio and television production. Many women and youths interested in educational programs offered by the center indicated that they had found the information through the radio magazine. Furthermore, the Research Center on Health (the organization that collaborates in the development of health issues for the radio magazine) has in 4 months dealt with 240 patients who arrived at the clinic as a result of information received on the radio. Surprisingly, we have even received Aymara visitors from the Peruvian border region of Puno.

La voz de las Kantutas also contributed to the diffusion of the health and educational goals of the center. This occurred through the devotion of air time to practical advice and information on the care and stimulation of children, on maternal and infant health, and nutrition. The central theme of the program approaches aspects of the living conditions of urban Aymara women in much the same way as outlined by our institution.

After 6 years, the project has achieved a close relationship between the communicational proposal and that of gender and neighborhood development. This goal is strongly influenced by the notion of participatory democracy. During these years mass media (radio and television) have been used to communicate experiences of women. In making more powerful the expression of Aymara women, the training is designed to maintain a fluid circulation between the different components of communication, always reinforcing the incorporation of an Aymara perspective in the process of communication.

As a result, a communication program was designed and incorporated into the 1990-1993 plan for the center. Its general objectives focused on the strengthening of the expressive capacities of urban Aymara women, the formation of public opinion on women's issues, and the systematization and broadcast of debate on the subordination of urban Aymara women.

Video: A Mirror of Ourselves

There is one television channel per 150,000 inhabitants in Bolivia. In La Paz, with a population of approximately 1 million, there are nine channels. As one can see from advertisements in the daily press, 75% of the programming on these nine channels are foreign produced. The 25% that are nationally produced are generally news and debate programs or musical variety shows.

The genres that have been developed in that small percentage of national production are very limited. The most elaborate tend to be news shows. Other programs, such as those directed to children, limit themselves to a series of video clips produced in the United States or in other Latin American countries such as Mexico, Brazil, or Venezuela.

What does this mean for women such as the urban Aymara in a city such as El Alto, where practically every household has a television set and the consumption of this medium is part of daily life? It means watching daily 19 *telenovelas*, mostly of Mexican origin, with the remainder from Venezuela and Brazil. From this massive consumption of melodrama these women are exposed to certain models of family relations, expectations of social ascent, and happy endings.

Video production at the Gregoria Apaza Center began in 1986. Video was introduced as an educational tool in small groups to review aspects of the history of the women's movement in the country. At the end of 1989, the center began to produce video reports along with documentary dramas. The programs, made by the women themselves, have a documentary frame that transcends anecdotal situations by presenting them as social facts. They represent situations in the women's own reality.

Upon initiating video production the center also began training Aymara women as video reporters (popular reporters) for participation in the documentaries. The programs began to be broadcast on commercial stations on a weekly basis.[10]

Video continues the communicational process begun by the center with radio, that is, a combination of the individual (in participation), the group (in reflection), and the mass (in broadcast). In this way, each stage in production can be used as an educational opportunity. Each moment of production has been of mutual learning for both actors and producers. The production of news and fictional video has allowed the center and groups of urban Aymara women the possibility of showing real images of themselves to the population.

The characteristics of the news genre permit women to examine the realities of their daily lives, while at the same time giving a space where they themselves are in the leading roles. The form taken by the videos incorporates codes from Andean culture: the language (Aymara), music, narrative rhythm, construction of text, and articulation of sequences.

The systematic broadcast of the reports has awakened much interest in the urban Aymara population, not only because of the themes but, more important, because the actors are barrio women. Yet a key point remains to be evaluated, as in the case of radio production: the reception.

The CPMGA does not have current and rigorous data about the effect of these television reports, other than through occasional visits, telephone calls, and letters that the audience sends to the center or broadcast station. Undoubtedly, as in the case of radio, an unbridged distance exists between the two components of our communication project. On one hand is the active participation of groups of women and individuals that learn and become empowered during the process of production, and on the other is the mass audience that receives the finished product through the media or in group session. This distance should be resolved from the point of design to the point of practice in the strategic communicational project being carried out by the women and the center. We can trust, as we have from the beginning, that mass is not opposed to popular.

Popular Reporters

The *pollera*[11] women are divided into hierarchies based on their economic situation and the extent to which they have integrated into the city. There is a difference between a woman with a *borsalino* hat, silk shawl, nylons, a gold *topo* and a long skirt and a woman from the country-side with a flannel skirt and leather hat and who speaks only Aymara.[12] This stratification, which originated with the Spanish conquest, is con-served in various economic and social ways.

Such is the case with popular *pollera* women, who through participation in some popular media have achieved fame as social communicators. Some have found political positions as councilors and deputies. The numbers of these women remain small, but these women have become much emulated role models.

For more than three decades, the radio has broadcast programs in the Aymara language with men and women from the popular sector as literacy workers, community promoters, and announcers. This has facilitated the formation of associations of popular communicators in native languages. In contrast, television gives little coverage to the urban Aymara woman. If it does, it is from a conventional perspective, through *telenovelas* and programs that reaffirm their traditional roles as house maids, ornamental objects, symbols of abnegation, and sacrifice.

To assist the participatory and popular direction of national radio broadcasting, the center supported the creation of a network of popular reporters, initially for *La voz de las Kantutas* and later for the program *Warmin Arupa*.

The team of popular reporters is made up of urban Aymara women from the northern zone of El Alto who have attended seminars at the center on basic orientation and training in the use of radio and television and in the strengthening of expression. This group of reporters consists of mainly single mothers who are daughters of immigrants from the province. Their ages range from 34 to 41. They have varied education levels and work in domestic and informal activities. Links with other community organizations are strong: All are members of organizations related to parishes, literacy projects, food distribution, or merchant associations. The reporters have said that their involvement in television aids them in acquiring useful knowledge for expression and participation in public events. One woman said, "It's helped me a lot because I've been trained. In my own group of women they say they would like to be like me. I'm strong-willed, now I'm motivated for anything, I'm self-assured and I say how things should be." The reporters also identify a more community-oriented result of their experience: They feel themselves to be spokeswomen for the demands of the zone and for the aspirations of other Aymara women: "It is we who make known the necessities of the zone on television. Other women like to see discussion of their problems on television."

There is a recognition of the undeniable increase in self-esteem and of the role these women can play not only in their own organizations but also in the barrio, the city, and society in general. There is also the recognition and empathy that the reporters awake in the audience. The messages received from a woman "of the people" is given a greater degree of acceptance: She is part of reality, of daily life, and for that reason is seen to be legitimate.

Communication is vital in a city like El Alto where the emergence of new social actors blurs the values of representation, power relations, alliance, contradiction, and leadership. Communication can affect the flow of these social elements, which, depending on the situation, join together on the force of electoral alliances and the possibility of political promises. In these conditions the assumption is that by strengthening the role of popular reporters we also strengthen female leadership in the city. But this is difficult to prove in the short term.

From the communicational process in which the center participates we are left with another concern: What is the potential of the popular reporters to affect change? It must be remembered that we are only speaking of a group of 20 women—out of a population of 30,000—who are in the process of claiming their own words. We also speak of a conflict that continuously appears throughout the process: Are individual achievements the engines of social change? In what way can the experience of communication include both dimensions—the individual and the collective, the public and the private?

Participation: Myth and Reality

The point of view of women participating in the production of radio and video has been assessed in two different evaluations.[13] According to a survey of Radio San Gabriel, the 59 women who had participated in the center's projects perceive it as an educational program that allowed them to understand various aspects of their reality and that reflected facets of their own daily lives: "It makes you realize what the reality is." "It shows things from our lives."

Participation in the program is highly valued, underlining not only the importance of self-expression and making known their reality but also the possibility of entertainment and losing the fear of speaking: "We ourselves direct our words."

They recognize the effect on both individual and group affirmation, with phrases such as "let's teach ourselves to respect ourselves" and "let's value our work." There is a consciousness of the need for social affirmation: "We know that we can do it." These perceptions are based on knowing themselves to be broadcasters of a message, educators of other women who, it is hoped, will "realize what their situation is and organize."

Participation in the program represents a social space for recreation, reflection, and sharing among women. They confirm that they learn to speak openly, gain knowledge of the experiences of other organizations from other zones, and achieve a greater knowledge of their own situation through the search for themes and information for the radiodramas. At the same time, they consider their activity as an incentive for the development of women in general, to whom they try to reveal different aspects of their lives as Aymara women with few resources. In the case of radiodramas, the reflection about real lives and their own experiences is considered educational and exemplary. The aspect of self-affirmation is constantly mentioned: They say they feel secure and proud of their work, of the fact that their voices are heard on the radio, and of their ability to express ideas and life experiences.

In general, we observe that women have a sense of ownership of the communication program. In the evaluation of 1988, the women declared how badly they would feel if *La voz de las Kantutas* disappeared. In 1990, they declared they would find the means to continue the project on their own, organizing and negotiating with the media.

Participation is a part of the myths and utopias much beloved by projects of communication and popular education in Latin America. In its mythological dimension it has been seen as a panacea, an infallible remedy, and an unquestioned necessity. In its utopic dimension it is an evasive dream, a winning ticket, but with a trick.

In the case of the project involving the CPMGA and the women from the *Villa 16 de Julio*, a basic certainty is that participation will be impossible if both groups of actors do not identify and practice common territory of participation, one that does not exclude actors such as women and youth.

A minimal agreement on a discourse that incorporates the strategic demands of women must be made along with the recognition that the interests of women are affected primarily by the well-being of the community.

Challenges and Perspectives

In a general sense, our project of communication supports grassroots organization and the community, contributing to a democratization of the mass media and the development of popular expression. Special emphasis is given to the expression of women, yet without exclusion of other ages and men. Two essential conditions for the achievement of this impact are participation through multiple training activities and the activity of selecting formats and genres that permit openness, flexibility, and an accurate picture of the present.

The open forum of *La voz de las Kantutas,* for example, contributes to popular expression and the democratization of media, permitting the spontaneous participation of those who have no other channel of communication. While the radiodrama has no direct relationship to grassroots organizations or the community, it is an important vehicle for the reinforcement of popular values and expression. This is because of the diversity of experience among its participants and because they do not lose sight of the problems faced in daily life.

Consequently, the themes explored by the program refer to, among other things, the rights of women; the cultural and gender identity of Aymara women migrating to the city; and poverty, work, and other conditions of daily life. The work of communication serves as an antenna that provides useful information to the institution about the social context in which it works. This channel of communication is fed by the reporters, actors, and visitors to our programs. They give information on events and on the problems and aspirations of the population. They provide the elements that help to better understand the values of urban Aymara culture.

However, the positive aspects and benefits of this communication project should not make us forget the challenges yet to be met. Throughout the process, we identified elements that cannot be dealt with overnight, especially in a small project carried out by an NGO with limited resources and reach.

A simple enumeration leads us to projections such as the necessity for links between production, broadcast, and reception, a link generally more clear in theory than in practice. Another challenge is the incorporation of cultural aspects in every part of the communication process. If one understands culture to be a series of material facts that daily alter the physiognomy and habits of a social space such as the city (Saravia & Sandoval, 1991), it is without doubt that the reconstruction and strengthening of the voice of women goes beyond training in expression and coherence of discourse. It goes beyond this because such a process must blend with ways of relating, the manner in which alliances are constructed, and conflicts declared. In short, it must blend with the basic and the daily relating of human beings, their common sense, and the ways they establish the rules of the game.

These challenges, together with the objective of establishing meaningful links between the impact of this process on women as individuals and social persona, give the communication experience a subversive dimension that goes beyond the physical use of words. In this sense, the possibility of expressing feelings, desires, nonconformity, and demands is not only an effect of exchange between women and the state but also, and primarily, a dialogue that women can establish with themselves and their reality.

Notes

1. The "indigenist position" proclaims the political proposal of the possibility of an Indian government and state—in Bolivia, a Quechua and Aymara state.

2. The CPMGA organizes activities for the promotion of women in the areas of training, economic production, services, research, and communication. The center works with various groups of women but mainly with immigrant Aymara women in the popular barrios of La Paz.

3. The Aymaras are indigenous inhabitants of the Andean areas of Bolivia. They were first conquered by the Incas and later colonized by the Spanish. Bolivia has almost 7,000,000 inhabitants, of which 1,156,000 are Aymara, according to the statistical projection from the 1976 census. From this number, more than 800,000 are bilingual (Aymara/Spanish) and almost 300,000, mostly women, are monolingual Aymaras.

4. El Alto developed as a suburb for workers, acquiring city status in 1976. It is located at 4,000 meters on a highland plain at the foot of snowy peaks, it geographically dominates the larger city of La Paz. Like many Latin American cities, called variously "young towns," "villas of misery," or "land invasions," El Alto consists of numerous barrios (208 registered), of which many are squatter settlements in the process of legalization. The majority lack basic

services such as running water, sewage systems, and conditions of basic hygiene. El Alto is a youthful city, as 66% of its people are below the age of 25. The number of children and youths that work is significant, as is the number of young women that work full time.

5. The diverse self-critical and analytical elements used to describe the experience are the fruit of the labor of many people, including the Aymara women, the residents of El Alto, and the people who work at the women's center. Through reports, evaluations, articles, and commentaries, they have facilitated the reconstruction of the process as well as identified the possible strategies for its enrichment.

6. Aymara women face discrimination because they do not use the Spanish language well. Most of the time their knowledge of Spanish is so limited that they cannot effectively communicate for daily survival—asking for addresses and speaking in government offices (see Ruíz, 1987).

7. The economic activity of most Altiplano women is noncontractual (73.5%). The rest of the women (26.6%) work under a contract. A total of 97% of working women are involved in commerce, services, or informal industry.

8. The miner's radio stations are located in the main mining centers of Bolivia. These stations function as support to the miners' social movement and are considered a model of the relationship between alternative media and the popular movement.

9. The changes also followed the recommendations of the external evaluation of 1988, which signaled the need to reach beyond the small groups connected with the institution. This challenge implied more involvement in shaping public opinion than with the education of closed groups.

10. The production of each weekly 10-minute report has the following steps: (a) training workshops for urban Aymara women, generally community leaders or those interested in the social issues of their community; (b) preproduction, which includes research and collection of information on selected themes and the writing of a tentative script; (c) production and filming of the images and pertinent interviews; (d) postproduction, which includes editing, final research, and delivery to television stations for broadcast; and (e) broadcast to a mass audience by a television station. The video is used as educational material to aid in the work of assessment and reflection among different small groups.

11. The *pollera* is the traditional Aymara skirt.

12. The division and stratification of popular sectors are complex problems with roots in the Spanish Conquest. The conquistadors struck alliances with some of the defeated, who in turn enjoyed a series of privileges.

13. The first set of data is from 1988, making reference only to *La voz de las Kantutas*. The perceptions of women from small factories and day-care centers and groups connected to the center are examined. The second evaluation, carried out in early 1990, looks at the radiomagazine and radiodrama and reflects the impact of the project on the participants of the workshops.

10

Shards of Remembrance:
One Woman's Archaeology of Community Video

DOROTHY KIDD

Every autumn, about this time, I reorganize my storage space in preparation for the coming winter. This year, I also unearthed some notes and
papers from a process video project in downtown Toronto. Begun in the
heady days of the late 1960s, our middle-class youth group described our
video work with a neighborhood group in the urban core as "social animation" with groups with little economic and social power. We had been
inspired by the Challenge for Change program that aimed to "encourage
dialogue and promote social change through the use of film" (Henaut,
1991, p. 49)[1]

As the documents stirred my memories, I reflected on that period as a
watershed for my own work and for the growth of grassroots media in
general, in Canada and internationally. Many of the strategies of grassroots
communications discussed in this volume were shaped then. The period
marked a major divergence away from the primary focus of the old left
and social democratic parties on the state-owned public media (and secon-
darily on their own party organs) and to the development of alternative
media[2] institutions and means of representation for the emerging social
movements (of people of Color, women, students, and first nations).

Since then, I have worked in a number of different media projects, with
women and other subordinate groups. The general aims of social change
through dialogue and animation have remained the same as in those original video projects. So too have the problems of understanding the specific
impact of these new ways of communicating in reproducing or transforming
the social relations within the group, community, and society involved. However, I have also witnessed some fundamental changes as groups have

developed production and distribution processes to match their increasingly complex analyses of power relations.

As my reflections continued, the days were becoming shorter in the Northern Hemisphere and winter was approaching fast. I decided to take stock of some of these issues by retracing their articulation in two or three projects on which I have worked in the last two decades. By then, I had turned the calendar to October. Two other dates, marking other longer historical cycles, began to shape this account, because they crystallized two of the competing logics within grassroots communications, that of social movements and of the nation state.

It is now less than a week until October 12, the 500th anniversary of Columbus's arrival in the Americas. Indigenous groups and their supporters from northern Canada to southern Argentina are protesting the quincentennial, making it into an occasion for continuing political education. They are using a variety of grassroots media, art, and street demonstrations to testify against the 500 years of exploitation of the Americas by European merchant colonialism and to reclaim their plural histories within their many ongoing struggles for self-determination.

It has been this kind of campaign, of social movements, that has contributed to the change in grassroots communication. The map of who is participating in social change and what they are demanding has been radically altered from the one that framed our work in the 1960s. The 500 years' campaign and others like it are using communication strategies that begin with the groups' recovery of their historical memories and the construction of new social identities in the present.

In the process of this analysis, they are naming social actors, both those whose heritages have been erased and those who would rather be left unnamed—the oppressive forces of the state institutions and those of the market system. Furthermore, much of this work is part of wider social and political campaigns. I will discuss some of the parallels in the communications strategy of a video produced for the Inuit women's association in 1990.

Then yesterday, another historical cycle wound its way around to my door. Two young people arrived: "We're here to enumerate for the referendum, to add your name to the voting list for October 26." This is the 125th anniversary of the establishment of the nation state we call Canada,[3] and the federal government (like an astonishing number of other national governments around the world) is urging us to vote yes to a new constitutional package.

At stake is a new map (Quebec may separate) and a renegotiation of power relations. The new package will restructure state institutions and the social contract—the power relations between social groups, including women, and, in particular, between the state and aboriginal or first nation organizations. As she leaves, the enumerator hands me a brochure: "Here's some more government propaganda."

After a dramatic refusal of an earlier proposal, the government has drawn on many of the techniques of participatory communications. It attempted to bridge what it conceived of as a "communications gap" between the people and the state through a year-long round of consultations and public meetings (televised over the public television network and the community station via cablevision). This process of incorporation of the participation of citizens was not designed to alter radically the existing relations of economic or political power. In the discussion below I revisit this problem of the use of participatory communications as a technique to maintain consensus for the status quo. Unless the outcomes of projects are evaluated within a wider analysis of the transformation of power relations in both the private and public spheres, participatory communications will be indistinguishable from the logic of national governments.

Changing the Vertical Hold?

Kay Parsons is speaking in the Toronto Municipal Council Chamber. I register her mix of East London (England) and St. John's (Newfoundland, Canada) in my headphones as she tells her story of her neighborhood and her way of life. "We want an opportunity to go on living the way we have been, getting on as best we can. . . . Instead, over and over again we've seen the politicians giving the zoning to the developers."

She notes the number of times she's watched her friends and neighbors move, after developers first assembled and then razed their working-class homes and replaced them with high-rent high-rise towers.

She finishes to a wave of clapping from the protesters who pack the hall, and the tiny video sound meter bobs wildly into the red.

Delegates from neighborhood organizations throughout the city take the microphone. Many who testify against the megaproject are women, putting the predominantly male councilors, officials, and developers on notice that they will return if they are not included in future development negotiations in their residential areas.

In the center of the auditorium, the councilors yawn and make notes for each other. As I flip the camera over to play with their upside down images on the monitor, one councilor announces he must leave to judge a beauty contest.

We—I, and another Euro-Canadian, and two overseas Chinese students—worked with Parsons and the English and Chinese residents' associations in the working-class neighborhood of Grange Park in downtown Toronto, the largest city in Canada. We were funded by a series of youth grants from the federal government at a time when the government was not only more generous but more tolerant of a variety of decentralized social action projects across the country.

Our aim was to give voice to views normally excluded from the state's vertical planning process. The unedited video tapes were played at public meetings as counterevidence to the government and corporate plans. They were also shown in people's private homes to mirror the views of various sections of the neighborhood to each other and for the cross-fertilization of ideas with other neighborhood organizations all over the city.

We felt that this testimony would help transform both the substance and process of the urban restructuring set in motion by commercial developers, city planners, and other government institutions. The video was our instrument to open the public and private discursive spaces for people who otherwise had very little economic, political, and social power.

The video work helped publicize and extend this local struggle to people in the neighborhood and other groups in the city. However, as our funding dried up, each of us moved on to other projects. I continued to work with the neighborhood organizations, which managed to satisfy some of their basic demands: to stop some of the expensive high-rise developments designed for urban professionals and to get more government funding directed to low-cost housing.

The Limited Scope of the Video Viewfinder

There were reports but no extensive evaluation of this video project and its impact on the resident associations' work or on the community as a whole. In hindsight, some trends are very clear and follow patterns noted more recently by critics of participatory action research projects (Thurton quoted in Rahnema, 1990). For a short period of time, the local government provided funds to bridge the communications gap among citizens, municipal politicians and planners, and real estate developers. Their efforts and those of projects like ours did, for a time, create better mechanisms for citizen involvement. There was some decentralization of power as new local leaders, many of them women and from ethnic minorities, emerged. Some basic needs of groups were met. However, these advances must be weighed in the context of what was more or less an unchanged local political and economic structure.

In the long run, there was definitely a narrowing of representation. Participatory techniques—such as the video work, block meetings, and area-planning meetings, which had involved many of the diverse groups within the neighborhood in speaking for themselves—were used less and less. Instead, the small number of community leaders (who had emerged in the organizing campaign) began to act more conventionally, as representatives of the neighborhood, in closed planning meetings. Combined with this narrowing of representation was the continuing economic pressure on working-class residents, many of whom were forced to move by rising rents or taxation rates on their homes.

While this lack of comprehensive evaluation was true of many of the independent projects such as our own, there was another kind of problem with the evaluation of those process video projects initiated by government departments and institutions. Challenge for Change described their projects as challenging relations of power at the level of communications, by allowing representation from those usually excluded from the dominant means of communications. The most famous Challenge for Change projects—in Fogo Island, Newfoundland, and in East End Montreal—were introduced to communities that already had high levels of community-based organization, and the media use reinforced the process of individuals and groups articulating their own social demands and, in reflection, realizing their commonality with others with the same interests (Henaut, 1991).

However, too often the assessments of the projects tended to focus on the technologies and processes of communication. Rather than a systematic analysis of the impact on the organizations and, even more important, on the audiences or the wider community, the evaluations tended to define success by the number of people who participated and the quality of their interaction in video making.

From 20 years away, it is much easier to see how projects like these fit within the logic of the Liberal government and liberal state of the time. Participation was not defined by the social movements active in the urban neighborhoods or rural villages but in the terms of liberal pluralism. Video was seen as an instrument of enfranchisement, bringing citizens on the margins of government decision making into the center, from where they would be better able to contribute to policy making.

In this view, democracy would ultimately be achieved by bringing representations of everyone to the screen. Democratization of expression[4] was circumscribed by access to the technology or media (at all levels of production, distribution, and exhibition). There was little acknowledgment of the limits to this discussion posed by the irresolvable conflicts of competing perspectives and power positions. This technicist idea of electronic democracy persists,[5] despite the best efforts of participants within government and social movements to extend access to the public to a wide variety of media, mainstream and alternative, in Canada and internationally. Access alone has not and cannot create democracy, electronic or otherwise.

Challenge for Change and other federally funded video projects were cut before these longer-term contradictions were exposed. However, several of the participants in these institutional and independent experiments (such as our own) went on producing media directly for the growing social movements of the 1970s that were concerned about women, Aboriginal people, and people of Color. The very creation of these alternative media networks embodied the recognition of a difference in logics between those of the mainstream government and commercial media. In the 1970s, other differences emerged between and within the social movements themselves.

Changing Standpoint

As are many of the downtown neighborhoods in urban Canada, Grange Park is a "reception area," the first place the majority of people land when they arrive looking for work. They come from the underdeveloped regions of Maritime Canada and the north, Europe, and more recently, the Pacific Rim; some come to attend school at the University of Toronto, the College of Art, and other educational institutions. Typical of North America, it is one of the oldest communities in Canada but has few buildings that have stood for more than 70 years. The new landscape, the multiplicity of roots, and the transience means there is no one collective memory and little in common among different groups beyond the experience of displacement and of contemporary urban survival.

The threat of massive land redevelopment and further relocation catalyzed the Chinese- and English-speaking homeowners. However, this was not the central concern of many of the tenants or of everyone among our video group. One of the Chinese members used the video to organize with other students about a land sovereignty issue in China. Some of the Chinese students with whom he worked were more involved in the struggles in their homeland than in the changes to their new neighborhood. Similarly, the other Euro-Canadian member became more involved in the campaigns of the student and left movements at the university and elsewhere.

For me, among the English-speaking residents, I began to notice that it was usually the women who were most active, as it was their responsibilities (whether on the first or second shift) at home that gave them an intricate knowledge of the neighborhood and ways to organize with their neighbors. I spent more time listening to their stories and, increasingly, to their other concerns. Many were immediate, involving welfare or employment, child care, and the education system. There were also many occasions when we talked about their roots and how they had come to leave their homes in Maritime Canada or in Europe. I started to realize how important it was to record their oral histories and with some other young white women began a project of collecting some of the memories of older women who had been involved in workplace and neighborhood struggles in the 1930s.

This review of my notes has reminded me of the work of archaeologists who reconstruct moments in history through the lens of their contemporary perspectives. Perhaps it is the present emphasis in North America on identity politics that has made me focus on the divergent paths we all took from that video project. However, even in the early 1970s it was hard not to recognize the differences made by gender, age, class, and race to who participated and what they said in the videos. We also recognized the problematic dynamic for each of us as outsiders to the neighborhood, until we each chose our own way to come in, if only a little closer.

Raising Consciousness, Activating Change

I found my own location in the burgeoning women's movement. It was a period in which the primarily young, white, and middle-class women's groups were asserting the right to make demands autonomously from those of men. No longer were women accepting that men would work for their interests or that women's demands could be unified with more general demands of progressive groups. This meant implications for those working in video and other alternative media, not the least of which was the importance of locating your own material interest in any and every organizing drive and of not speaking for others.

A few years later, I worked on another video whose process embodied consciousness raising, in which we and other groups of women were engaged. Intending to make a series of videos about violence against women, our team of four young white women found ourselves talking for hours about our personal experiences, and through this dialogue, we began to discuss how our personal life experiences were situated within a wider analysis of the oppressiveness of patriarchy.

I see this practice continuing as women of all backgrounds in Canada use video to make visible what had been beneath the surface of private discussions and suppressed in the public discourse—the pain and joy, values and dreams. Our videos about violence against women played on the idea that the personal can be political, as we named the structures and institutions that legitimate and reinforce the violence against women. This naming of collective experience, and of the struggles against constraints and oppression, reflected a growing feminist awareness that women's identities are not fixed but are socially constructed.

What, in hindsight, we did not recognize was the multiplicity of oppressions within this collective experience, specifically how our understanding of violence differed, depending on many factors: the violence in our family of origin and our class, race, and sexual orientation. As Kawaja discusses (Chapter 9), women of Color video makers, in fighting to document their own experience, are incorporating a much more complex understanding of power differences among women in their contemporary videos. Kawaja also notes the contribution of techniques of collective social analysis from popular educators.

Beginning at roughly the same time, in the late 1960s, popular educators in Canada derived their practice of conscientization from the work of Brazilian educator Freire. They also recognized the importance of the psychosocial dimension of experience and of collective reclamation of historical memory.

In writing this chapter, I found instructive the words of hooks (1989), an African-American feminist who is a follower of Freire: "In the process of learning to speak as subjects, we participate in the global struggle to end domination" (p. 18). In an essay that discussed contemporary critiques of identity politics, hooks suggested that consciousness raising can radically challenge mainstream definitions and processes of identity creation. Naming needs to be linked to action, or there is the danger of creating conditions for "even greater estrangement, alienation, isolation, and at times grave despair," or depoliticization through lifestyle politics (hooks, 1989, p. 32). Her solution is the Freirian one—to define and describe identity within an analysis of the concrete material reality, offering strategies of politicization and transformation.

hooks and other feminist educators (see Ellsworth, 1992) are moving beyond the earlier Freirian-inspired work, in which there was little recognition of power differences among the oppressed, particularly between women and men, and between facilitators and participants. hooks suggested that consciousness raising that does not link individual identity to an analysis of the complex structures of domination can and has allowed white middle-class feminists to participate in "misnaming," disregarding race and class, and their own privileged relationship to exploitation.

She described how differing levels of social power among a social movement can constrain transformation and allow the radical venture to be incorporated into the market system. As a writer, she warned artists to be wary of speaking to audiences that have more social power, for that can lead to their expression being overdetermined by the needs of the more powerful. Women and minority artists must consider whether their work will be used to reinforce or perpetuate domination (hooks, 1989).

As Kawaja (Chapter 9) also suggests, much of this cyclical process of reflection and analysis turns toward a third integral component: that of action. Some contemporary videowork is centered in campaigns: The videos themselves articulate the multifaceted experiences of subordination and of analysis around a particular issue. Such was the aim for the making of a video by Pauktuutit, the Inuit women's association, and the Inuit Broadcasting Corporation.[6]

Ikajurti: Recovery of Midwifery
in the Canadian Arctic

We've flown all day today, from east to west, joining several of the bigger dots on the blank white space that represents northern Canada on the map: Iqaluit, Rankin Inlet, Yellowknife, Cambridge Bay, and now we're in the most northern community on the mainland, Spence Bay. We go from pressurized air cabins to anonymous-style airports to our billet here in a townhouse in Disneyland, the local name for the new subdivision. Up the carpeted stairwell, Canadian Prime Minister Brian Mulroney looks out at us from a Christmas card family snap shot, reminding me of all the gray suits and brief cases that filled the seats on the plane. Yet beside that photo is another view of the Arctic.

A map that literally turns my southern urban perspective upside down, it shows the world from North to South. And as I look closely at the detail in the foreground—at the communities among bays, rivers, and islands— Nunavut, the Inuit homeland, takes on a new meaning. The white mass thinly ribboned by double-ringed dots, the southern cities, are in the background of this map.

I'm here with three other women, two Inuit, two of us Kallunaat (white) to record Nipisha Lyall's experience as a birth helper.

I guess you would call it training on the job. My first delivery I was very nervous. I tied the cord first and then I cut it. My mother was there to tell me

what I should be doing. My mother was my teacher on this, telling me what
to do and I had to learn instantly. . . .
    I will just talk about my own experience of delivering children. My husband
would be the one supporting my back and two women supported me by
holding my arms. Traditionally we kneeled down. This was from the advice
that came from my mother. This was the way I had most of my children.

Both Nipisha and her sister Bessie Asavak were birth helpers until the
English-trained nurses took over. The nurses came in the 1950s and 1960s,
when the federal government removed the Inuit from the land. Nursing
stations were set up in the new colonial settlements. In only a generation,
the Inuit knowledge of birthing was almost lost. Now, most pregnant
mothers must fly out to large metropolitan hospitals in those double-
ringed dots of southern Canada, because the nursing stations no longer
provide birthing services.

This videotape, *Ikajurti: Midwifery in the Canadian Arctic,* was made
in the different dialects of the Inuktitut language for Pauktuutit, the Inuit
women's association. At their annual general meeting in 1987, their first demand was to bring birthing back to the communities. The idea of the video
was to promote discussion of the traditional knowledge and ways of
dealing with birth, of the contemporary problems with the modern medical model and delivery system, and of the possible alternatives. The video
would be translated into different dialects of Inuktitut (with English subtitles)
to encourage full participation among all the Arctic communities.

It is the older women who are most concerned about recording their
memories. Several elders tell us how they learned and carried out their
work as birth helpers. During their earlier years, birth was a time for
celebration in the family and wider community: Women were respected
for their contribution and for their hard work. The elders also alluded to
the violent disruption for themselves and their culture when that knowledge and practice was erased, when the Euro-American practice of medicine
took over. There was no longer the same respect for the women, either by
the European nurses or by men and other community members.

In *Ikajurti,* women analyzed how the system had failed them, how it
was that young mothers often had to stay in the southern territories—
within an alien language, diet, and environment—to wait to give birth. They
spoke of the problems of the Euro-American medical model: Its focus on
the operation of highly expensive technology and of the predominantly
male experts who work in the large centralized facilities of southern Canada.
They also demonstrated the alternatives that women are developing—

relearning birth support skills and bringing them back to their community, involving men and their other family members in the process of the entire pregnancy and afterward.

[Music up and under Maina Kenoayuk.] The baby is coming out from the mother to its own surrounding. It feels it is in its own world. The baby goes out to the father, being there surrounded by loved ones. One can feel its feeling. But when they come out down south, no one we know is there. Only strangers. We used to have to come out to the world as if with no home. This one here was born free.

Ikajurti was first played to the annual general meeting of Pauktuutit, and then broadcast via satellite throughout the north over the Inuit Broadcasting Corporation.[7] While made for broadcast, it used the same strategy as alternative work, of reclaiming history by recovering the indigenous knowledge system of women, and the social roles and responsibilities that have been suppressed. The video assisted the women's association in naming some of their social issues and concerns, within a representation of the forces that stand with them and against them. It has been used as a discussion piece within Inuit communities and as an instrument to reinforce Pauktuutit's representations to politicians and government officials. But the video technology was only one instrument of many.

One of the lessons that the Ikajurti video again underscored for me is the importance of recognizing the power differences between and among social movements, in this case among women. While much of the video was made in a language and with people and communities that are not mine or that of the other Kallunaat crew member, we had the advantage of being from Canada's dominant culture and of working with a technology about which we were more familiar and more in control. There is no doubt that had the video, or even this account, been made only by Inuit women, it would have been very different. For example, one of the senior Inuit crew members told me that the final version had too many white doctors, and I have to agree.[8]

Conclusion

The process of the last 20 years of working against the grain of the official story—filling in the details of the diaspora in the colonial and contemporary history of Canada—has made questions of media use much more complex. Reclaiming so many different women's stories not only makes it clear that there is a plurality of experiences and analyses but also visibly shows how the privileging of one account can act to silence or erase another. (In *Ikajurti*, we used some archival footage showing just that: A white nurse at a government clinic raises her voice to make her point to a woman whose language she doesn't speak, while the Inuit patient maintains her silence.)

If nothing else, the Canadian referendum has shown that there is no such thing as a "women's position." Individual women and women's groups are competing with the male-dominated institutions and with one another, negotiating power differences—of race, class, sexual orientation, and dis/ability—and differing visions of the future. Any assessment of the impact of women's media work must take these differences of power and perception into account. This will require a constant inquiry into how decisions are made to leave some stories out of the script as well as some acknowledgment of where each story is situated in the wider frame.

I get ready to put these documents back into my closet, in preparation for teaching a women's studies class on participatory communications. They won't all fit, as there are now so many more examples of women's creative representations, stories, analyses, and campaigns. Still few enough thorough evaluations, but I consider ways to turn these reflections toward evaluating and enriching the work in community radio I'm engaged in now. A strategic evaluation seems increasingly urgent as the growing privatization of our mainstream media put pressure on the little space maintained by alternatives such as these. Perhaps this combined intelligence will make it more possible to evaluate these works from an autonomous viewpoint, not that of government or market funders. What kinds of public and private transformation are these projects encouraging for those who engage with them from inside and outside the radio?

Notes

1. Challenge for Change/Societe Nouvelle was jointly administered by the National Film Board of Canada and other federal government departments.

2. I use *alternative* to mean the wide variety of grassroots media uses outside the commercial- and state-operated media.

3. The word *Canada* comes from the Mohawk word for "village."

4. For more thorough critiques see Riaño (1990), Rahenema (1990), and Thede and Ambrosi (1991).

5. The most recent example is in coverage by the North American media of the triumph of capitalism over Soviet-style Marxism. They often refer to modern telecommunications as

the motor, or more appropriately modem (Witheford, 1992), of electronic democracy and electronic revolution.

6. In 1983, Rosemary Kuptana (then president of the Inuit Broadcasting Corporation) likened "the onslaught of southern television and the absence of native television to the neutron bomb. This is a bomb that kills the people, but leaves the buildings standing. Neutron bomb television is the kind of television that destroys the soul of a people but leaves the shell of a people walking around. This is television in which the traditions, the skills, the culture, the language count for nothing" (Inuit Broadcasting Coporation Position Paper on Northern Broadcasting, Ottawa, 1985). The Inuit Broadcasting Corporation was set up in the early 1980s after a decade-long struggle to control the southern television being beamed into their communities by satellite. It provides several hours daily of public affairs and cultural programs in Inuktitut from several centers.

7. It was also played on independent stations in the south and at film festivals. There are also campaigns for changes to the medical model of delivery and a return of midwives in southern Canada.

8. In Canada, there is a very full discussion going on about who can tell what stories and under what circumstances. Women directors at the Inuit Broadcasting Corporation and, further south, from many different Aboriginal nations are fighting to tell their own stories, their own ways. In this case, all the Inuit Broadcasting Corporation women directors were busy, and I took on the project with the understanding that I would act as a codirector with an Inuit codirector. However, this did not solve the problem.

11

Being Women in the Popular Radio

MARITA MATA

To the mothers, the grandmothers, to those who silenced their desires and necessities, and made possible these voices of today.

With this dedication a group of Colombian intellectuals opened their collective and polyphonic work of reflection on women. To have chosen the same dedication to begin this chapter is obviously not by happenstance, but neither is it so specific a choice. In *Insurgent Voices* (Laverde & Sánchez, 1986), that collective work, as in other productions, silence and its opposite —voice and words—name women.

The testimony of Domitila de Chungara (Viezzer, 1977) announced the innumerable spaces in radio that identify the voice of women[1] and that Our Voices[2] synthesized in its choice of name. The Peruvian raido program *Pass Me the Voice*[3] resounds with this process of appropriating the word and expresses (as do many other sources) the journey between feminine submission and dignity, alienation and self-identity (AAVV, 1987, Alfaro, 1988b).

To propose a conquest of voice and to assume the ownership, the peculiarity of one's voice, seem to be paradoxical attitudes coming from the *charlatanas* (talkative women, chatterboxes), the gossipers, and the *cuenteras* (confidence tricksters); women so often identified with parrots. Paradoxical attitudes coming from the mothers who are the first and immediate transmitters of voice to the child to whom they murmur and tell stories.

I was invited to participate in this book on the role of women in popular communication to reflect on women's presence and work in the space of radio, and I promise to speak of that. But first it seems necessary to me to refer, however briefly, to the question of language. A language that, as I have tried to suggest, appears in communicative practices and conceptual elaborations as the constitutive space of the feminine, the place of being a woman.

Feminine Word and Public Word:
Tension or Identification?

Numerous feminist approaches to the theme question the paradoxical association of women with a silenced subject. Gossip; women's stories; fairy tales; the advice of old women, witches, and healers; and the talk of companions—in doorways, in markets, and at the doors of churches—are thematically and enunciatively comparable instead to a minor tongue. This is a tongue unfolding in domestic space whose referents are situated in the private sphere: familial, affective, and personal and made of dreams, beliefs, and illusions. It is a tongue whose "disability" refers to the existence of another more valued tongue, that which names public themes connected to reason, power, and socially legitimated knowledge. The dialect carried out in the forums that each society recognizes as the scenes of the construction of opinion, of norms and decisions.[4]

If, as Moser and Levi (1988) indicate, "gender refers to that which is socially essential in the fact of being a man or woman" (p. 45), to the way that relations between the two sexes are socially constructed, we can recognize that no language exists that accepts uses differentiated by gender in the same way that occurs in the speech of particular social groups, in slang, or even in regional dialects. What would exist in each case would be two languages—the feminine and the masculine—as occurs with the genders: "one does not exist without the other . . . they go always as a pair" (Scott, 1986, p. 27). This reveals, then, their mutual incompleteness, their complementarity, without allowing one to naturally infer any kind of hierarchy between the two.

Illich (1990) made a provocative analysis of the destruction of a society articulated through the function of gender and its substitution for the economically indistinct but profoundly unjust and sexist industrial system. Illich pointed out that the perception of reality distinct to each gender finds expression in language. At the age of five, girls and boys generally dream differently, even though no anatomical difference is found in their speech organs. Upon passing from gibberish to speech, they adopt the form and style appropriate to their gender, even when playing among themselves (Illich, 1990).

Yet, as Illich (1990) hypothesized, "the common speech of the industrial era is lacking in gender" (p. 11), tending toward the imposition of a genderless neutral language, which characterizes the masculine speech. A series of studies reveal the gender differences of language and their disappearance under the illusory and ideological creation of a language that establishes asymmetrical inequality—domination. Before, one could recognize ambiguity and complementary inequality in the language of individual voices that named reality from their own particular social attachment to one of the genders that make up the human animal. From this series of thoughts, and others from history and politics, it interests us to retain those that think of feminine language as a minor tongue (in the sense I have indicated) and consequently as a repressed and subordinate language.

Rivera (1991) remembered that "the famous first epistle of Paul [in Corinthians] ordering silence for women in the Church is no more than a link in the chain, of which the phrases of Aristotle on the silence that women should keep are as well, simply, another more ancient link" (p. 129). Amoros (1990) indicated that in Greek thought "women appeared as excluded from logos, the space of *aner agathos*[5] which carried the discourse of the exchange of reason" (p. 19).

Reviewing Judaic tradition, then that of Hellenic and Pauline Christianity, and finally that of the Enlightenment, Amoros (1990) revealed women as the subject of the transcendent, far-reaching word and consequently their exclusion from the world of reason. In Enlightenment thought, she concluded, women are not a social subject:

> Their will is contained before all pacts, or as it were precontained in the pact. It is a precivic space that requires the mediation of another interpreter that is not herself, but the carrier of logos, who is a subject of the social pact between the diverse interpreters of logos: patriarchies and heads of families. (p. 28)

This trajectory that runs from antiquity to the establishment of bourgeois capitalist society (which makes the home and the private world the "kingdom" of women) is inseparable from that which converts feminine language into the intimate and domestic, the affective and practical. A language in contraposition to the rational, public, and speculative discourse appropriated by men. The footprints of gender are erased from this rational discourse, which assumes its centrality as the speech responsible for all communication between autonomous social subjects.

In this sense, feminine silence is not thought of as the absence of words but basically as the exclusion from a determined space and as a veto: a disqualification to name that which exceeds the area socially assigned to women. Movements for the vindication of the words of women tend then to seek to expand the universe of public speakers, to conquer a new social space, and to obtain recognition of women as full individuals, equals, actors, and citizens or with no necessity to seek the protection of or be protected by a male interpreter or mediator.

The exercise of speech as a way to recuperate dignity, as a step from the condition of being reified to that of a subject with full rights, is the exercise of entrance to the public scene and of the extension of socially determined linguistic competency. It is the construction of a new identity: that of women who assume roles of social representation and direction, leadership and participation, which are traditionally assigned to men.

Does this struggle to gain access to dominance of the established genderless language make possible a new feminine identity, liberated from male oppression and the self-marginalization that all similar situations provoke? Is discursive indifference the desired object of all these efforts to break the silence and utter our own words? In certain cases, in the reflections and practices inspired by what has come to be called the feminism of equality, yes (Amoros, 1990). But in many other cases, the issue is more complex.

> In respect to us, pulled between the timidity of entering a liberation movement for women and the feeling of a path without return, we mutter excuses, explanations, justifications. In what language do we speak? (de Oliveira & Harper, 1980, p. 40)

For the more dogmatic representatives of the feminism of equality, these types of questions on the issue of language lead to the dangerous "differential essence" of women. This threatens a reappearance of biologism, through ideas of sexual specificity, and to a certain idealism that is incompatible with the political struggles necessary to reverse inequalities between men and women.

From other perspectives, however, to ask oneself about language is one way of escaping assimilation into the masculine world. It is also the only guarantee to be a recognized social subject. That is to say, the way of escaping the:

> secular pagan and then Christian tradition which held that women, to become visible in society and in history, had to convert themselves into men.

To become what the classical and early Christian fathers called *mulier virilis,* "virile woman," a combination of female sex and male gender, a liminal and unclassifiable being, and as such much less dangerous to patriarchal order than a new model of gender. (Rivera, 1991, p. 128)[6]

In this sense, and by returning to my initial considerations of gender and its linguistic manifestations, the search for a woman's voice alludes not only to the right to express oneself in equal circumstances and with similar conditions of possibility as men but also to the elaboration of a discourse that recovers not essential but socially and historically constructed marks or footprints and recognizes them as valid. This discourse deserves to be spoken publicly, even though it derives from territories that are personal, private, and intimate, and exactly because of that, it recovers ideas of the integral human being. It is a word dignified because it identifies, permitting assimilation with some and allowing distinction with others, and which from difference seeks to construct equality.

Alfaro wrote of her experience of education and communication with migrant Peruvian women. She noted the feeling of not knowing how to speak that these women had and their wish to learn from her (and university activists like her) how to enter exclusively male domains. Alfaro (1988b) wrote:

> The [masculine] domination relates to the opposition between public and private spaces. The familiar words of women are valued, even shouted out. In the markets and at home feminine words are loud and expressive. They are listened to in the arena of personal dispute and in the exclusive relationship between client and merchant. Yet in assemblies and meetings this is not so; words are those of men. Feminine participation is limited to their presence and their vote, or to commentary between individuals. (p. 239)

However, as one can infer from other passages of Alfaro's reflections, the possibility of self-expression for these women questions notions of egalitarianism and instrumentalism. This is not a matter of access to new technical knowledge, the dominion of a code and of certain rules of social behavior, but that of encountering themselves in their own speech and from there seeking possibilities of interlocution in the wider scene:

> Because private speech is social silence, and liberation demands the questioning of those barriers which move women to public adventure without taking into account the value of that acquired in daily experience, private speech

must be converted into social speech. This is not about the other, public speech, but about amplifying the social and political force of daily life and its lessons. (Alfaro, 1988b, p. 144)

Feminine experience becomes, from this point of view, the territory of a new speech. Yet as this very experience negates the productive value of the feminine, the territory of reproduction, and service to others, it constitutes a territory to be renamed. From here the words of women are not mere positive verbalization but a creative act that must clear out, destroy, recompose, and make oneself.

Like all creations—even in language—this is the work of multidimensional individuals, placed in specific contexts, in particular times and spaces. The notion of the position of the subject (Mouffe, 1984) helps us to go beyond simplistic reductionisms and substantialisms. Each person is committed to a multiple game of identities. This recognition alerts us to the temptation of considering feminine speech as if it were the speech of women who do not identify themselves with other referents: a specific social sector, a color of skin, or a national or generational culture.

If silence and its opposite seem to mark women's efforts to achieve a valued identity, it is no less certain that other oppressions and restrictions make the question more complex (Sojo, 1988). For popular women, public speech is doubly removed from them, as they are women and poorly spoken, servants and minimally educated, intuitive, affectionate, irrational, and poor, and they share with their men a conquered language and economic and social oppression.

Feminine Speech and Popular Communication

Nothing lends itself to feminine speech, struggling against social and male discriminations and its own undervaluation, as much as popular communication.

> *I come from a silence*
> *old and very long*
> *from people who rise up*
> *from the depths of the centuries*
> *from people they call*
> *subordinate classes.*

I come from a silence
that is not resigned . . .

I come from a silence
that will be broken by people
who now want to be free
and love life;
who demand the things
that have been denied to them.

[From the song "I Come From a Silence"
by Raimon Pelegero Sanchís. Reprinted
by permission. Original text in Catalon.]

These verses of the Catalonian Raimon help me to say that beyond techniques and methodologies, resources, and means, what we in Latin America call popular communication has much to do with this unresigned silence, with these collective words that for so long have named when, where, and how one can do it; this is the reality of the popular groups. It is a speech that upon naming this reality—stammering, fragmented, and contradictory—makes it visible, identifiable, and meaningful (Mata, 1983).

Thinking of communication as a set of exchanges from which norms, values, ways of being, and identities are processed and from which interests, knowledges, and powers are shared and legitimated, we come to recognize communication as a key ground for the production of different meanings of the social order. That is to say, a ground on which different actors propose their own meanings of this order and their own ideas of what is real, and these ideas compete for hegemonic meaning. We can agree with Muñizaga (1983) when she affirmed that "the communication system of a society is constituted of a network of potential or actual opportunities of speech" (p. 9) and that "the speeches available to a society are the result of a communicative practice in which the means of power and social discipline are present, through the silencing of some expressive zones, the highlighting of others and the hierarchization of all" (p. 12).

Understood this way, a brief analysis of the communicative structure of Latin American societies reveals the nonactualization of a series of discourses that necessarily lead to the exclusion of some speakers. While some actors can display their discourse before society in different spaces and opportunities—giving these actors cohesion, legitimation, and power—others lack this possibility. And what is more serious, those others, impeded historically from participation in the production of public discourse, do not often demand their right or recognize their capacity. In this way, exclusion becomes internalized and naturalized, and it is only with difficulty recognized as part of the social and economic oppression that subordinate sectors of society suffer.

Despite this, an attentive look reveals the presence of multiple groups that offer resistance from their position of subordination and work to change this exclusive order. In the area of labor and production there were historical struggles by workers and peasants that used various means of action and social expression. Today, in the framework of significant socioeconomic redefinitions, we find the proposals of various groups: women, urban dwellers, workers from the informal sector, youth, seniors, and indigenous peoples. They resist different forms of social marginalization and develop alternatives in the areas of production, work, culture, and daily social life. They organize at the local level and beyond and present their demands to public or private authorities.

In this dynamic of confrontation, which assumes characteristics peculiar to each reality, excluded groups communicate in diverse ways. They begin to form their languages, begin to produce new discourses: It is not a discourse about the others but of us, a discourse that transforms nonrecognition into legitimacy, exclusion into presence. I could give multiple examples of these expressive practices: newspapers and neighborhood press networks, small community radio stations or program time bought on large stations, videos and audiovisual material used as a means for the debate of problems, marches, paintings, posters, pamphlets, and songs. These are speeches that name poverty, marginalization, injustice, and the initiatives to overcome them. These initiatives use all media available in a society that believes that what is not seen in public barely exists.

It is this ensemble of practices that many of us call popular communication, by which new communication actors—the peasants, the unemployed, women, indigenous peoples, street vendors, the illiterate, the inhabitants of poor neighborhoods, and the marginalized youth—make themselves visible to both society and themselves. It is a precarious and contradictory communication of exclusion, struggle, and the search for a self and a space to recognize oneself—what could be more appropriate for feminine speech! Yet, as with feminine speech, popular communication might become pure desire for egalitarianism or an echo of an already institutionalized discourse. Instead, popular communication must become a link marked by experience, a set of practices that permit the self-validation and identification of popular actors.

Popular identity is not some immutable or pristine essence, but refers to the way in which those actors respond to the hard question "Who are we?" This is inseparable from the question about the others that confirms identities by difference. The answers to the question are historical, given that identities form, disintegrate and recompose, through multiple processes in which those who compete choose or reject different ways or sources of identification (Romero, 1987).

From a sociological point of view, among these sources stand the recognition of the experience of popular subjects, originating in social practice and transformed in the representation of themselves. These are the representations that the other, the elite, create about the popular us, the most convincing versions of society that are formulated in the various institutions and spaces of power to ensure the process of social reproduction. Included here as well are those representations of the existing social order created from a critical or alternative position.

From a communicative perspective, it is in the area of discursive production where a repertory of possible identities unfolds. The mass media interpolate popular sectors in certain ways, naming them and representing them in determined ways and designing for them possible areas of symbolic interaction. These are possible cultural behaviors that popular sectors can choose to ignore but that are offered as a horizon.

Without a doubt, the mass media are the central source speaking to the popular in our modern societies. This is part of a set of operations that the media carry out to achieve acceptance, to form those social subjects as their audiences. Between the offer of meanings and their effective acceptance on the part of the popular sectors is strung the warp on which those sectors weave their identities. This is not the only source, but certainly the most privileged, given the centrality in our societies, the popular level of mass-mediated consumption, and the relative weakness of other sources of interpolation such as, for example, political and educational institutions.

It is in this context that the different communicative practices of a popular character develop into other, or alternative, means of identification. For example, these are found in the recovery of the image of the citizen for the popular world, a citizen named and placed in dialogue with the powers of society. Without denying the existence of the marketplace, popular subjects are represented as a workforce subject to their own laws and not as mere consumers. The poverty suffered and its causes are represented together with the innumerable individual and collective actions taken by the people to combat it. Yet these alternative routes to identification do not exist in a vacuum: They compete, contaminate, and differentiate with hegemonic proposals. In much the same way, women's speech emerges from the undervalued place it was historically relegated to and in conflict with the masculine speech consecrated as the norm. But these practices also do not exist in a vacuum: They compete with, are contaminated by, mimic, or sharply differentiate themselves from hegemonic proposals. In the same way the words of women create themselves in their historically undervalued place, in conflict with the masculine language that is consecrated as the norm and that still speaks to us.

Popular Radio: A New Voice on the Scene

In the Sierra Norte of Peru, between the peaks and hamlets of Cajamarca, there are *campesinos* (peasants) who farm, tend animals, build corrals to protect themselves against cattle thieves, and weave hats. They have also built their own radio transmitters by dismantling old receivers and experimenting with broken transmitters. Sometimes the radio waves cover up to 10 kilometers, other times less, if they are blocked by hills or trees. If batteries run dead or equipment breaks down, then these radio stations have to stop playing the music so loved by the inhabitants of the zone, and the messages exchanged with the audience are also silenced until the owners of the equipment travel to the capital or the coast to buy replacement parts. The same occurs when owners have to attend to urgent work or family business (Gogin 1990).

The radio stations obviously function outside of official approval. They are the informal Peru appearing in the field of communication and which, in Lima, pours forth from speakers installed in the barrios and popular markets. It is there where the voices of leaders, women, neighbors, and youth inform themselves, gathering together and acting out their daily dramas.

In Brazil, these speakers are found throughout the periphery of Sao Paulo. The eastern zone of this enormous city houses close to 3.5 million people, the majority of whom live in slums and tenements in conditions of simple survival. About 3 years ago, there, where people lack just about everything, *Radio de Povo* grouped together about 40 of these popular radios—generally a pole with four speakers installed in the parish or community center of each barrio and sector. Each radio covers a reduced, local space, through which neighbors speak and listen to each other. Between them, these radios cover an extensive suburban area and move around as well: six cars with speakers show up at protests and gatherings to strengthen the local population's voices.

Many kilometers from Sao Paulo, in the Venezuelan Andes, there are no speakers or farmers that dismantle and build to convert receivers into transmitters. Yet the voices of campesinos from southern Merida state are heard through Radio Occidente, a 10 kilowatt transmitter owned by the Catholic church. The same occurs in the Peruvian Amazonian through *La voz de la selva*, in the southern Dominican Republic through *Radio Enriquillo*, in the Ecuadorian mountains through ERPE and *Radio Latacunga*, and in southern-most Chile thanks to *Estrella del mar* and *La voz de la costa* (whose transmitter had to be moved each time the authorities attempted to stop it, often with the help of the poorest as happened in Bolivia with *Radio Tarija* and with the Peruvian *Onda Azul*).

This list of radio stations includes 30 more in those same countries and in others such as Mexico, Guatemala, Honduras, and Costa Rica. They are managed by the Catholic church and are usually found in rural areas, working to encourage the expression and participation of the popular sectors. In general, Catholic stations have a long history, relatively good equipment and facilities, and the possibility of receiving financial help and training for their staffs.

The character of the once-powerful Bolivian miners' radios is quite different. Few of these stations survive today, after the new economic policy begun by the government in 1985 weakened the State Mining Company, closing mines and relocating workers (Salinas, 1988). The experience of community stations in Argentina is also different, given that they exist on the fringes of legality. They arose mostly after 1984 as a result of the restoration of democracy and through the initiative of neighborhood organizations, church and educational institutions, and youth groups that wanted to challenge the centralization and concentration of mass media in the hands of a privileged few.

The above review of popular radio is not to be taken as an inventory, only as indicative of the fact that popular radio broadcasting in Latin America is diverse, heterogeneous, and changing. Powerful transmitters with daily programming of up to 18 hours and with complex organizations connected to other larger organizations—such as the church or a nongovernmental organization—are found along with small grassroots groups, which have different modes of management and social intervention. Any attempt to characterize them as homogeneous organizations would be highly simplistic.

However, among such diversity there is something in common, something substantial that allows these experiences to be placed in the area of popular communication. These are more or less successful attempts to allow popular subjects to communicate among themselves and with society, without the restrictions implied by the manipulated participation (for simple informative coverage or to increase ratings) offered by the hegemonic system of mass media. These stations represent one of the most permanent and consolidated strategies in South America to make popular words present in the public scene. They are contributing to the creation of a popular discourse and an organized action of solidarity that is working to reverse situations of injustice.

Another series of features are common among these experiences, even if in each case the outcome depends on the political and cultural conceptions of each group; the particular contexts in which they work; the greater or lesser articulation and activity of the popular movements connected to the work; and the religious, party, or institutional affiliations. For example, there are educative and cultural practices, facilitating a systemic analysis of reality, of issues, for forming critical judgments and proposals for action. They are spaces for the production of a particular popular knowledge that recover and validate people's history and experience as well as incorporate notions and habits that permit participation in increasingly complex social and economic realities. They are spaces for the symbolization of life that put into question the beliefs, ideas, and tastes of the popular sectors.

There are also common practices defined by their service dimension, including facilitating basic communication between distant subjects, supplementing mail inaccessible to the illiterate or telephones that do not exist, and providing information on the many and important themes of daily life. Last, they are political practices, intervening in the social realities in which they work to carry a discourse and confronting the powers that conspire against a dignified life for the popular sectors, individuals, and groups on the margins of the system of decision making, and the mechanisms for the distribution of wealth.

The ways to make these dimensions a reality are multiple and varied, not only with respect to the reach or management of the stations but in relation to the medium of radio itself: programming styles, production, relations with audiences. But in this area, there is also a common emphasis—the use of formats and methodologies to encourage the emergence of a new radio broadcaster, to facilitate the direct participation of popular subjects as interviewees, correspondents, and program producers.

The Place of Women in Popular Radio

In 1990, out of 61 institutions affiliated with the Latin American Association for Radio Education (ALER),[7] only 2 were directed by a woman. This is not a situation limited to ALER, whose Catholic affiliation does much to explain such a statistic. The Bolivian miners' radios were always managed by men, given their direct connection to the mining unions. Until recently, there were no women in positions of management in community radios in Argentina. In general, women are also not found in programing positions but as secretaries or receptionists and, as happens in the majority of mass media, working as announcers either alone or with men.

We cannot be surprised by this situation. Latin American popular radio is not an island; it reproduces the male hierarchical order in institutional terms, underlying the placing of women in service roles and their slow and difficult access to autonomous tasks and management positions.

Having noted this and recognizing it as an issue of primary importance, we return to what constitutes the substantial finality of the majority of popular broadcasters: to permit and favor the emergence of popular subjects as announcers in the public scene, through access to the territory of mass media, which is usually monopolized by the voices of power and their intermediaries. This is a role that implies the direct speech of these subjects as well as their discursive representation and their incorporation as actors in a reality constructed from their feelings and thoughts.

Diverse studies on Latin American popular radio indicate that women recognize that the medium has helped them to lose the fear of speaking.[8] In all cases, this willingness to speak appears connected to two basic dimensions of the work carried out by the stations. On one hand is the incorporation in programing of themes basic to the everyday life of women as themes worthwhile of a mass audience: their activities in the home as wives and mothers. On the other hand is the incorporation into the radio discourse of women as agents of social transformation, as actors in processes that at the everyday level (the basic necessities related to family survival) empowers women to be involved in the development of community-based organizational practices.

In the first case, either in programs targeted to women or directed by them or in other educational spaces, the everyday life of popular women is transformed into material for reflection. The characteristics of this life so often disregarded become the object of analysis and proposals from "experts" in the area but also by women whose experience is given equal validity alongside professional knowledge. Señoras are interviewed in the market about how they prepare foods bought in bulk to economize; wives and mothers (through sociodramas) share ways to confront male authoritarianism. Women who discover in popular radio that their affairs, those discussed with relatives and with no relevance at the level of informative agendas, are material worth speaking of. Speaking becomes easier when the presence of a microphone does not imply a necessity to enter the area of knowledge of the others, in which woman historically has stammered or shut up.

In the second case, given the importance that popular radio has placed on grassroots organizations and the diffusion and strengthening of collective experiences, the activities of groups of women, or of women in neighborhood movements and organizations, occupy an important position. The placing of women as equal social actors in the public terrain has an important historical dimension: Numerous popular radio stations begin to read the past in terms of the roles played by women in crucial moments of national or regional history, as individuals or collectively as *campesinas* (peasant women), *palliris*,[9] or mothers. And speaking becomes easier when, no matter how minor an action a woman carries out, words are pronounced in a space where women are not relegated to the kitchen or bedroom.

Yet the loss of the fear of speaking and the appearance of feminine themes and voices in radio do not necessarily equal the presence of women's words. The public and private worlds remain divided in the majority of cases. Women are spoken to as inhabitants of either one or the other but rarely as subjects that pass through both in a particular manner.

In many cases, the weight of class and economic determinations in the construction of social relations minimizes the importance of the predominant sexist model. This occurs especially when radio stations are not connected to groups or organizations of women who carry out their work with a perspective of gender. In general, popular radio has made great progress in recognizing the oppression of women as one injustice facing society. Yet a specific feminine discourse is often accused of being sectarian, antimale, or feminist, which, in those cases, stands for "ultra position of petit bourgeois women." This is an attitude and ideology that is understandable if we remember how the institutional power of popular radio reproduces the masculine model of social organization and covers or minimizes the oppression of women behind a global class oppression. In others, or sometimes at the same time, the fragmented representation of women is produced by the imposition and/or adoption of a logic valued for its communicative and political efficiency, that of argumentation unwilling to accommodate anything not based on reason.

To participate in radio is not easy, even more so for women. Not only because of a lack of familiarity but because they have made us believe that our word is not valuable, that only the educated, the cultured and men can speak. That's why many times we don't want to be leaders, because we don't speak well, nor use impressive and difficult words. And we're always afraid and prefer that others speak for us. And some people take advantage of this passive attitude and without consulting us speak for us. . . . But we have to know what we want, what we seek and talk for ourselves, because in this way we can be sure that we're not being used, control what we are saying and when we should be quiet. . . .

We have to begin with what we know how to do. And we're very good at dramatizing, telling our problems with socio-dramas; we do it with such emotion that we're very convincing. . . . Even if we have to speak in assemblies, to tell the news, denounce, etc. But always by telling a story, because we know how to get ourselves listened to that way. Our children are witnesses of how we know how to dramatize and tell stories. (AAVV, 1987, p. 40)

This excerpt from a workshop of popular promoters of communication from different Lima neighborhoods highlights some of the elements often absent in the radio speech of popular women. Constrained by typical radio formats—the news program, magazines, interviews articulated through questions of opinion, and debates—and by expressive forms derived from rational methodologies that have predominated in the area of popular education (see, judge and act, for example) women are required to "moderate" the expression of their feelings. Women are compelled to substitute anecdotes with notions; formulate clear, distinct opinions; disregard intuitions; and specify sources instead of valuing what is generally the source of their knowing: conversation with others.

These constrictions impede the participation of women in popular radio by devaluing what has been culturally configured as features of feminine thought and speech, as essential features of female identity. What becomes difficult as well is the assumption that difference is the requisite for the presence of women in the mass media and, by extension, in the public scene. This reveals one of the limitations typical not only of radio but of all practices of popular communication—the fruit of a restrictive and reductionist view of popular subjects.

The representation of the popular in radio for a long time privileged among many popular actors only one leading actor—the social class—and privileged, among various contexts of representation, varied spaces where popular actors develop their existence, only a few restricted scenarios—those delineated by labor relations and organizational practices—and privileged among multiple conflicts (sentimental, familial, generational, etc.) that run through popular life only one of socioeconomic character—the contradiction between capital and work or between bourgeois and proletariat. Within this way of representing the popular, women were workers; domestics; *pobladoras*; peasants; and fighters for a salary, for services, and for land. Even more, they were wives and mothers, responsible for the tasks connected to the reproduction of the workforce. But rarely were they partners to a man or the owners of a body and a sexuality, which was tangled up in taboos, or a person who in the function of maternity constructs in a distinct manner relations of affection. Women were not all of this because men were not affectionate and sexed subjects who carried paternity as an affective and cultural trait.

A content analysis of popular radio programming shows a predominance of social, economic, and political themes. The world of feeling and sentiment, the difficulties of becoming individuals and relating with others, the area of desires and personal expectations only appears occasionally. The heart is given time only at night, with melodic music accompanied by smooth-voiced announcers. Emotion, dreams, and affection are reserved for private spaces as though human beings from any social class are not also guided in the public sphere by passions, aspirations, and beliefs.

Today in Latin America there is a questioning of these ways of representation and construction of the popular in radio. They reject discourses articulated only in function of enlightened or rational matrices of thought, discourses that ignore the symbolic, mythical, and dramatic dimensions of feminine and popular culture. Yet some women, especially the young, still feel that their worries, dreams, ways of thinking, and problems are absent in popular radio.[10]

Upon the conclusion of a self-evaluation of the program *Our Life,*[11] produced for and by women in Lima, the authors stated:

> The evolution of the program today is found in the political dimension, demonstrated by the growing dialogue and interlocution with public authorities and private enterprise and including the presence of popular leaders and correspondents of the program. This role of the program as an intermediary in political dialogue, and as the possibility of the public legitimation of popular women has been highly successful: it has seen the direct participation of ministers and mayors and the promotion of women leaders who have conversed with the public through the telephone or by testimony collected in the barrios.
>
> However, this has not been as appreciated as the radio soap operas, advice and music produced by popular women. This is probably due to the lack of clarity and simplicity of the language and intellectual formation of the news, the disregard for emotion in favour of a more formal and calculated tone.
>
> Correspondents and leaders have to work on their radio discourse, and announcers have to tutor authorities and leaders on the culture of the

listeners, making them change their register, to put some emotion into social and political discussion. (Pinilla, Macassi, & Alfaro, 1990, p. 61)

Recently, upon finalizing research in Peru on *Radio Cutivalú,* we concluded that peasant women recognized the station as an educational resource; it provided the possibility for knowing, understanding, and receiving suggestions for action. At the same time, we perceived that the demands of women listeners basically centered around spheres whose social dimensions did not overshadow more individual concerns: family planning, the possibility of assuming control over their own bodies, drug addiction, and the threat of seeing the destruction of their children. Among the women, as well as some men, they chose to listen to two particular female announcers. These two are capable of sharing female sentiments and modalities usually judged as not developing a critical sense in the audience and are able to transmit adequate information to the audience, adding to the debate on the problems facing popular sectors in the region. They use a maternal and teaching language that insistently articulates advice and recommendations, a cunning that converts the gossipy "They say that . . ." into a resource to share disquieting truths in reference to their own emotional states about what is happening and what they communicate to listeners.

The Path to Be Walked

Despite inequalities (the uneven presence of women as radio producers), popular radios in Latin America have contributed to the legitimation of women as speakers. This is even though their own voices, capable of naming not only the feminine but naming the entire world in dialogue with the masculine, are still but a whisper.

Access to microphones and mass media technologies will make popular men and women technical equals. But it is an equality that by erasing differences perpetuates male injustice and supremacy. Because of this, being female in Latin American popular radio is a difficult task. It signifies breaking through barriers that split the public from the private as spheres belonging to one gender or another and restoring complexity to the human condition, and to men and women a complementary dignity.

To accept this task is to accept that there is a pathway ahead. I have no travel guides or recipes, because I do not believe they exist and because a review of the most significant radio experiences barely indicates the route to follow.

Yet this does not impede me from imagining trails, directions, and tracks. Some have been suggested by the reflections of popular women that I have been able to gather from what I call "popular memories of reception." This is the means by which radio (the object itself and its commercial broadcasting) becomes part of the culture of these social sectors. Others are suggested by my own experience as a woman wanting to speak in a world of words that although apparently neutral bears the mark of masculine domination.

Upon reconstructing the popular experience of being a radio listener, I found that for women this was an experience associated with an imagination of familial dignity and liberty. In countless testimonies (independent of age or when one began to listen to radio) the activity of listening is a means to leave the tight framework of the four household walls. At times, radio is characterized as allowing one, through radio theater or music, to be freed from the restrictions imposed by fathers or men on independent entertainment that is outside of the home and that requires an escort. In other cases, radio is the means to inform oneself on an equal level as men, who return to the home daily enriched by information obtained in the exterior context. As a consequence, this permits women to dialogue with men in better conditions.

These experiences bring me to consider to what point popular radio has neglected listeners in general and women listeners in particular. To what extent has the question "What do women experience as listeners?" been simply left behind. It is a space of dreaming, a means to give free rein to fantasies and desires, without stopping the washing and ironing. Yet it is also a resource to speak as women on a far and wide world that, especially on the popular level, seems part of the masculine dominion. What are the fantasies and desires that popular women want to feed through radio programs? What are the themes that they feel are important? This is exactly what must be researched. We must assume that beyond the facts offered by studies on what popular women consume (and that provide only a partial view of what women are offered by the market), we must recognize popular listeners and work with their demands and tastes to construct alternatives that represent them.

In the same way, and because of my own experience, I suggest that we study, beyond the issue of radio, the question of feminine discourse: How we speak, how we elaborate notions, how we argue, how we play, how we articulate the global and the particular, how we weave reason with sentiment, and how we relate data with our perceptions and experiences. The recognition of speech is the recognition of self. What do we know of our language, which can be lost when taking control of it only means to speak like the others?

Recently, in one of those shows mounted in all countries to award journalists and radio and television programming, a very significant thing happened in my city, although many readers would think it had little to do with the question of women and popular radio. So many awards were given and the televised time was so short that winners limited themselves to receiving trophies without speaking. There were, however, two exceptions. The only two women to receive awards for production and hosting television programs broke with established protocol and said that they could not remain silent on such an occasion. One woman spoke to offer the trophy to her parents for all the support she had received from them. The other remembered her husband, with whom she had shared a successful career as a radio theater actress, and her children, who work with her today.

And I, the television spectator, asked myself what this feminine transgression (which very much annoyed the show's producers, so concerned with following the schedule) was really saying. Many things, surely, and different for different viewers. For myself, as a woman, this unforeseen taking of the microphone, of speech, spoke to me of the female capacity to recognize the necessity of support for us to be able to work and the feelings of guilt and remorse when we divide ourselves between the home and the world. It spoke to me of the will not to leave outside of profession and notoriety that private and intimate dimension that constitutes family and affection. It spoke to me of being a woman in popular radio: a ground to gain in which entertaining, dreaming, speaking, and informing oneself should not be limitations but simple access to the mass and public space. It would be an entrance from what differentiates us by gender—that is historically and culturally—and also restores to us the right of parity with men.

Notes

1. There are radio programs with this same name in radio stations as far away from each other as *Radio Santa Clara* in Costa Rica and *Radio Onda Azul* in Peru, to name only two examples.

2. Name of a Costa Rican women's collective working on communication issues.

3. Name of the radio program produced by the Training, Promotion and Diffusion unit of the "Movement Manuela Ramos" in Peru.

4. See Prost (1990), who examined the "sites for feminine and masculine words" (pp. 119-120).

5. Expression for the perfect male.

6. See also Bidegain's (1986) reflections about the masculinization required for women in academic and ecclesial environments to be accepted as thinking beings with the ability to intervene publicly and institutionally.

7. This association, created 20 years ago, gathers radio stations, centers of production, and educational nongovernmental institutions that produce radio programs in almost all the Latin American countries. Of Christian inspiration, its goal is to contribute to the development of the popular radio in Latin America. A total of 80% of the affiliated radio stations are institutions related to the Catholic church.

8. In particular, we are referring to the results produced by the research carried out in collaboration with ALER about the workings of *Radio Enriquillo* (Dominican Republic), *La voz de la selva, Cutivalú* (Peru), *Radio Yungas* (Bolivia), and other studies developed by the Association of Social Communicators, Calandria, Peru.

9. In the Bolivian mines this is the name given to widows or abandoned women working independently in the leveled ground, gathering leftovers that contain mineral particles.

10. This type of perception was identified in my research on *Radio Cutivalú*, a radio station in the Peruvian north.

11. A program conducted by the Association of Social Communicators of Peru. It is broadcast through commercial radio stations that have a popular reception.

PART IV

Women as Sociopolitical Actors: Building Organization and Strategies of Communication

The chapters in Part IV bring a relational perspective that explores issues of grassroots communication, women's organization, and social movements. We look beyond the structures of communication (the communication means), the product, or the content to discuss grassroots communication as a strategy. At an institutional level, this includes strategies of participatory research, community development, and mobilizing initiatives. At the organizational level, it includes strategies for popular education and action.

In this context, a number of relationships are reviewed: between women's grassroots communication activities and women's organizations; among the communication proposals, the organizational structures, and the models of leadership; among gender alliances, the women's movement, and the feminist agenda; and between the strategies of communication and the alternatives provided by structures such as networks and **coalitions.**

More specifically, some of the chapters in this part address the relationship between communication strategies and political action for social change. They also identify how specific communication strategies address the social, political or institutional work in a specific area such as the environment, research, economic development, housing, and food provision. The notion of empowerment is reviewed, looking into the ways in which goals of women's empowerment are tied to the acknowledgment and further recognition of the knowledge and expertise of women regarding these areas.

Communication as Strategy: Forms and Issues

The design of an overall strategy of communication includes alternatives to disseminate ideas and information and ways to impact a target group. The strategy contains a plan for action that is based on the desires and needs of the participants and the goals of the organization implementing the strategy.

It is in this perspective that organizational proposals such as coalitions, alliances, and coordinating bodies represent an organizational effort to promote better information, mobilization, and communication. They constitute communication sites to provide channels of communication and decision making as well as instruments for change. Overall, they are proposals that attempt to address the power and leadership alternatives for social change-oriented initiatives.

Networking has been regarded as an important communication strategy that redistributes power and mobilizes, decentralizes, and disseminates information. An important contribution of a network is its capacity to support local struggles by linking them with wider issues of regional, national, or international organizations. Technologies such as computers, teleconferences, and faxes have become instrumental in the setting up of networks by allowing individuals and groups to connect through time and space.

The relationship between knowledge, power, and technology is crucial in the definition of this type of communication flow. The assumption is that the horizontal or circular structures provided by these networks defies the vertical exercise of power and redistributes it, while using the technology for a wider reach and a more friendly use. In Chapter 12, Mensah-Kutin introduces a Pan-African research and information-sharing project, the Women, Environment and Development Network (WEDNET). The article focuses on one specific country, Ghana, but brings forward the key issues for researchers from eight African countries. The network has three purposes (a) the documentation and legitimization of women's indigenous knowledge, (b) the attempt to link researchers for sharing of information and resources, and (c) the development of effective communication systems and strategies for disseminating information to impact policy makers, to share information with NGOs, and to associate grassroots users with the research findings (WEDNET, 1991). The network is an example of how women are building their own communication bridges, sharing knowledge and concerns, and developing research and communication strategies. Mensah-Kutin argues that research networks that implement participatory methodologies can potentially re-create positive images of women.

One area of concern for the researchers involved in this initiative is encountering the most appropriate ways to diffuse research results to women and the ways of empowering women's indigenous knowledge and environmental alternatives (Rosemary Jommo, personal communication). The question is how a communication strategy can provide the adequate structures and communication channels to empower women's knowledge and how it can be accomplished through the dissemination of research results and information (Rathgebher, 1989a).

Electronic networks are currently promoted as useful tools to facilitate community organizing. Annis (1990, p. 5) argued that their widespread use has generated an "information revolution at the grassroots," facilitating an increased "connectedness" of the poor. However, there are a number of concerns regarding access and control of these networks. Balka (1991) argued, for example, that "their value as an organizing tool is not guaranteed simply as a function of their use." The supposed decentralization of access and control and the deprofessionalization of production associated with such a network (Annis, 1990) are relative and very much mediated by the individual's capacity to access the technology and its language. What can instead happen is an unbalanced distribution of technical skills and, therefore, the tendency of those with the technical skills to control the information flow. Balka's research on the use of computer networks by feminist groups in North America showed the impact of this imbalance among those with and without computer skills.

In Chapter 13, Taylor elaborates on other alternatives for networking and linking women at a national and international level. She explains how the organization Single Mothers Against Poverty in Newfoundland, Canada, used teleconferencing to share concerns and experiences, for mutual encouragement in the process of personal and collective empowerment, for problem solving, and to reach the larger community and the government. The chapter provides an exploration of how a process of economic development is seen as a process of communication and of individual and group empowerment. The potential of a technology like teleconferencing to create information bridges and encourage empowerment processes is analyzed as well as its limitations in providing the same kind of personal and interactive experiences that interpersonal communication tools can facilitate. Taylor's argument for the need to recuperate women's interpersonal communication skills and communication tools indigenous to their cultural traditions is supported by Mensah-Kutin, who shows that the success of the Ghanian WEDNET researchers in acknowledging that women's knowledge about the environment is rooted in traditional informal channels of communication. These are channels that women have used to create community awareness and transmit knowledge about various aspects of their lives, knowledge included.

Both chapters agree that the major constraint for the implementation of development alternatives has been the disregard of indigenous alternatives and knowledge with respect to natural and social resources. This point returns us to Part II, where this gap was identified. In the institutional and mainstream development context analyzed in Chapters 12 and 13, this disregard has resulted in the continuous destruction of key environmental resources for the community (forest and fuel wood in the Africa case and fishing in Newfoundland) and systems and methods of living.

Social Movements, Women's Organizations, and Grassroots Communication

Another connecting idea of the chapters in this part is the involvement of women's organizations or women's media production in larger social movements that use protest, defense of rights, and social demand for change to become active subjects of social change.

Alfaro's chapter on women as social communicative agents and the interview with Lloyd (Chapter 14), one of the editors of the South African women's magazine *Speak,* examine some of the motivating factors for participation. Alfaro identifies how social motherhood is the motivating factor for the participation of women in the various struggles in Lima's barrios. Through their participation in the production of radio soaps or in the movements for a "glass of milk" or "popular kitchens," women recognize themselves as women and as mothers but also as belonging to a social motherhood—a motherhood that connects women, their organizations, and their communities. While acknowledging the importance of social motherhood in participation, these authors suggest that this is not the only goal of women's movements. However, progressive political organizations and social movements have tended to perpetuate the idea of women's participation in supporting and secondary roles. Women have regularly been isolated from positions of leadership in mixed-gender organizations, and their key roles as equal partners in processes of change have been frequently disregarded.

Women's joining of social movements brings an increase of work and social and domestic responsibilities. The burden of their participation needs to be acknowledged. An increase in women's participation in organizations is not generally accompanied with a redistribution of their tasks within the family or community. Paradoxically, many progressive movements have failed to address these issues, either regarding the increase in women's work or the unchanged status of couple relations (inequalities between heterosexual couples, battered women, etc.). Alfaro's analysis of the challenges posed to women's organizations when they achieve their social goals provides a stimulating discussion: There is a need to look beyond the goal of women joining organizations. Once there is a strong organization, the challenges are to democratize and redistribute power within the organization itself, in relation to larger organizations and mixed-gender structures and in changing the forms of leadership. Lloyd mentions how within the African National Congress (ANC) and the Congress for Democratic Elections in South Africa (CODESA), as in various other organizations, women are bringing these issues to the front. *Speak,* as a women's magazine, plays a leading role in providing space for both women and men to discuss and present their views about these issues.

Conflicts of leadership and democracy within the women's organization and overall within the women's movement is one area of continuous discussion and concern. In fact, as Ford-Smith (1989) pointed out, the fetishizing of the grassroots organization sometimes covers up the irresolvability of a number of conflicts, the power of intervention of outside actors, and the presence of informal power structures. As Alfaro discusses in Chapter 15, the structures of communication and tools of information acting within the organization itself have often failed to address the entire constituency of these organizations. The continuance of informal power when the structure is vaguely defined as horizontal, collective, and democratic represents a key constraint to the development of these organizations both in terms of their internal communications and in the way they establish outside relationships. Kishwar (1990) asserted that the importing of structures like collectives to non-Western women's initiatives proved to be mistaken. In organizational settings where there is a heterogeneous group, the collective structure cannot guarantee either equal responsibilities or continuity. Moore (1986) criticized collectiveness as an end in itself, as it just becomes anti-dialogue, anti-participatory, anti-democratic activity.

Alfaro (1990) noted, for example, how the general assembly, considered as the ultimate form of democratic organism, tends to function with informal power and leadership that allows for little real participation. With the formalization of the structures, the communication becomes one of a more rational and articulated communication, for which there is little space for personal feelings and emotions, for resolutions of conflict, or for crises of everyday life (Ford-Smith, 1989).

Collective decision making and collective media production seem to work well with very small groups that have a strong sense of group membership, with limited and tightly defined aims and objectives. Within larger groups these processes tend to become lengthy and inefficient. In structures where the roles of leadership are not clearly defined (because of the principles of horizontalism and egalitarianism), processes of participatory media production can increase informal practices and mechanisms of authoritarian power, especially when the manipulation of media such as radio or video fosters a feeling of power for its user (interview with Stuart, 1990).

From Group to Movement: Women's or Feminist Movement?

Depending on the view and position regarding the women's movement and its agenda and different communication strategies and positions in regard to mainstream media, social demands and organizational alternatives are foreseen. In the case of Latin America, Alfaro identifies how approaches to gender and communication have had two points of departure. The first is in feminist concerns about the manipulative capacity of mass media to foster gender inequalities, and the other is in popular communication approaches that see women's and popular organizations as the field to question inequalities and as strategies to defend life in conditions of economic or political hardship.

The connections between local and regional, Western and non-Western women's organizations, women's movements, and feminism seem to be a constant source of tension and challenges. Lloyd suggests, for example, that the women's movement has evolved in South Africa not within a feminist movement or within an antisexist movement parallel to the movement against racism and poverty but in the active presence of women and their views in the political and social movements. The identification of feminism as a movement with northern origins has brought a number of questions and concerns for women in southern regions as the label does not necessarily identify the type of experiences, goals, and concerns of these groups. In India, for example, some scholars and grassroots educators have emphasized the need to look at the indigenous roots of women's movements in their own history and not just as a contemporary feminist movement. The presence of informal social networks and togetherness among women has been in existence for many years and is an approved form of organization in India (Ghadially, 1988), as is the case in Africa of women's organizations and associations that have been in existence since precolonial times (Moore, 1988; Stamp, 1989).

One editor of *Manushi,* an independent women's magazine in India noted the constraints of adopting a feminist label: The prioritizing of some struggles and forms as the agenda of a women's movement is difficult in a context where the identification of other social struggles, the need for alliances with other oppressed groups, cannot be reduced to a women's issue or to gender subordination. This is echoed in some of the remarks made by Lloyd; however, she also notes the increasing acknowledgment by women of the centrality of gender issues. The type of women's organizational processes we are describing here have emerged as a response to a number of economic survival and defense of rights issues rather than around the identification of a gender inequality. This identification is something that with time and the growing and maturity of the organization, women may address. Taylor mentions how the identification of the differences of resources between men and women has been a painful process for Thai women. Struggles for equality of women are seen by Lloyd as more difficult, because "it's not a struggle against an outside enemy, it's a struggle against our brothers, fathers, husbands, and comrades."

Strategies of Communication

The chapters in this part contain a number of methodological proposals to readdress some of the questions formulated throughout the book. Taylor explains how the use of a variety of communication means such as video, teleconferencing, and interpersonal communication represent effective ways to explore social resources, gender roles, economic distribution, and changes in tradition. The processes followed by women in rural and urban Newfoundland and in the Mahasarakham province of Thailand demonstrate the power of the communication to work on a variety of levels, from identifying obstacles for personal development and empowerment to looking at the group and community level, the women's economic and social contribution, and the impact of modernization in the community.

Mensah-Kutin's chapter sensitizes us to the need to implement participatory research methodologies. Research is seen as a communication process that requires a communication strategy that identifies indigenous forms of communication. This issue is of relevance for research carried out in Third World societies, because, as Meena and Mbilionyi (1991) pointed out, their dependency from external donors carries the danger of an external agenda, which emphasizes the policy-making and reformist aspects of gender and social issues and grants limited space for political activism and social change goals.

In her review of the responses and communication strategies of Latin American women to the economic, social, and political crises Alfaro illustrates, how the support of these initiatives raises communication dilemmas that have not been carefully considered. Beyond the training of women in media production, video making, radio broadcasting, and or coordination of meetings, the communication work must look at the ways that communication with others (the state, the political parties, the other classes) is established. This includes carefully considering the ways the images of women leaders are going to be managed in the mainstream media and how to counteract the level of exposure and risk that this presence of women in mainstream media might entail.

The first chapter in this part is by Mensah-Kutin and discusses the communication strategies used by the Ghanian WEDNET researchers in their research process and in the dissemination of information. Chapter 13, by Taylor, discusses the use of teleconferencing, interpersonal communication tools, and video in the process of economic empowerment of women's groups in Newfoundland and in the Mahasarakham province of Thailand. Chapter 14 is based on an interview with Lloyd on the work of *Speak,* a South African women's group that publishes a magazine. In Chapter 15, Alfaro presents an analysis of women as communicative and social agents, exploring their social maternity and leadership. The chapter reviews the popular communication experiences in Latin America with a special focus on the evolution of women's neighborhood and market associations in Peru. This chapter closes the book, as it presents a holistic analysis that identifies research, political, organizational, and communication avenues that shape participatory practices of communication. The self-critical tone of the chapter provides the reader with a number of open issues that suggest new research agendas and communication strategies.

12

The WEDNET Initiative:
A Sharing Experience Between Researchers
and Rural Women

ROSE MENSAH-KUTIN

In Africa, there is an increasing awareness that rural women's poverty and marginalization is the result of structural inequalities they experience in the development process. In recognizing the general impoverishment of African peoples, there is an increased acknowledgment that African women are even worse off in social, political, and economic terms.

The development of colonialist policies have ignored the very core of traditional African practice. In Africa, the imposition of Western frameworks of socioeconomic development and growth rejects all that is truly African, adopting foreign modes of thinking and behaviors that have brought untold hardship to the continent's populations, especially women.

An example of policies on the food production sector will explain this point. Before the colonial period, African women were key food producers. Yet when cash crop production of cocoa and coffee became a major policy of the colonial government (especially in the Ashanti[1] region of Ghana), women were ignored while men were encouraged to migrate to undertake farming in cocoa. Women became responsible for the traditional subsistence sector that, though crucial for household survival, continues to attract little or no support from governmental policies.

In recent years, considerable interest has been generated in women and development issues. Governments and international agencies now recognize that integrating women effectively and fully in the development process is not just a question of equity but one of necessity for national and international progress (Dixon-Mueller & Anker, 1990).

With reference to Africa, action by women's groups, researchers, and concerned individuals has brought to the fore the need to take into account the crucial role and position of women in the society. At different levels, efforts are being made to analyze socioeconomic, cultural, and political issues from a gender perspective.

The question of the environment is one issue subjected to such an analysis. The worsening condition of the environment has become a matter of great concern for African countries that depend heavily on their natural resources for their livelihood. In some areas of Ghana for instance, more than 80% of the forests have already been lost (Ministry of Energy, Ghana, 1991).[2] Agricultural practices that involve deforestation and overfishing are also issues of great concern. The cost of losing the environmental resources in Africa is a high one.

In an effort to understand the complex nature of the environmental question, a methodological approach for research was developed by the Environment Liaison Centre International (ELCI)[3] under its research project the Women, Environment and Development Network (WEDNET).[4] Under this initiative, it was hoped that a clear appreciation of the environmental situation in Africa could provide the basis for effective planning and policy-making objectives at the regional, national, and local levels.

The unique quality of the objectives of WEDNET is in its emphasis on women's knowledge, especially the indigenous knowledge rooted in African tradition that has been ignored or changed over time. It is essentially an attempt to look at women's roles and perceptions of environmental issues. In the long term, it looks at the African culture and reclaims it for sustainable development.

Because culture itself is closely linked to communication, this chapter examines the extent to which Ghanian researchers of the WEDNET initiative have used traditional and other forms of communication to study women's experiences at the grassroots level. It establishes a link between women's media (interpersonal communication, dance, indigenous drama) and the use of these tools for developing awareness about the environment. Furthermore, this chapter assesses the extent to which the researchers of the WEDNET initiative have taken into account grassroots women's mode of articulating their views and the ways to use adequately these modes of communication to elicit information about the environment.

The chapter is divided into three sections: The first gives a brief summary about the media, traditional forms of communication, and women's roles and positions within it. The second gives background information about WEDNET itself, and the third focuses on an analysis of the WEDNET research as was undertaken in Ghana. The information in the third section is based on interviews conducted among the Ghanaian researchers themselves.

The Media, Women's Concerns, and
Traditional Forms of Communication

Ghana's pattern of development, like other countries in Africa, has been characterized by an unequal relationship in the world capitalist system in varied historical forms (Nyong'o, 1989)[5]. In practice, there has been a near destruction of the traditional ways of thinking and behavior, impacting negatively the economic sphere as well as the whole political and cultural fabric of the society.

In regard to Ghana, much damage has been caused as far as the indigenous culture is concerned. The mass media have been the focus of development campaigns and policy in a context where more than 70% of the people live in the rural areas and lack formal education. Furthermore, there is little or no access to radio, television, newspapers, films, or books in these areas. Thus messages transmitted through mass media are often rarely accessible or meaningful to the population who produce the bulk of the country's food.

The development of mass media not only has ignored the basic tenets of Ghanaian culture but has also been promoted without adequate involvement of women. The positive contributions of women to society have not been included in the institutional capacity of mass media. Instead, building on some of the negative aspects of traditional male/female relationships, media messages are often demeaning to women. This is worsened by the lack of proper understanding of the implications of such messages by women themselves, because the majority of the women in the rural areas lack formal education.

Mlama (1989a) referred to the portrayal of women in the African media as being the same as that in capitalist cultures; the woman as a sexual plaything, a commodity. She also pointed out that the other culture that sees the woman as a toiler, a producer, a pillar of society's welfare have had little space or time in these media (see also Chapter 4).

It is to re-create these positive images and roles of women that a research objective such as the WEDNET initiative was undertaken. But before one gets into what was actually accomplished, it is essential to establish some of the basic principles of culture and, therefore, of communication in the

African traditional context. These principles served as part of the approach adopted for the WEDNET research.

The belief that there is a traditional mode of communication that is
positive in its portrayal and closeness to women is rooted in the belief in
an authentic African culture. Moemeka (1989) gave prominence to the
idea of the reality of an African culture, which is distinguished from African
ethnic groups or from Western, Eastern, and other cultures. He accepted
Turnbull's (1963) and Levine's (1966) characterization of African culture
as ethnic pluralism and diverse as well as Ricard's (1970) view of a cultural
marginality or the dualism of the African culture. Cultural marginality or
dualism refers to the idea that there are certain cultural patterns that are
distinctively African and not specific to any ethnic grouping. Yet as a result
of cultural interaction between Africa and the West (which is unequal and
Western dominated) these patterns have been influenced to the point at
which they have been transformed or modified, becoming neither African
or Western, taking on a kind of in-between character. He further defined
culture as that which determines the code, context and meaning of communication, where communication refers to what occurs in traditional or
the rural African context.

At this rural or grassroots level, the media of communication are accessible to women and carried out in family and village meetings, the marketplace, the village school, funeral occasions, and social forums. Through story
telling, songs, dances, discussion, and drama, these communication forums
serve as important channels for dissemination of information about the
social, cultural, economic, and political life of the people. Looking at the
forms and channels of communication, it is clear that in the African context,
interpersonal means of communication is what is closest to the people.

As outlined by Moemeka (1989), there are five basic principles underlying the clear identification of African peoples with this interactive form
of communication. These principles are true of the general African situation as well as the particular Ghanaian context. Specific communities will,
however, define these principles, taking their own socioeconomic reality
into consideration. These principles are the importance of the community,
the capacity of the individual to be useful and sensible, the sanctity of
authority, the respect to be accorded old age, and religion where there is
no clear distinction between ordinary and sacred matters.

As women have been marginalized in the mainstream media, they have
learned to create, for themselves, forms of communication at the grassroots level that have evolved from the principles outlined above. These
efforts have rightly been recognized by Lihamba and Mlama (1986) as

being very important in creating the condition for making women active participants in their development as they find them more familiar and easily identifiable culturally.

Background to WEDNET

It is a tragedy not only of the Ghanaian case but of Africa as a whole that the basis and forms of communication that are appropriate to women's experiences have been neglected. The overemphasis on formal planning through the mass media has often led to the projection of views and concerns that have little or no relevance to the local socioeconomic condition. In the case of women, as they are already disadvantaged in such situations, what they know and can offer toward change are often ignored.

Recent scholarship on women's roles and positions in society and on gender issues has brought to the fore the need to recapture tools of communication that are more accessible to women. This is seen as a way of ensuring that mainstream planning and decision making take them into account.

The WEDNET initiative was conceived with these concerns in mind. It is a project that was launched in 1989[6] by the ELCI, with financial support from the International Development Research Centre (IDRC)[7] through its Gender and Development Unit (GAD). The project was formally launched in June 1989 at a meeting in Nyeri, Kenya. At this forum, researchers from different academic disciplines and information and communication specialists came together to develop methodological approaches to undertake research and networking.

There are three interrelated aspects of WEDNET. One component endeavors to link up the researchers in a computerized network for purposes of sharing information and other resources. Another aspect is focus on the publication of a newsletter, *WEDNEWS,* which serves as an ongoing medium of information on activities within the WEDNET and other issues coming from the wider development community.

The major component of WEDNET is research attempting to cut across several academic disciplines in 10 different countries in subsaharan Africa. The theme of the research is women and natural resource management in Africa. The assumption is that African countries are currently faced with the common problem of deteriorating environmental conditions. A problem that takes on specific forms in particular ecological and socioeconomic contexts and that requires the identification of both similarities and differences to outline strategies for improving the African situation.

The common framework of investigation under the research project is that the environmental crisis in Africa and the poverty of African women are not distinct phenomena. This situation is the result of global and regional policies that force African women to transfer their own precarious socioeconomic conditions onto the environment to meet their immediate subsistence needs while jeopardizing the sustainability of the environment. This has led to the trivialization and undermining of what women know about the environment.

Hence, the overall purpose of the WEDNET research is to document and legitimize women's indigenous knowledge in the traditional and contemporary contexts as part of the search for strategies to halt the degradation of Africa's environment and bring about sustainable development. This clearly links up with the theme of traditional forms of communication at the grassroots level. Women's knowledge about their own environment is hardly to be found in the mass media of communication. This knowledge is rooted in traditional, informal channels of communication that have been used historically by women to create awareness and knowledge about the environment and other aspects of socioeconomic life.

Gender, Communication, and Environmental Issues

Two main subthemes under the framework of the WEDNET research have been considered in Ghana. These are women and forestry resources in Ghana, by Schandorf, and gender and access to land: the interface between land tenure and land use management in Ghana by Manuh and Songsore.[8]

This section outlines the main findings of the research and examines the extent to which various aspects of grassroots communication mechanisms informed the research undertaking. The methodologies employed will also be examined to establish their connections with women's own way of articulating their views and knowledge about their environment. To a large extent, the studies undertaken in the Ghana case combine issues of gender and communication to examine aspects of the environment that are critical for a sustainable development.

The study on gender and access to land shows women's deep concern about the deteriorating condition of the land and its resources, which in the past served as the main source of livelihood. It indicates that ensuring household food security is the major concern of the participants in the study. There is also the increasing need for cash to meet pressing social and economic needs. However, the ability to ensure food and derive other revenue is increasingly threatened by ecological change and population and demographic pressures, leading to a decline of soil fertility and production.

In one of the study areas—Barekese, in the southern part of Ghana—where some forest cover still remains, there is a lesser dependence on the market for food purchases, and it is possible for some households to engage in cocoa production. However, in both Barekese and Ahwiaa (the other southern study location) migration, especially by men, occurs and is increasing. This is more severe in Ahwiaa, which has lost all forest cover and has become derived savanna because of demographic pressure for land for housing. As a result, even indigenous people are forced to rent land under different arrangements, and many women are abandoning farming. This has wide implications for food production nationwide. In addition, the study identified customary law as the operative legal regime, although there is selective use of the state legal system. The study also noted widespread knowledge of the Intestate Succession Law,[9] but actual application is limited. Finally, the research identified women's extensive knowledge and concern about environmental degradation and their willingness to support efforts toward reversing the trend.

With reference to the study on women and forestry resources in Ghana, the knowledge that was identified and documented was immense, and the methodological approach was extremely rewarding. Major conclusions of the study are yet to be drawn, but the findings so far show the willingness of women to come together and discuss their own problems and suggest ways of solving them.

As far as the evidence goes, there is much to say about gender and class identities in the study areas. In the study on access to land, particularly, it is clear that there exists evidence of differentiation among households between indigenous and nonindigenous, between men and women, and among women themselves. While the general level of the village community precludes very sharp differentiation in the living conditions of most villagers, the materials used in house construction, the size of holdings and receipts from production vary among groups and individuals. Many women depend on others for land rights and so are nonautochthones who rent land for cash or do sharecropping. Women generally need to contribute labor on husbands' farms to be rewarded with a share of farmland ownership, which is not often transferred until after the death of the husband.

The wives of migrant farmers/laborers have the least land rights and can often not even spare their labor for own-account farming. The implications of these for rural differentiation and conflict are immense but are left to the villagers alone to handle. There is an awareness of these differences, and poorer women are often more articulate about their problems.

What is clear from these studies is the general powerlessness of women in the face of the worsening environmental condition. The study locations differed in socioeconomic, ecological, and linguistic backgrounds. Yet the situation of women is similar: powerless and poor yet conscious of the need for change and a better future.

How was it possible to uncover the hidden agenda of women's relationship with environmental questions? In the study on gender and access to land, the villages of Barekese and Ahwiaa, near Kumasi (the regional capital of Ashanti) were chosen.[10] As a contrast, the Upper West region in the northern sector of the country was also selected.

While the Ashanti villages are essentially matrilineal in character, the Upper West is predominantly patrilineal.[11] In regard to ecological systems and historical backgrounds, differences are obvious: the north is in the savanna belt, and Kumasi is in the forest zone.

Despite these differences, the researchers were able to investigate how men and women are able to secure rights to land in different tenure regimes in the study areas. They were also able to establish the extent to which particular tenure regimes impinge on the long-term stability and sustainability of vital resources and the emergent lines of conflict between the different tenure regimes and their reflections at the levels of gender, class, and state.

The other research on women and forest resources management was also undertaken in the Saboba-Chereponi[12] district in the Northern region of the country. The objective here was to examine whether there were different management practices of forest resources with reference to women. Though detailed findings of this study could not be provided, it was clear from this study that the women's condition is worsening because policies of government have ignored the wealth of women's knowledge about the utilization of trees, seeds, and the environment as a whole.

It is important to establish at this point that the interests of the researchers themselves were in direct relation to the topics for study. In spite of their different academic backgrounds, they shared the common interest in issues of gender and its implications for land use and forest resource management.

From this common perspective, the researchers believed that the undertaking of the WEDNET research was going to increase their own sensitivity to gender and class inequalities in the development process. More important, they acknowledge that focusing on women's knowledge and natural resource use and management cuts across the efforts to deal with the various aspects that determine the lack of recognition of women's position in society. Thus, from the onset, the communication aspect of the research was seen as being a fundamental issue: "I believe that if research is to be of any use it should identify who its audience is, the levels and the ways to disseminate information," said researcher Manuh (personal interview).

Recognizing the importance of mechanisms of communication, the researchers attempted to achieve effective ways of communication. Dialogue with persons working in existing administrative structures was seen as the way to reach out to the grassroots women who constituted the study participants.

At the local government level, there were, for example, the secretariat of the Committees for the Defence of the Revolution (CDRs) and the National Council on Women and Development (NCWD).[13] In addition, there were nongovernmental organizations that served as key institutions for reaching out to women in the data collection exercise. There are also traditional structures that coexist with the governmental structure. These consist of the chief and traditional councils, which have important roles to play especially in the rural areas. There are also grassroots organizations such as the 31st December Women's Movement (DWM)[14] and the town development committees. All these represent vehicles for community mobilization in support of initiatives aimed at improving the situation of women.

The identification of these institutions as essential channels through which women can be reached shows the extent to which the researchers gave recognition to existing structures that were relevant to the people at the grassroots level. Researchers were committed to deal with the reality of their study participants. They acknowledged and established a relationship with authority figures in the institutions and at the different levels in the communities as a basis for securing access to the views and opinions of the women. Without adequate government recognition, NGOs have improved the situation of women, especially through income-generation activities. They have, therefore, become important channels through which women can easily be reached for dialogue and action. These organizations constituted an important source for the researchers.

In both research projects, the methodology linked up with the basis of communication in the African context. The focus was on the interpersonal channels of communication through structures that recognize the importance of the individuals and the community, the role of the chief and other opinion leaders, and the significance of religion, structures that encompass all aspects of life. Such collaboration and cooperation were ensured in the data collection exercise.

The awareness of the need for fostering effective means of communication as a condition for participatory research is further borne out by the choice of persons to serve as facilitators. In both studies, there was reliance on facilitators (who were mostly women and who had some experience as far as the subject matter of the research was concerned) from within the communities themselves. Meetings with village chiefs and other notables (symbols of authority) to explain the purposes of the research helped in deciding on the right choices of persons as facilitators.

However, sometimes making the right choices was not easy. In areas where peace prevailed in the socioeconomic and political setup, it was easier to identify with whom to communicate what issue. When the reverse was the case, it was more difficult. For instance in Barekese, there were no chieftaincy disputes or conflicts, and all the government structures were in place. But in Ahwiaa, there were two factions, and it was necessary to take this into account not to get caught up in the dispute.

With the assistance of the facilitators, participants in the study areas were selected. Language[15] was not a problem, as the researchers themselves could communicate in the language spoken in their particular study area. In the case of the women and forestry study, the facilitators often acted as translators. Because facilitators had been recruited from the study area, the women who participated in the research trusted them.

It is however interesting to note that women sometimes did not want to discuss matters relating to land disputes, given their peculiarly weak position of ownership and control of land, especially in the northern sector of the country.

Recognizing that communication can be facilitated when it is a two-way approach, the researchers adopted a participatory method of research. They identified with the people and respected their opinions and views on the subject matter. Thus it was more of a bottom-up rather than a top-down approach. There were interviews with knowledgeable informants, with women's groups, and at the household level, where detailed life histories were gathered. In addition to the direct interviewing among the people at the grassroots level, other sources of secondary data were sought from published works.

While it was easy to create the necessary condition for effective communication, there were situations in which the researchers had to deal with specific traditions and values in their efforts to communicate with the women. Ardayfio-Schandorf, in her study on women and forestry resources, was faced with the problem of how to mobilize women in the study area. To come to terms with this, she relied on the already mobilized women's groups as ready focus groups to develop initial communication. In the gender and access to land study, Manuh had to deal with the issue of decision making and power concerning reproduction. This was sometimes problematic, especially among nonliterate women, since culturally to speak openly about sexual reproduction offends popular morality and the sense of decency. Conscious of this fact, she tried to use female facilitators. Also the fact that she herself was a woman often helped to relax her audience and to ensure that there was effective communication. Again, in such situations, interviews were conducted with the individuals alone or in the presence of other women if this was the choice of the participant.

Thus the key communication strategy was based on the consciousness that the researcher was taking up the time of the grassroots participants. In spite of the need for operating on the same plane as the women, the researchers' perceptions of the research benefit was not necessarily the same as the women participants. The researchers and the women shared the common objective of seeking answers to women's position in society, thus there was a kind of equity between them. The WEDNET study shows the importance of combining issues of gender and grassroots communication mechanisms to discuss developmental questions.

The researchers did not see their audience as objects of study but as subjects whose active involvement and participation in the discussion of the subject matter could bring out critical issues that ought to be addressed by policy makers. By giving recognition to the validity of their perceptions and modes of thinking, ordinary women could easily identify with middle-class women to discuss problems affecting their very survival.

As researcher Manuh said, "I believe that by discussing issues with grassroots women, some perspectives are opened up. As a middle class woman who enters these communities, the messages can be contradictory, although the manner of communication helps towards some empathy" (personal interview). For her, one of the joys in undertaking the research was when after interviewing a woman for nearly 2 hours, the woman turned the discussion to herself and contraception. "We could talk as women about the powerlessness of many women over their sexuality and reproduction," she recounted (personal interview). In this instance, the researcher realized that she was being educated about the woman's maternal condition and it struck her how many of the methods of contraception were new to her (the researcher) and how the assumptions that all women live in houses with privacy, running water, and bathrooms were inappropriate.

Yet it was not the mere fact of being a woman that helped to facilitate the communication process at the grassroots level. The main factor was having a sense of recognition of grassroots women's own reality, according them with respect and understanding in the discussion of developmental issues.[16]

To evolve strategies for ensuring that there are opportunities for a continuing sharing of experience and knowledge, links have been forged with some of the study participants and some of the areas have been revisited. In the event of the development of a project or program to address some of the problems at the locations, such women will constitute a ready target group.

Conclusion

This chapter has shown that grassroots women are aware of the problems they face in their daily survival strategies. While their concerns have been ignored over the years, a research initiative such as WEDNET is an important contribution toward finding a suitable medium for identifying these environmental problems and women's views and knowledge about the environment.

The WEDNET research shows the rewards of establishing a horizontal and emphatic relation with women at the grassroots level. Here, traditional interpersonal modes of communication are very crucial as they respect the reality of rural communities. In this research process, a common identity was evolved with grassroots women in spite of the researchers' middle-class background. This identity provided a basis for the articulation of issues on the environment. Discussing the real issues at stake and using forms that are close to women are the beginnings of finding solutions to African women's precarious socioeconomic condition and to the environmental situation.

Notes

1. Ashanti is in the southern part of Ghana. The Ashantis were formidable in the struggle against colonial rule. For more information about the Ashantis, see Rattray (1923, 1929).

2. The Ministry of Energy is responsible for coordinating all energy sector activities in Ghana.

3. The ELCI was established in 1974 to promote the ideals of sustainable development; it is headquartered in Nairobi, Kenya.

4. WEDNET researchers have conducted research using a common methodology to uncover different aspects of women and environment. Topics include forestry, land tenure system, and medicinal plants. The framework is one of participatory research.

5. For more information on the world economic system and Africa's position within it, see Frank (1980) and Goncharov (1977).

6. The project was to be of a 3-year duration.

7. The IDRC is a research funding agency based in Ottawa, Canada.

8. Elizabeth Ardayfio-Schandorf is a senior lecturer in the geography department of the University of Ghana at Legon. She works on women and energy and other developmental issues. Takyiwaa Manuh is a senior research fellow and the coordinator of the Development and Women Studies (DAWS) program of the Institute of African Studies (IAS), University of Ghana at Legon. Jacob Songsore is a senior lecturer in the geography department of the University of Ghana at Legon.

9. This law was promulgated in 1987 to rectify the situation under customary marital arrangements where wives and children suffer unduly when the man dies intestate.

10. For administrative purposes, Ghana is divided into 10 regions: Greater Accra, Western, Central, Eastern, Volta, Ashanti, Brong Ahafo, Northern, Upper East, Upper West.

11. Traditional forms of inheritance in Ghana consist of the matrilineal and patrilineal systems. The matrilineal is practiced by the Akans, while the patrilineal is practiced by the other ethnic groups in the country. In the matrilineal system, a person inherits from the mother's line, while in the patrilineal, the individual inherits from the father's line. In both systems, the rule of primogeniture is observed.

12. Apart from the various regions in the country, there are districts that constitute the focal points in the country's administration. Starting from 1988, the number of districts increased from the original 65 to 110. Each district is headed by a district secretary.

13. The CDRs are organs for popular participation at all levels and were established when the present military government of Ghana, the Provisional National Defence Council (PNDC) came into power on December 31, 1981. The NCWD was set up in 1975 to advise the government on all issues affecting women in Ghana. It has assisted women's groups in collaboration with both government and nongovernmental agencies to improve their socio-economic well-being.

14. The 31st December Women's Movement has been working with existing women's groups throughout the country.

15. Although there are more than 90 ethnic groups in Ghana, these can be classified into two major language groups. The Kwa linguistic group embraces almost all the population in southern Ghana, while the northern part is inhabited by the Gur linguistic group (Dickson, 1969). Within the Kwa group, the Akan are by far the most numerous, accounting for 44.2% of the total Ghanaian population. Among the Akans, the Ashantis (where Barekese and Ahwiaa are located) are in the majority.

16. In this respect, Songsore, the male researcher in the gender and access to land study mentioned that "women at the grassroots level were happy to find alliances among men" (personal interview). Due to limitations of space, I have not further elaborated on the aspect of alliances with men.

13

Communicating for Empowerment: Women's Initiatives to Overcome Poverty in Rural Thailand and Newfoundland

SHARON TAYLOR

This chapter presents a descriptive account of the quality-of-life improvement initiatives taken by a collective of rural women in the province of Mahasarakham, in northeastern Thailand, and a group of single mothers from Newfoundland, Canada. It focuses on an ongoing Canada-Thailand institutional linkage program between Srinakharinwirot University in Thailand and Memorial University in Newfoundland.[1] The objective of the project is the application of a women's empowerment process, focusing on self-empowerment and the development of group strategies for social action.[2] The ultimate aim of the project is strengthening and furthering women's abilities to identify and overcome barriers to their economic, political, social, and spiritual development. The project incorporates various communication tools in the strategies to achieve this aim. The communication tools include participatory video, women's interpersonal communication, and teleconference.

The empowerment process described in this chapter was developed 5 years ago with the Single Moms Against Poverty (SMAP) of Newfoundland. The organization is composed of single mothers on social assistance who live in Newfoundland and Labrador.[3] The group evolved from a workshop on the impact of poverty on single women and their children. At the experiential workshop, the women identified their fears and disappointments about being poor parents. By the end of the workshop, the participants decided to continue seeing each other as a group because it had helped them finally bridge some of the isolation and emptiness in their lives. Teleconferencing was suggested as the means of enabling this ongoing communication throughout the province as the women had limited incomes with virtually no money for travel.

For the past 5 years, SMAP has been applying the women's empowerment process with rural Newfoundland women through teleconferencing, interpersonal communication, and video. Through this process women have identified key principles of the empowerment process: the need to relearn and reclaim women's ways of being and their capacity to dream, and imagine (Johnson, 1987). This central component is seen in relation to the needs of, first, naming and identifying women's internal barriers to overcome internalized oppression and, then, applying themselves to the tasks of creating new ways of organizing society.

In response to this, safe and nurturing small groups that support consensus building have been built. Women and disadvantaged groups must work together to find commonalities across cultures to challenge the present barriers to empowerment (Taylor, 1990). Single moms have identified that empowerment is about creating conditions in which their needs and those of their children can be met, moving beyond economic self-sufficiency toward political self-reliance (Peck, 1987). This includes challenging systemic subordination to mobilize and organize a new agenda for society as a whole. The strategies adopted are those identified by Mies (1986) and Leonard (1989), which empower women and the disadvantaged by identifying the unmet needs and by addressing key issues through participatory approaches to development. Development, according to Freire (1970, 1973), has to be from the roots, educating both the disadvantaged and advantaged in participatory decision making and planning.

The Thai women make up a group of approximately 60 village and academic women from Mahasarakham province.[4] The village women had been approached initially by women from the university to assist in bridging the gap between the university and rural Thailand in women's resources and development. They have been adapting some of the tools of the empowerment process used by SMAP while also developing some of their own. The Thai women, usually in groups of 3, have been visiting Newfoundland women regularly over the past 3 years. A total of 10 Thai women visited several hundred women throughout Newfoundland and Labrador, including the single mothers group. During this time, they discussed the tools they are using for empowerment and identified common and divergent development concerns. Because the process is ongoing, it is difficult to evaluate the impact and success of the women's endeavors. However, what can be offered is a number of suggestions concerning the potential of electronic, visual, and interpersonal communication media for promoting group processes and social action.

My role in both groups is that of facilitator, or enabler. I had the good fortune of being a facilitator for SMAP since its inception. The opportunity to work with women in northeastern Thailand developed in 1988. Over the ensuing 4 years, I have been involved with the cross-fertilization, ongoing growth, and analysis in both groups. The process has been enriching and empowering.

This chapter describes some of the communication tools used by both groups of women, including teleconferencing; women's interpersonal communication; and participatory video for personal, political, social, and economic empowerment. It highlights the contribution of women's initiatives in capturing their analysis, strategies, and skills. Finally, it emphasizes the value of exchange between women of different cultures.

Tools of Communication for Empowerment

Teleconferencing

Single Moms Against Poverty (SMAP) has used teleconferencing as a tool to link group members across the province. Initially, it had a regular booking with the teleconference center and met every 2 weeks, until a lack of funding diminished the frequency.[5] The Thai women do not have access to teleconferencing at this time, but when they visit Newfoundland they are active participants in the provincial teleconference sessions.

The objectives of the group sessions by teleconference were to provide an opportunity for SMAP members to share concerns, ideas, and experiences; to analyze and assess sources of the difficulties they were experiencing; to encourage each other; to problem solve; and to raise the consciousness on the part of communities, professionals, and government about their role within the increasing levels of poverty and alienation experienced by single mothers in the province. The focus of most of the sessions was not on group process but on the empowerment of the individual women attending the sessions.

The first series of teleconferences organized by SMAP was highly structured, partly due to everyone's anxiety about using this new tool. Women were encouraged to visit centers before their first teleconference, to meet staff, see the equipment, and develop some familiarity with it. Child care and transportation were arranged by the local single moms' groups.

The women had varied reactions to the system during the early teleconference sessions. While some women came prepared to talk as openly as they had at the original workshop, others felt pressured to speak before they were ready. Women new to the system were encouraged to bring a friend for support when talking about feelings of social isolation and alienation. This had the effect of increasing the size of the group, as women who came to provide companionship stayed to participate and later brought other friends. As the teleconference sessions evolved, the participants began to talk about women's intuition and how it represents a source of personal power. The group then started to develop skills in strengthening their connection with such intuitions. It was at this point that meditation was introduced to provide the interpersonal and face-to-face interaction that teleconferencing could not offer. Meditation was seen as further assisting in encouraging group bonding in dealing with conflict resolution and with personal and group processes of healing that require face-to-face contact.

Women's Interpersonal Communication Tools

Interpersonal communication tools have been employed by women's groups in the project to discover and change core beliefs that have limited opportunities for women's growth.[6] These tools have been equally useful in building relationships in women's groups and in the community. Some of these tools include the act of changing consciousness at will, visioning, visualization skills, active listening exercises, consciousness-raising rounds, meditation, feeling-sharing rounds, self-criticism with response, group bonding exercises, consensus, decision making, rituals for energizing and action, chants, and songs (Johnson, 1987; Starhawk, 1988; Stein, 1988).

The women's groups in the project also used other tools indigenous to their culture such as reading runes or tea leaves for guidance in Newfoundland and drumming as meditation in Thailand.[7] Although the Thai women have been using meditation since early childhood, they were unused to the idea of using meditation in a group, as a problem-solving tool or for enhancing group process. For Thai women, meditation constitutes a connection with the eternal, a reminder of their true essence, and as such it is used daily to assist them in the linkage between spiritual and the physical. The Thai women feel that meditating regularly in the women's group had, in fact, strengthened the credibility of the groups in the eyes of others in the village. Newfoundland women, on the contrary, acknowledged they were initially embarrassed and afraid when using meditation, especially in small communities where the activity could be misunderstood. While they enjoy meditating and seek out the opportunity to meditate in small groups, they are careful in disclosing the importance of this activity to outsiders. Meditation has assisted Thai and Newfoundland women in organizing their personal and group growth. In both regions women began the exploration of such values and beliefs by recalling messages given to them as very young children, as adolescents, and as young women. The messages both groups of women had received from peers, parents, and siblings were startlingly similar.

Although these women still feel trapped by the messages they received as young children, they also see the beginnings of change in their belief systems. Furthermore, their own personal and group behavior is changing in ways that are challenging the belief system in the community. Both groups agree that processes of this nature are timely. There are times when women have to endure the knowledge of their own oppression until they have the support and the means to confront the system oppressing them. In addition, both groups have seen the need to work with the community/ village as a whole to identify the values and beliefs being passed on to children and the implication of these beliefs for their children's development in the changing world. They identified the need to create consciously community and village values that enhance self-esteem and provide a balance for the future of both sexes.

Visualization in this project is used to assist women to explore and change their feelings about themselves in situations where they feel powerless and inadequate. For example, both groups were negotiating with government agencies in their countries. To prepare for these negotiations, the women's groups imagined the event happening. The group would begin with a relaxation exercise, then the future event would be described by one of the women as though it had already happened. Others added their visions of the future event. This was followed by an acting out of the guided imagining by the women. Visualization was also used to help the group when they became blocked on an issue. In this situation, a group member would take the group through a relaxation exercise and then use an imagining that emphasized flowing and connectedness—for example, the flow of the river to the sea. Women who used visualization said that they felt strong and balanced when meeting with government officials.

Participatory Video

The Thai women have been using small format video as a participatory communication tool for the last 3 years. Participatory video is used as a means to reflect the lives of people back to them for discussion and planning. The Thai women, both rural and academic, learned to use the equipment with facilitators from Newfoundland who applied participatory methods in the teachings of video. In this framework, development support communication is seen as a tool in participatory action research and participatory development. Communication media such as video are seen as, "powerful means in a process which enhances self-awareness, self-confidence, and self-empowerment through objective reflection, consensus, community action, structural change and participation in development" (Williamson, 1991, p. 286).

The Thai women have complete control over how and when the video equipment is to be used as well as the final decision on the use of the subsequent videos. Thai academic and village women have worked together to create videos on the development of their women's cooperative, reclaiming women's role in the economic evolution of the community and women's stories of their foremothers. Video has been used to monitor group process: decision-making, problem-solving, and leadership styles. Video has been particularly helpful in monitoring the balance between tasks and relationship building in the Thai group, as it has frequently enabled them to focus and follow issues that would ordinarily be overlooked. For example, the communication styles within the group, which were usually indirect, were monitored and discussed when the group reviewed videotapes of previous meetings. Now the group members are practicing a more direct communication style.

In this project, video has been used as a group process. Emphasis is placed on the process of production rather than on the end product.[8] The Newfoundland women have used video to transmit knowledge from one community to another, to raise the consciousness on poverty-related issues, and to enhance communication skills. They had not used video as a tool for monitoring and enhancing group process and were anxious to learn more about this from the Thai women.

The use of participatory video by these groups has shown that there are limitations to the use of video in the empowerment process. A key issue when using participatory video is that of ownership and location of equipment. At the moment, the university women control the video equipment in Thailand. The village women can and do request it for their use; however, the fact remains that the university owns and controls the video equipment, which is, of course, a reflection of the distribution of power and the obvious gap between village and university women. The key task for the users of participatory video is to identify the possible and most adequate uses of this tool for the fulfillment of the group and community expectations.

Although participatory video can be an effective and creative tool in the empowerment process, its use in a group process does not lend itself to quick-fix solutions. To be empowering and participatory in a group context, a high degree of trust, openness, and commitment to process must be first established. Video, by its very nature, motivates people to become involved, promoting direct communication and effective information sharing (i.e., between villages and between villages and government departments). Video has assisted the women's groups by promoting self-awareness and consciousness raising through the process of reviewing videos to explore attitudes and behaviors exhibited by individuals and groups. Through taping and screening, video has fostered a varied and interesting group or village experience that validates and promotes bonding. The particular effectiveness of video as a teaching aid in both formal and informal settings is well documented in this initiative. In particular, the video has enhanced group process by providing insight and by visually documenting areas such as leadership, decision making, conflict resolution, problem solving, value clarification, group structure, group maintenance patterns, and communication skills.

Capturing Women's Contributions
Through Participatory Communication

The purpose of reclaiming women's economic contributions in their communities is to gain insight into the complexity, subtlety, and impact of women's work. The reclaiming of women's economic contribution validates the historical role of women in the maintenance and development of economic self-reliance in the family and the community. In the group process followed in both countries, women have set up a process of identifying and recovering these roles.

Reclaiming Women's Contribution in Thailand

The Thai women decided to use a combination of video and written interviews to capture the contributions of community building made by their foremothers. They developed questions that explored the changes and evolution of the role of women in the community. Initially, interviews were done by the academic women. However, because most of the interviewing was completed in a relaxed, informal mode, the village women soon felt comfortable enough to interview each other. Some of the women wrote their interviews, which resulted in a collection of women's stories about women's roles in community building and family maintenance. Both this collection of stories and the videotaped interviews are presently used in group discussions to focus on the past and present strengths and skills of women. They are also used in the process of planning the future role of women at a local, regional, and national level.

The videotaped and written stories constitute rich sources for an analysis of the self-imposed limitations compared with those imposed by others. Strengths and resources are more often revealed indirectly through descriptions of their community tasks or the events they participate in rather than through explicit statements that reflect ownership of strength. For example, a village woman described how she had worked as an assistant to other weavers until she had saved enough money to buy a loom and start her own business. She was amazed when the group identified the skills she had demonstrated throughout this process: setting objectives, commitment to goals, planning, organizing, budgeting, and support building.

The process of collecting stories has proved very enjoyable and a motivator for the active participation of older village women. The trust and intimacy developed among the women involved have reinforced group membership and processes of empowerment. Thai women are taking a holistic approach to developing a community economic profile in which they identify the complex interplay of economic, political, social, and cultural factors in economic development. This view is evident in their stories, songs, and dances. They have been creating pictures of life in the village, describing what has happened in the past, what is happening presently, and what they expect in the future. This holistic view of economic development challenges the restricted focus on economic growth and redistribution of the traditional development initiatives that are targeting rural Thailand.

To this end, women have videotaped stories, songs, and discussions about village life in the past. They decided what they needed to know about the past that would be helpful in understanding the present. They questioned differences and how these differences came to be. Both older and younger women came together to discuss differences in women's behavior, for example, what was acceptable in the past but is no longer acceptable and which changes in women's roles are depicted in songs and dances. A number of questions were formulated during the meetings: How did these changes occur? What else was happening at the time? Did women resist change? Did they encourage change? How? What changes have they appreciated? What are they afraid of? What changes have been limiting? During the meetings, the women performed the dances of who they are in their community today. Everyone (including men) who came, stayed and participated.

Up to this point men had been involved in the project in a very limited way. Women began the process of envisioning the community's future with drawings and paintings done at home with their children, husbands, and parents. While the men engaged in such discussions (drawings and paintings at home), they were generally not involved in the group activities. At first, they came to watch group activities. Later they joined in the drumming and finally in the dancing. They are now beginning to participate with women in looking at the videos of the dancing and identifying changes from the past. They are also beginning to explore community values with women, to celebrate through dancing, and to identify the group and community's resources. However, there is still hesitation among the men about involvement, particularly in the analysis of values and roles in their community.

Currently, women have divided into teams and are videotaping a profile of their village. They are videotaping the village and surrounding area, identifying existing and potential resources and problems. In this process they have identified human resources in the community (weavers, singers, mothers, cooks, builders, farmers, dancers, poets, and children) as well as physical resources (buildings, water, and straw). Slowly, the resources of men are beginning to be identified as are the perceived distinctions between the resources of men and women. The videos indicate that this is an uncomfortable process and perhaps a threatening one. There is less laughter and joyfulness than is usually found on the other videos.

The videotapes show an interesting pattern in the cycle of activities. The village women take the lead in deciding the focus of activities and the pattern that has emerged indicates that they have an awareness of the impact of exploring sensitive issues. The videotapes indicate that when the discussion becomes labored and complex—for example, in envisioning women's and men's role in raising children in the village 5 years from now—one of the women will send one of the children for a drum and the whole group begins to drum and sing. When the struggle is with values that are particularly difficult to be direct about, the singing and dancing may continue for a week. This is particularly difficult for some women who are more task oriented and would like to have concrete results to show as evidence of their involvement in the community. The process of reviewing the videos has been particularly helpful for identifying limitations to group process because of the attitudes and positions of the women themselves. Initially, women were somewhat hesitant about participating in this kind of analysis, but now they often point out where they have become directive, aggressive, or passive-aggressive. Usually, this is done with physical touching and laughing. However, it is rare that a younger woman will confront an older woman, even in this fashion.

Reclaiming Women's Contributions in Newfoundland

The focus of the provincial group became the economic empowerment of single mothers. They began to consult with local groups to formulate a plan that would enable single mothers to gain control of their own economic situations and to contribute to economic decision making and planning in their own communities. At conferences, teleconferences, and workshops, SMAP members explored the skills and strategies used by their mothers and grandmothers in maintaining and developing families and communities.

They found that modern-day women seemed to have forgotten the instrumental role their foremothers had played in the economic and social maintenance of their families and communities. Discussions with women in small groups revealed that historically women assumed responsibility for the community for long periods of time when the men were away fishing in Labrador or working elsewhere in Canada. In effect, most of the mothers had functioned as single mothers for long periods of time. However, it was important to make the link between the single moms of today and the kind of responsibility, problem solving, and decision making of the women who had functioned as single mothers in the past.

The single moms' discussions with older women in small groups uncovered some of their ideas about the reasons for women's changed status. The change in the northern fish stocks and federal policies meant that men were away for shorter periods of time and frequently did not go away at all. Consequently, men remained at home for longer periods and gradually took on more responsibility for community development. Agencies involved in community development frequently focused on male leaders for the organizing of community councils and rural development associations. Incorrectly, it was assumed that women played a role in the family but not in the community.

These actions disregarded Newfoundland traditions, which are based on the work of the family as an economic unit and the maintenance of the community as a unit. Even when they were living in the community, men were frequently away fishing late into the evening, and as a consequence, women were responsible for organizing community events—weddings, "times," church suppers, and so on—and community responses to families or individuals in need.

Single moms also identified other factors that possibly contributed to the change in the role and status of women. The influence of mass media such as television and the emphasis on privacy, for example, affected people's tradition and definition of roles by gender. The young women, because of their research, began to develop an appreciation for the knowledge and skills of the older women. They became more aware of women's work in the past: of the long days, of the existence of community wells, of families bringing their containers (kerosene cans and molasses jars) to the store to be refilled. They found out more about the contribution of children in earlier days, who helped in the vegetable gardens, tended the sheep, or worked in the fish plant after school, sharing their energy and resources with the family.

From Local Group Communication to International Exchange

During the visits between Thai and Newfoundland women over the past 3 years, they have raised each other's awareness of the similarities and differences in development issues between rural areas of Newfoundland and Thailand. These women maintain that the obstruction of indigenous alternatives for societal self-expression and progress is the major obstacle for development. The following is a summary of some of the women's observations during the process of participatory communication.

Acceptance of a Passive Self-Image of Inferiority. Rural people in both areas have been labeled poor by urban experts, becoming objects of sympathy and paternalistic intervention. Many people, particularly in rural areas, have internalized this self-image. Perceiving themselves as inferior, they have sought to be developed by their superiors, surrendering their own values and their own accumulated knowledge and wisdom. This surrender has not always been without a struggle. They have suffered not only economic impoverishment but also a loss of identity and the ability to develop authentically within their indigenous cultures.

In rural Newfoundland and Labrador, for example, the fishing people have consistently confronted the federal fisheries bureaucrats with their traditional knowledge of fish and fishing grounds; however, the government officials have consistently rejected the wisdom and knowledge of these people. Recently, the Federal Fisheries Department announced that cod stocks have been seriously depleted and has admitted that its "experts" were indeed wrong about the size of existing cod stocks. These mistakes, while having little impact on the well-paid experts, have proven costly to the fishing people of Newfoundland and Labrador. They have lost their fishing grounds to foreign overfishing and zealous use of advanced fishing technology by large corporations. Similarly, in Thailand, rural people were dismayed by the rapid demolition of the teak forest and the potential of flood damage to farmland. Their concerns were largely ignored, and today they too pay the high price for technological advancements in the teak industry.

Uprooting of Self-Reliant Styles by Development Initiatives. Traditional development programs have often uprooted communities from their traditional lifestyles, which valued self-reliance, economic plurality, and the collective maintenance of family and community. This view of development places little value in the contribution of work that is crucial to human and community survival—childbearing and child care, water and fuel collection, family health care, homemaking, ceremonies, celebrations, and community maintenance activities that are generally executed by women. Today women are urged to become more visible in the production of goods and services, which constitutes the focus of government and mainstream development programs. There are projects and programs in both countries that have had as their goals the economic development of women. Yet few of the development experts seem to have questioned who will maintain households, provide child care, and generally support family and community when the females become official producers. There has been little or no effort in either country to involve men in the holistic development process, which involves such issues as health, education, and child care. Nor do funding sources promote the inclusion of women's invisible work in national indicators of economic growth.

Role of the Elders. Discussions between Thai and Newfoundland women revealed differences in their experiences. The Thai women observed that generally rural communities in Newfoundland no longer had a place for their elders. The indigenous people in Newfoundland and Labrador were closer to the Thai tradition of seeking wisdom from elders. The settlers in rural communities in Newfoundland and Labrador indicated that they too had valued the wisdom of their elders in the past. However, federal programs that emerged in the 1960s and 1970s had removed elders from communities, placing them in senior citizens' homes in larger centers.

This was done to provide better care and access to health services for the elderly. However, the Newfoundland women noted that not only had the community lost a valuable resource but the elders frequently died shortly after the move.

Domestic Activities. The Thai women were obviously impressed with the level of male involvement in child rearing and housekeeping activities in rural Newfoundland. The Newfoundland women indicated that the males in the household generally helped when asked, but that women were primarily responsible for the organizing and maintaining of family and household.

As observed by the Thai women, the circumstances of childbearing, child rearing, and household maintenance were different in rural New-foundland. Community healers, for example, are no longer acknowledged, as there is little interest in learning their knowledge of local plants and healing. The Thai women also noticed that the mother in the family was primarily responsible for the health and well-being of the children. New-foundland women indicated that the extended family had been extensively involved with child rearing in the past, but that with the modernization of small communities, most people were working in fish plants and had lost sight of this role. Even after the fish plants shut down, extended family support only emerged in times of crisis.

Sources of Income. Rural women from Thailand are engaged in economic pluralism, deriving their income from several sources such as farming, fishing, and weaving. Thai women perceived rural women in Newfound-land as dependent on social welfare programs and community develop-ment make-work projects, which diminished self-esteem and created competition for too few jobs within the community. They also expressed concern over the large numbers of single mothers in Newfoundland. From their point of view, the development of government programs eroded the role of males in Newfoundland families, because they were no longer identified as primary providers for the family. The Newfoundland women disagreed with this analysis. They pointed out that with such changes women were less likely to stay in abusive relationships as other choices were available. They conceded that these choices continued to be limited and agreed that the existing system undermined male involvement in child rearing responsibilities and diminished the status of single mothers in their community.

Thai women visited Newfoundland at a critical point in the history of the province. The province's only university was in the process of ending its historic role in the empowerment of rural people. Memorial University would no longer have an extension service that would link the resources of the university to rural Newfoundland. The implications of this move to rural women was a primary concern during their discussion with the Thai visitors. The Thai women reported that the universities of Thailand were becoming more aware of the importance of exchanges between university and communities and in fact were reaffirming their roles in women's development and in rural development generally by developing extension services.

Conclusion

The use of communication tools such as teleconferencing, participatory video, and women's interpersonal communication skills have enabled women of different classes and different countries to explore their assumptions about themselves and each other. They have provided an opportunity for these women to assess their own role in the victimization of themselves and other women. The process of learning to apply these tools of communication has been empowering in itself. Furthermore, the occasion to analyze the historic and current contributions of women in the maintenance and development of family and community was a vital part of the empowerment process. Throughout, the communication tools provided an opportunity to review the concept of women in development as conceived by funding agencies and governments and as experienced by women themselves.

Overall, both groups of women discovered several similarities in their experiences, particularly regarding the difficulties created by problem solving. Women in both countries valued the reviewing and reclaiming of values and traditions that enhanced the growth of community. They also became more concerned with values and lifestyles being imposed by outside sources.

The discussions have assisted women in identifying the strengths and difficulties experienced in their work with women in development. Finally, the realization that their struggle, while varying in degrees of difficulty according to the place, has essentially the same aims and objectives. This constitutes a reminder to the women involved in this process of the reason for their commitment to struggle for change.

Both groups are beginning to identify concrete results from the strategies for social action by using teleconference, participatory video, and women's interpersonal skills. The single moms group in Newfoundland has assisted in the production of a video on poverty, which is being used in schools, universities, and government agencies to raise consciousness about women in poverty. They have worked extensively with the provincial Department of Social Services and have successfully advocated for increases in single mothers' social services payments. They have had teleconference sessions on issues such as housing and have worked with Newfoundland and Labrador Housing to increase the allotment of housing for single mothers. Presently, they are engaged in a participatory action research project that also employs participatory video to identify the barriers to education for single mothers. In some communities, single mothers have representation on economic planning boards and rural development associations.

The women in Thailand have established a woman's center in their university to teach women's interpersonal communication skills, to engage in participatory action research, to provide support for female faculty and students, and to ensure links between rural and academic women that focus on common goals and barriers. The academic and village women have used participatory video to incorporate the realities and concerns of village women into university curriculum and research. They have used participatory video and women's interpersonal skills to create a women's cooperative for weavers.

It is evident, however, that both groups of women are challenging their own core beliefs, are committed to building a common vision, and demonstrate daily dedication to their vision as evidenced through the consistently high level of participation in group activities. They have built and are continuing to build support systems, locally and globally, that are committed to the growth of women. They also approach their work with a lightness and joy that is reflected in their songs, dancing, and dramas. Above all, the emphasis both groups have given to self-love is perhaps the greatest measure of success. Each group has developed and incorporated exercises that accept, validate, and nurture the individual within the group. The focus has been on the importance of each woman finding her own truth and consistently over time loving that truth. The dedication to this focus has enabled both groups to provide a sanctuary for each woman while working together to eradicate poverty for all women.

Notes

1. This project, funded by the Canadian International Development Agency, aims at strengthening the capacity of Thai University for community outreach to women. It further develops the communication links between the university and rural women through the use of small-format video, teleconferencing, and participatory action research. The project has a particular emphasis on identifying the barriers to women's education and economic development. As a result of this project, a core interdisciplinary team at Thai University has been created. It has set up a women's center to sustain and expand project activities.

2. The empowerment process centers on understanding women's subordination and in creating the conditions under which disadvantaged peoples can meet their daily needs and actively participate in the development of structures that realize social, political, and economic rights. It is a long-term process that requires changes in the behavior of both women and men. This process focuses on women's growth as individuals and in society, identifying and respecting their values and rights. The empowerment process includes the formation of common community visions, the development of commitment to these visions, and the practice of discipline or daily dedication to activities that realize these visions. A key component in this process is the creation and maintenance of support systems committed to the empowerment of women. For further elaboration of these ideas see Freire (1970, 1973), Johnson (1987), Leonard (1989), Mies (1986), Peck (1987), Starhawk (1988, 1989), and Taylor (1990).

3. Newfoundland and Labrador, on the Atlantic coast of Canada, cover an area in excess of 100,000 square kilometers and have a population of little more than 0.5 million. The climate ranges from arctic to maritime temperate, with most of the people living in rural coastal villages. Fishing, forestry, and mining are the core of a resource-based economy, struggling to keep pace with the relative affluence of the rest of Canada.

4. Mahasarakham is one of Thailand's smaller provinces and has a population of around 30,000. It is located in the northeast and its economy is based on rice farming and silk weaving.

5. The Memorial University teleconference system is a provincewide system consisting of four circuits that allow people at teleconference centers all over Newfoundland and Labrador to attend meetings or engage in educational activities. Each center is equipped with a teleconference kit, which consists of a speaker and a push-to-talk microphone. The system is audio only, and there are approximately four to eight microphones in each center. The speaker in each center is what provides the sound. The teleconference centers around the province are usually located in vocational high schools and hospitals. The teleconference system used by the single moms is available 7 days a week. The single moms chose to meet by teleconference on Sunday afternoons, because the cost was lower at that time and this time was convenient for most participants.

6. Core beliefs are central to the overall direction individuals take in life. These beliefs are the basis for the value the individual places on herself and other women, activities toward change, self-esteem, expectations, and so on. Most of these beliefs are formed in early childhood and are not a part of an individual's conscious reality.

7. Runes and tea leaves are oracles that women in Newfoundland have traditionally used to access knowledge and wisdom.

8. Such emphasis can easily be switched from process (i.e., community and group building) to product, if the project follows the goals and priorities set by funding agencies, institutions, and project personnel.

14

Speak Magazine:
Breaking Barriers and Silences

LIBBY LLOYD

The *Speak* collective is part of breaking the silence about the lives of women, particularly black women workers and women in the rural areas. We've been part of that struggle for the past 10 years and we believe that media is an important weapon in the fight for a society free of sexism and racism and where the wealth of the country would be shared by all.

Libby Lloyd (at the AMARC Conference, 1992)

Speak was started by a group of women activists from community organizations that were fighting for better housing conditions. We started with a newsletter called *Speak* to look at the issues that were happening through women's lives, to give women workers and women in the rural areas a voice, and share their experiences of organizing. Community groups at that time had started to organize around housing issues, around rent issues, and access to housing. Women from the different organizations started meeting, feeling that they specifically had to look at how these things were affecting women. They decided to launch a newsletter, both so that other communities could learn from their experiences at organizing and so that they could share and look at the mistakes they have made. So it was very much looking at organizing.

At first, it was all volunteers. None of them was a journalist; none of them had any media experience. Everyone who is still with the collective talks about how they sat on people's lounges and knew nothing about how

EDITOR'S NOTE: This chapter is based on an interview with Libby Lloyd, one of the editors of the magazine *Speak,* which is produced by a women's collective in South Africa. This interview was conducted by Dorothy Kidd at the fifth conference of Community Radio Broadcasters (AMARC 5) in Mexico in 1992. Extracts from a paper that Lloyd gave at that conference complement the text.

to do things. They used to produce 200 issues, and it came out twice a year. They had one issue in English and one issue in Zulu. Then, they made a decision, about 2 or 3 years after they had started the newsletter, to hire people, to actually stop being a volunteer organization. Part of it was because they had a lot of people that when they bought a newspaper would be surprised and say, "Ah, *Speak* is still around!" It was coming up very infrequently and they thought it should come up more often. So, one person was hired, then two people were hired, but there was still a lot of volunteer work. Now, we do not have any volunteers working for the magazine, but we do have a volunteer committee that decides on policy. Everyone who writes now gets paid, including members of the community.

Recently, we have broadened our audience, or we have broadened it rather than changed it. Initially, the audience was organized women, women from within organizations and unions. We want to appeal to more women now, not just women who are politically involved. We are trying to draw in women who are not necessarily in organizations and women who are in other kinds of organizations, like church organizations, not just political organizations. We are also broadening the issues we cover. For example, there is a top commercial radio woman, Shado Twala who is very famous. She has a jazz and talk show. Before, we would never have thought of interviewing her, but we put her on our front cover because we are trying to appeal more widely now. We also have competitions now to draw more people in.

Our feeling is that we need to broaden the content and increase the number of testimonials from individuals and groups. In the beginning, it was very much about organizing, health, advice articles about how to get child support from fathers of children. We have always had that. But things have changed, people have other things in their lives besides politics and wanting to know about advice. So, we run a lot of lighter stories. We even have a gossip column! Gossip is normally about people in the political parties, what some of the men have said about things.

Speak is for opening controversy over issues. We did, for example, a story on beauty competitions. This is something very different for us to do, but we felt that there is a huge thing going on around beauty contests and we could not pretend that it did not exist. For the first time, we have had a black Miss South Africa, so a lot of people are now saying that beauty contests are fine. Before the issue was that they were racist, it had nothing to do with the concept of these competitions. We interviewed a number of women from the organizations and half of them said "We have to fight"; they said they were against the whole idea. We feel that if this debate is raised in *Speak* it will be raised in those other organizations as an issue and at least they will debate it. Through *Speak* we get a lot of resources and are able to read numerous publications, and we want to give women access to these resources through the magazine, so they can have informed debates. Individuals and groups will work with us to tell us their stories because *Speak* is trusted. It was started by people who were community activists within those communities. People know people in *Speak* and the response is that when you go somewhere, even among women you don't know in rural areas, and you say "I'm from *Speak*," immediately people open up to you about what is happening. With women in unions we have probably had stronger relations than with any other group. They felt that *Speak* was an important avenue for sharing experiences. They use *Speak* in workshops, so they have always been prepared to sit and tell us what they think should happen.

One of the constraints we face now is the cost of the magazine. We are trying to compete in the mainstream with the magazines that advertise stockings and cosmetics. Even the magazines claiming they are for black people in South Africa do not write about women workers, or give them a voice, or even realize what their concerns are. It is difficult to compete when other magazines have a glossy cover, so we have a glossy cover and we always try to have an active picture of a woman, not a beautiful picture. Cost is a huge constraint. Advertising is also a problem. There is always debate about advertising policies: What do you do and how do you get it? Advertisers are not going to advertise that easily.

Distribution is a problem in South Africa for all of the media. We are all on with a big major network that would never have us before. They are owned by the mainstream media, and their publications come first. They also tend not to go to the more rural areas where our magazines would sell, because the magazine is inexpensive and is about women's lives. Now, it is sold on the street in the book shops where people buy the magazines. When *Speak* started, we distributed it ourselves at the meetings. It was also distributed by shop stewards in the women's unions, and by organizers within the community.

There is something missing now (although we do not miss working seven days a week). We miss the selling in meetings, because when you are selling a publication you see people respond then and there. They will come and discuss something they want advice on, and you get an immediate feeling of what is needed. Although we do sit in on a lot of meetings, it is not the same interaction as when we sold the publication personally. Now we have started coming out monthly as of May this year. Since then it has become a lot more difficult to receive feedback. We used to be able to spend more time on each article working directly with women.

Collectively Produced Articles:
The Magazine as Facilitator

There is one civic organization, a squatter organization, that has asked us to go work with them on an article. They see it as a means of education. They know what they want to consider. There are a lot of issues: wife abuse within the civic organization, child sexual abuse, not enough women in leadership in the civic organizations.[1] They want to discuss these issues. They believe women in other civic organizations can learn from their experience of setting up a separate women's structure within the civic.

This civic is a very organized community, in which there is a housing project set up on collectively owned land. There are issues coming up now around land. For example, a woman was given a plot of land, she lived with someone and he built a house. Who does it belong to? They want to discuss these issues. They believe that the women in the civics can learn from their own experiences, and they have recently formed as a separate structure within the civic.

They asked us to come in for the first meeting and essentially what we did is sit in on one of their normal meetings, just listening. Everyone knew why we were there. There must have been about 100 women. They were just raising the issues that they usually raise. What we did was raise questions about how to change this. People were talking a lot about the awfulness of child abuse in the community and not focusing on how they thought they could stop it. They chose several women to work with us. We would interview these women, and they would take us to different places.

They would have a say of what went into the article, because many of them were raising things about men in the civic. They do not want men to know they are concerned with such issues, because they fear a breakdown in trust. So for safety, it has to be carefully done.

Opening Spaces for Controversy:
Sexism and Leadership

These days we have been told about the will of the people and how they have fought against repression. These days we also have been told about the violence in our society now, about how the street has been washed with the blood of our own people. But women's voices, particularly the voices of black working-class women are not heard. There is silence, for example, about how women experience the violence that is going on in our country. There is silence about how very often it is women and children who are killed in this violence.

Libby Lloyd (at the AMARC Conference, 1992)

Speak has a commitment to nonsexism. We challenge sexism in our organizations, in our society, in our homes. Leadership of organizations have not really responded to our criticisms that they are sexist. I am not sure why—maybe it is not an issue to them. More women are standing very strongly and saying we do not want to be toys anymore and we are sick of our supposed comrades having political discussions with us only when they want to go to bed with us. And they are raising this within the unions. So we are reflecting this also, what they are saying.

We are starting to do more critical things, interviews with men, challenging them on their ideas. It is not always easy to ask their approval of what is being written. But I think that because *Speak* has been around for 10 years there is a trust in the magazine within a lot of organizations.

Before, we used to focus on African National Congress (ANC) aligned organizations. Now, although we write about women in other political organizations like the Pan African Congress (PAC), we are also more critical and challenging of the liberation movements. Most of the independent progressive media have decided to distance themselves from political organizations to be more critical. Before, it was necessary for us to give a voice to the ANC and the PAC, because these mass democratic movements never had a voice in any other media. Now they do get a voice in the mass media and so a lot of the independent newspapers and magazines are stepping back and being more critical of those organizations. There is a lot more open discussion.

I think we are lucky in South Africa because people have learned a lot from other countries' experiences, and there is encouragement at the leadership level—although not always at the grassroots level—for media to be critical and to have a diversity of opinion. People will sometimes say that they are glad "you're being critical of us."

Women's Participation in Negotiations

Negotiations have been a big thing internationally. But on the ground, some people do not even know what is going on. It is so removed from everyone. It is not really an issue at all. We reflected some of the debates around participation of women in the negotiations, which has been taken up very strongly by women across the political parties. If you go into some areas and ask, "Do you know CODESA (Congress for Democratic Elections in South Africa)?" which is what it is called, they do not even know what you are talking about, it is very removed.

I think the negotiation process has had an impact on the organizations purely because people are aware that they are writing a new constitution. Women have come up very strongly saying that they know it is only the first step, but they have to get some sort of legal equality written in. It is not going to change our lives, but we need to do it now. Women, again from across political parties, have set up a coalition to collect demands from women to include in a charter for women's rights. I think it is from the experience of other countries in southern Africa where—as in South Africa—women were being told to not bring up the women's issues because it would divide the struggle and it would all be sorted out after liberation. People have learned that that never happens. That women will be parachuted back into the kitchen after liberation, and they need to fight very hard now to make sure that there is equality for women at least written into constitutions.

There is in South Africa the Women's National Coalition (WNC) that is very much a coalition of women who do not agree on the political issues at all.[2] Even some of the issues like abortion—whether or not it should be legalized. But there is not a big national women's movement in South Africa. There are more women who have formed organizations within their own organizations. There is the ANC women's league, there are the African women's organizations within the PAC. Inkatha has a women's forum. But there is not an autonomous women's movement. When the ANC came back, there was a long debate about whether or not the women's league should separate and become a national organization, separated from any political structure. It was decided to stay within the ANC, although a lot of women felt it was the wrong decision. They felt that often you sort of suppress the issues you want to raise because of the political implications of revealing stuff. If you talk about real issues, about the fact that one ANC member beats his wife regularly, you are undermining your organization and your first allegiances are to a league within the organization.

Times of Change

> I consider feminists to be women who recognize they are oppressed as women
> and who are prepared to fight for basic rights, privileges and choices which
> women should have in a society. (*Speak Magazine*, 1992a, p. 5)

Speak has always raised women's issues very strongly. There have always
been women in organizations doing so. The magazine was set up because
there were no other media that did it. Now, things are changing. Before
many African women would never admit that they were feminists, even
if they were expressing feminist ideas. Feminism was labeled a Western
and bourgeois ideology. Progressive organizations gave it these labels and
women found it difficult to say, "I'm a feminist." But this has changed.
We did an article about three months ago and interviewed women who
had always been in the forefront, always expressing these ideas. All of
these women said, "Yes, I am a feminist." It was interesting. There has been
a whole change in the way people are seeing and viewing their demands.

We were the only magazine focusing on women's issues, and we are
still the only one that writes in simple English that is accessible to people
who speak English as a second language. The other progressive media do
not take women's issues seriously. It is the same with the mass media,
although they may run some progressive articles. Every now and then in
those publications you will see atrocious headlines like "Unions wooing
working girls." They just do not have any consciousness of it. *Speak* is
really the only magazine in South Africa that is doing what it is doing.

> And also sadly male comrades in our organizations say, "We have to work
> slowly with these traditions, we don't want to alienate our membership."
> Tradition is supposed to be something sacred, something we can't challenge.
> Even though at the moment in South Africa we're trying to change so many
> aspects of our lives. One rural women, Xoliswa Tom, said recently, "The
> traditions that are sacred often are oppressive to women. The ones that were
> related to the behavior of men have all gone."
>
> *Libby Lloyd (at the AMARC Conference, 1992)*

Relationship Between Sexism and Racism

We see everything in terms of race, gender and class. That is the sort of
analysis we are coming from. In the magazine, although we raise women's

issues, we look also at racism and class exploitation, and how women are feeling that now. How they experience those forms of exploitation as well as the patriarchy. We feel this is very important. *Speak* runs political issues that might not have anything to do with women's issues but we feel it is important for *Speak* not to be seen just as a women's magazine that is only going to raise women's issues, but that women have also to be part of the political process. Sometimes when those complicated agreements are reached that we do not fully understand, we spend time simplifying them so they will be accessible. In this way women can take part in the political process, outside of just the women's forums.

Women have demanded strongly from all the political parties that there must be a gender advisory committees set up at the top to advise every working group and discuss every issue and check all the racial issues that were coming out. Also individually, women within the organization were pushing very hard that some of them change their delegations to include women.

Radio Project

In August 1992, *Speak* launched a Radio-Audio Project (RAP). The airwaves are opening up in South Africa, and we at *Speak* felt we must grab the chance now to make sure women's voices are heard, both on the air and in discussions around how to restructure the broadcasting sector.

The RAP has several aims. We are not planning—at least yet—to set up our own station, but we want to produce programs for both community stations that are starting to go on air and for the state public broadcaster. We are also producing audiocassettes on women's poetry and musical and educational cassettes. We are, for example, planning to produce a cassette to educate women about how to vote in preparation for the first nonracial elections in our country. It is important that women vote. Cassettes will be playing in clinic waiting rooms, in advice offices—everywhere women are waiting. Training is also important to us. We believe it is crucial to help train women in communities so they can grab the chance to have a voice on community stations, otherwise such stations will only be controlled by men.

There is silence about the ways recently women have broken down the barriers of race, language, and class and have launched a campaign to draft a women's charter, knocking from village to village, from door to door to collect the demands of women for a new South Africa. There's silence about how we're fighting against being seen only as the mothers of revolution and have not been recognized as taking part in that revolution as well.

I think that all of us notice that the struggle for equality of women is a difficult one, is more difficult than the struggle against racial and class oppression in many ways. It's not a struggle against an outside enemy, it's a struggle against our brothers, fathers, husbands, and comrades. What we want to make sure is that we use radio effectively to help us to win the victory in our struggle.

Libby Lloyd (at the AMARC Conference, 1992)

Notes

1. There is a civic organization in every community. Everyone can become a member. It is made up of residents in an area. There are smaller groups of street committees.

2. The Women's National Coalition (WNC) is made up of a wide range of organizations. It was launched with the aim of drawing up a charter for women's rights. This campaign was given the name "Operation Big Ears" (*Speak Magazine,* 1992b).

15

Women as Social Agents of Communication: Social Maternity and Leadership

ROSA MARÍA ALFARO

This chapter describes a process that has been followed by a collective of Peruvian communicators called Calandria,[1] in 12 years of efforts to support popular movements. This is a summary of our communication discourse built on years of practice and theoretical reflection. The following analysis on women and communication has two points of reference: (a) the responses of Latin American women of the popular[2] classes to the economic and political crisis of the 1980s and the ways that these women use communication to find meaning in their lives and (b) the process followed by social communicators who sought to build an alternative relationship with women and an alternative sense of professionalism in the service of development. Within both sets are found the dialogue between thought and practice; theory and action; communication, culture, and society. Latin American thought on communication has assisted us in analyzing these processes, aiding us to see beyond our own experience to understand the context.

Approaching communication from a gender perspective has origins in two frameworks in Latin America. On one hand are the **feminist** concerns with mass media and their manipulative capacity to foster inequality between sexes. In the 1970s feminists condemned this manipulation and began to use alternative media produced for and by women. Alternative communication offered a method for generating critical consciousness for change within a women-controlled space that could challenge masculine power. Some feminists directed their message to all women, without recognizing differences of class or culture and assuming a universality of gender that united or reconciled other secondary differences.

On the other hand, those involved in popular communication supported the social struggles of women of the popular classes within a framework that identified women as social actors. This approach emphasizes the primacy of women's organization as a strategy to defend life (e.g., for socioeconomic survival and against repression and violence) and also as an arena to challenge inequalities. Some communicators working from a popular communication approach did not include gender in their framework, but there were those who attempted a more integral process of liberation by connecting social and communication experiences, including relations between women and men.

During the 1980s, feminist and popular communication frameworks ran parallel without many chances of encounter. However, the social and cultural histories of Latin American countries soon demonstrated that these frameworks were only partial, and that there were no absolute truths. The 1990s have given birth to rich and unsuspected points of encounter as well as new challenges and areas of work. It is this beautiful encounter that I will be discussing, even though it is sown with violence, death, hunger, and desperation. Although the principal protagonists in this reflection are women from the popular classes, other groups of women are not left out. Although the analysis is nourished by the experience of all Latin America, the Peruvian example has been taken as a model by other countries in the region.

There have been two key events in the development of a perspective on gender and communication in Latin American: (a) the meeting about alternative communication for women, organized by the Latin American Institute for Transnational Studies (ILET) in 1983, and (b) the seminar titled "Communicative Identity and Alternative Proposals for Women," organized by the popular education network Between Women of the Latin American Council for Adult Education (CEAAL) and our Association of Social Communicators of Peru (Calandria) in November 1991.[3] The first conference emphasized critical analysis of the mass media and the ways to introduce alternative messages in those media. The second evaluated our work from a gender perspective and developed ways to understand how messages are consumed and perceived by audiences.

This new theorizing about women and communication does not lose sight of the concrete social practices that made such understanding possible. This is particularly relevant in Latin America where our approach began as a practical proposal of political activism derived more from ideological than purely academic considerations.

Popular Women Leadership During the Crisis

In the 1970s a new broad-based women's movement arose in the popular neighborhoods of Latin American cities and later in rural areas. The backdrop for this movement was the economic and political crisis and the complex cultural processes of adapting to a new urban culture.

In Peru, these social movements of women began as simple agreements among collectives to receive and distribute food aid given by churches, national governments, and international aid agencies. The initial requirement was for the poorest mothers to participate in community projects or handicraft production. Their participation was rewarded with oil, milk, and grains to complement their families' diets so affected by poverty. While the initial organizing was almost as a survival instinct, it led to solidarity among these women.

A second instance was the experience of the *olla común*. The *olla común* refers to the collective preparation of meals for several families with the organized participation of women. These collective strategies initially developed as forms of institutionalizing self-help between women and were influenced by government assistance agencies and Christian groups. The *olla común* sometimes goes by other names: mother's clubs, popular dining halls, family kitchens, etc. The *olla común* experience was double-edged for these women. On the one hand, it provided them with a level of internal organization that improved services by collectivizing the purchase and management of food and its preparation and distribution. But this participation was always circumscribed by a traditional feminine responsibility. At the same time, this experience engendered a greater commitment and investment of work that obliged women to leave the home and participate in collective processes that were either unknown to them or previously conducted by men. New leadership opportunities arose for women. Their motivation was sustained by maternal responsibility and the social situation.

Yet despite these collective efforts to combat the impact of the crisis[4] on the popular sectors, the crisis continued with no immediate short-term hope of change. The need for collective solutions for food provision became a permanent situation that required the establishment of better internal organization and better relations with other women with similar aims and also with the governments, NGOs, and the Catholic church. These ties were often initiated by the institutional bodies but developed with the decision and experience of a self-sufficient women's movement. Without having foreseen or imagined it, women entered into negotiations, and this became an important component of their community's work.

In a parallel manner, women sought to assist their spouses economically by going out to work as domestics by the hour or seeking work in the informal sector of the economy, especially as street vendors and through participation in small-scale public markets. This entry into the workplace was also an important source of new knowledge as women assumed a central place as providers in the family. This led some researchers to recognize these women as family heads (Del Pino, 1990). The percentage of single or abandoned mothers grew rapidly.

This process defined new ties between the public and private worlds of women of the popular classes as dimensions not separated but interconnected. The domestic world ceased being private when eating took place in groups and when public pressure was generated, demanding national laws and budgets to distribute the food. In Peru, this was achieved by the organizations of the *vaso de leche* and the *comedores populares.* Women went from being recipients of donations to becoming active organizers. The significance of this transition was their commitment to the construction of a social identity as women and, indirectly, the repossession of their dignity.

During those first years, the nongovernmental organizations and some sectors of the church worked with an alternative communication proposal centered on two basic principles: the validation of the popular voice and the generation of a popular discourse of self-determination. The consensus for this proposal was sustained in the social processes lived by women, their urgent communicative demands and also in the sensibilities of communicators in their approach to the formation of leaders. Women needed to learn how to express themselves and defend themselves against meddling and poor treatment. Popular communication gave them the tools to do so, although with more ambitious goals related to social liberation.

During this period, newsletters were produced that included community's news and testimonies as well as participation in radio broadcast and seminars that used sociodrama as a method for education and for the promotion of self-esteem.[5] Recently, both videos and photonovellas have been used.

The priority in this process was to work with the low self-esteem of women. Popular communication methods provided the tools to participate and speak in public spaces and assemblies and the mass media, encouraging an increase in self-esteem. It demonstrated to women that their experiences and their forms of communication had as much coherence and value as other knowledge that has more legitimacy. The epoch of participation was discovered, and this was a time of dramatization and testimony but also of protest, marches, and mobilization. Through the validation and exercise of popular speech, women sought to be participants in making decisions and in affecting public opinion.

Some of these popular communication experiences allowed dialogues of mutual recognition between the women and the social communicators and activists; these were times of social romance that we will never forget, as it formed a part of ourselves. During this process we discovered the immense communicative capacity of women from the barrios: the way they told stories that seemed to come alive in the telling; their ability for theatrical improvisation; the importance of daily communication through gossip and endless conversation with friends and neighbors; the mutual tensions, agreements, and disagreements of friendships between women; and the multiple networks of contact that produced an incredible vitality in the barrios. These women's communication dynamics demonstrated a vision of life centered in the construction of relationships.

At the same time, a social discourse was needed that would integrate and give meaning to the women's movement and that would face the complex processes in which women were forced to live, especially when relations with parties and the state intensified. Autonomy associated with self-determination became the preferred discourse that claimed the need for popular organizations to be united to seek benefits or protest. This generated an idealization of the organization as the only field of liberation for women. The alternative communication proposals that arose from this discourse led to organizations working through the media, without motivating women who were not organized to work with the movement.

However, this proposal proved insufficient, not only because it did not address transformations toward gender equality, but also because it lacked sufficient consistency to deal with the many and profound personal and group conflicts affecting women at the grassroots and their organizations. The daily life of women of popular classes and its many tensions were scarcely touched on or were dealt with in a simplistic manner.

The fact that women leaders were negotiating with parties and governments gave rise to a rapid and poorly processed confidence both in themselves and in their abilities to communicate and lead social mobilization. This newfound self-esteem of women in their work in the public arena was not necessarily backed by any profound organizational and personal changes. Communication with those they claimed to represent at the grassroots was precarious. A feeling that all could be achieved—even a change in the government's economic policy—grew among the women's movement. Popular communication programs encouraged a sense of omnipotence among women leaders, creating problems and misunderstandings, even of a political nature.

The self-determination was exclusively in the public arena and in relations and negotiations with the government and the parties. This provoked a rapid process of confidence in developing a forcefully public voice for these women, but it did not work in understanding the communication with others groups and sectors, or even among themselves. The women's movement did not have the support of and relations with other political institutions and movements, and over time, these sentiments of omnipotence were undermined. This has, in many cases, provoked feelings of pessimism, disappointment, social fragmentation, and self-absorption.

Social Maternity:
Motivations of the New Heroines

Being a mother was the principal motor driving the formation of the women's movement. These women could not resign themselves to see their children suffering from hunger and malnutrition without reacting, and they soon understood that these problems were shared by many. They had already participated in collective work during the formation of barrios during the 1950s to the 1970s, as well as in the more paternalistic aid programs in the 1980s. Being a mother meant situating and concentrating the meaning of their gender identity in that role.

> As such, it is not only a category of personal and psychological order, but is prolonged through life as a social and cultural process. . . . In the maternal relationship they face different paths of encounter and relation with the real world, through an ethical perspective. . . . Nor is it only a social role, but the meaning of their existence. . . . Outside of maternity their essence loses equilibrium and destroys itself. (Alfaro, 1988b, p. 138)

Women of the popular classes both value themselves and are valued by society as mothers. Their maternity is lived as the best and most dignified of relationships.

Protecting their children came to define a broader arena than they were used to. The subject of children came up very strongly in the discussions and decisions of many groups. This created a new consciousness as women began to take responsibility for all children, fighting and organizing not only for their own but for other women's children, marked by necessity. Even childless or aged women would commit themselves to the organizations, indicating a realization of social maternity. The initial resistance to participation in public kitchens had been because it signified a public recognition of one's poverty. This resistance disappeared, however, with the rise of the reputation of Peruvian women's abilities and the satisfaction (not always acknowledged) of maternal sentiments.

The act of participation also signified the enrichment of processes of socialization interrupted by their domestic roles and that Guzman, Portocarrero, and Vargas (1991) called resocialization. The meetings or assemblies became newly conquered spaces for communication, outside of the home, to converse about everything; to explore with each other; and to share facts, gossip, stories, and emotions. At the assembly, women distanced themselves from their domestic roles, facing new adventures, receiving information, assuming responsibilities, struggling with political arguments, electing leaders, budgeting, censuring, deciding about tasks, and making political definitions. The execution of these tasks of internal politics and, to some extent, of macropolitics meant that women were developing new political roles and discourses. It was in these associations where the real changes for women occurred.

Organized popular mothers gave birth to "the meeting" as a place that symbolized their selfhood and their acquisition of real powers in relation to men. A wide variety of educational opportunities such as "talks" were developed as the women participated in workshops and popular education sessions. These nonformal educational experiences also signified the restoration of education to women whose traditional schooling had been interrupted by their burden of their work as women or by poverty.

As women's organizations became more institutionalized and established a diversity of relations, they faced a new task: to understand and deal with politicians, NGOs, and international institutions. These experiences brought both personal and neighborhood conflicts. On one hand, spouses and partners began to protest their going to meetings and the time they spent at organizing. On the other hand, local politicians and leaders began to have conflicts with these women's organizations, which were confronting their male power, their formality, and their male passivity. Women began to recognize their rights and who they were as women, adding to the development of self-esteem and a recognition of gender identity.

The video *Mothers United by the Glass of Milk* was produced by a group of women from the barrio (*Villa Maria del Triunfo*) with the assistance of Calandria. It presents the conflict with spouses over time spent organizing. In the video, this conflict is resolved when a *señora* congratulates a husband for his good wife, as she has helped many other people's children.

The video shows how and why men felt so affected when their partners acquire some independent social standing. In one town, there was almost a civil war between the men and women, because the women had not asked permission from the male neighborhood leaders to carry out an economic activity. Men had even drafted a request that the women be charged by the police, which one of the women intercepted. In the end, the activity was carried out and reconciliations were made in an atmosphere of a fiesta.

Conflict and Leadership

Women went from being mothers of their children to being mothers of society, later recognizing their condition as women. However, this step was not sufficiently integrated to lead to a true questioning of the unequal nature of the established roles for men and women. Nor were the women able sufficiently to adjust their personal worlds to these changes. The distance between leaders and the grassroots grew greater with time, because inevitably only some women could specialize in the leadership role.

One of the results was the establishment of organizational norms and their respective rituals that were formalized in meetings.[6] Different types of tensions and distances emerged among the women, coming from a lack of understanding of formalities. In assemblies, for example, decisions were not taken through open discussion, but rather one listened to information previously decided on by the leadership. After complying with the ritual of voting, the leadership believed that a collective agreement had been reached. But what was really occurring was the formation of authoritarianism among the women.

In these processes of centralization (in Peru and other countries), a generation of women was formed that represented women from the popular classes and that was dedicated to political struggle and negotiation with the state. These women emerged as leaders of the popular dining halls, the glass of milk movement, the peasants' federations in Peru, the feminine circles in Venezuela, and the native women's movement in Ecuador. However, the pressure and urgency with which the crisis pushed these women to join the movements meant that the women's learning process was compulsory, disordered, and difficult to grasp. This public political role presupposed a personal revolution and an enormous investment of emotional strength and enthusiasm. This pressure led to the emergence of superwomen and omnipotent heroines who were noted for their vitality and passion but were not always democratic. Political parties were quick to recruit these women, originating ambivalent processes of hidden militancies that could not satisfy.

This change from a traditional woman's role to a new one that no one had foreseen happened in a rush of frantic activities without support to process the change. The women also did not have enough support in terms of popular education and communication, so they had to labor with incomplete information and underdeveloped understandings and analysis.

For a time, popular communication programs supported and praised these women in alternative radio programs, NGO magazines and videos, and some left wing newspapers. However, only a few NGOs committed themselves to this wider grassroots movement beyond offering support via media training and broadcasting. Their enthusiasm over the growing presence of women in public and social life clouded the vision of these supportive professionals, intellectuals, and activists. The NGOs applauded these new amazons and their emergence in the midst of the old fold of popular workers, farmers, and local movements, but there was also a quick-change strategy that revealed the women's lack of understanding and ability to deal with the very serious conflicts and organizational problems of the period. The discourse on self-esteem and autonomy continued unmodified, as women leaders attempted to revive utopias that had long since been discussed and discarded by earlier social movements. In many cases, they projected autonomy as a closed self-sufficiency that did not require dialogue.

If social maternity led to a greater public role, it did not necessarily lead to a decrease in domestic work or to changes in relations between spouses. What did occur was a growing respect among men for their spouses and the vitality and capacity for work among women's organizations. Yet this respect was achieved only by taking on new tasks and pressures at home, work, and in the organization—all of which conflicted with each other. The leaders had trouble communicating what they were going through with their families and with the rest of their community at the grassroots. Social motherhood signified an advance, but it also complicated their personal lives, especially with their children.

The entrance of women into the political world was premature and, therefore, full of conflicts. Social maternity did not necessarily lead one to a solid identity as a citizen and to a clear appreciation of democracy.[7] Women who joined political parties became second-class members, rarely did they enter positions of leadership, and they suffered from a lack of trust and marginality. The parties were unable to accommodate their female identity or their social experience and provided little education to integrate them into the organization.

Conflict and Leadership Among
Popular Women

The first obstacle for organizational processes of women of the popular classes was the attempt to recognize each woman as an individual. This at the same time was its best possibility for change.[8] Lamentably, in each group a collectivist ideology existed that tended to deny differences and uniqueness. The only differences recognized were those of power between the leadership and grassroots. The personal was often hidden, seen only as a special interest or a "personal problem." But the personal dimension inevitably appeared in relationships among the membership, which became loaded with antipathies and sympathies, alliances and rejections. This was the origin of much internal tension and real wars, the sources of which were both personal and political and reflected a poor dynamic between the personal and the collective from the beginning. Amid all this, the democratic process became loaded down with many interpersonal conflicts that began to have more influence in the organizations than their overall objectives.

Another factor of organizational analysis is the form in which power was constituted in women's organizations and what this meant in the construction of new leadership. Two contrary motions occurred simultaneously. On one hand, there was the discovery of a surging vitality that could explain internal relations and the development of organizational means to meet their daily lives. On the other hand, authoritarianism with its logic of efficiency, as a pragmatic political model allowed the attainment of better benefits. These two logics, which lived side by side without touching, did not generate organizational development.

Relations with others (men, politicians, NGOs, the dominant classes) were rapidly begun in a precarious and even rigid manner. "The other" was perceived for their use, service value, or as the destination for complaint. It was not possible to construct an equal relationship between those who were so different, who put at risk the women's own world. Instead, women denounced the society that did not understand them. Less effort was put into comprehending this society and incorporating women of the popular classes into more structural struggles for change. This is not to deny the importance of what has been achieved but to recognize a problematic paralysis in facing the new challenges and the ways that women's popular organizations have yielded to the instrumentalization of others. The concern here is not that relations were defined by conflicts and indifference, because in some ways that corresponds to a stage in organizational growth. Rather, there was a kind of organizational deadlock, perhaps set in motion by other insoluble problems such as social insecurity, growing poverty, and violence, all which weighed heavily on women.

The popular communication strategies programs supporting women at the grassroots were not able to assist in the transition to a more complex dynamic. The communication programs developed by NGOs and communicators helped to elaborate the speech of these women, valued it and gave it legitimacy. But their communication strategies also contributed to making complaining the way to establish communication with other sectors and the way to generate pity or **clientelism** among the grassroots. Women's leaders appearing in both media (alternative or mass) used this style of communication, with no consideration for making their media discourses a scenario for transformation. The discourse of autonomy was not able to become a discourse about the relations with others, but rather it was self-absorbing, a resource or strategy of internal security. Working cooperatively was less emphasized than working for one's own group, even if the first is the prime factor of a more social and communicative development.

The educative and communicative proposals in the area of formation of leadership and training did not address the need to resolve the problems presented by the incorporation of women into organizations and public life. It was thought that organization was the change itself, even though more cautious looks indicated that it was only an opportunity to reorganize the internal world (Santisteban, 1989). Others who were more skeptical pointed out the profound "scars of poverty," which were seen as deterministic and unsalvageable.

Women's grassroots movements are experiences of great social and human quality. Although highly significant, they have not consolidated into strong organizations (Aldana, 1991). They depended heavily on individual leadership that contained the collectivity with all its strength and was unable to resolve the numerous power and value-driven conflicts that arose. These experiences could not legitimate a new democratic political culture that could be useful to understand and direct women's political participation at a macrosocial level.

New Challenges: Use of Mass Media

The social tensions in Peru in the early 1990s has compelled the women's leaders, with the aid of some NGOs, to use the mass media. Obtaining their participation and preparing them have been key to developing new alternatives for better dialogue with the media and public opinion.

There are two different sects of actors who are part of this dialogue: the journalists or professional social communicators and the audiences. The popular leaders have been trained with professional advice from NGOs such as Calandria in the preparation and conduct of press conferences. This training has made them think about the audience: Who are they? How can we speak to them and reach them? What communicative strategies are needed? Impressive gains have been made in the practice of organizing press conferences, in optimizing media opportunities, and in developing friendships and alliances with some journalists. There have also been some journalistic competitions on the topic of women's popular organizations.[9]

We have made the training of press secretaries in women's organizations a priority. Women are not only trained in communication skills for internal democratization but also in the importance of participating with their local media to build a stable relationship with their local communities and the mass media. We also consider here the formation and training of women correspondents.

These new challenges motivate women to look outward and to become concerned about unorganized women and the political repercussions of their communicative work. They are also motivated to consider the female media consumer and take into account the individual, familial and spontaneous situation in which she processes the media.

It is at this educational level that the first steps have been made, because the presence of women of the popular classes in local and mass media is still not ensured. There is also a need to evaluate the impact of their messages on public opinion, and their growing involvement in political life. This work has just begun and much remains to be accomplished. More is needed to work with the discourse of the leaders and their comprehension of media, as some still maintain a fatalistic and apocalyptic posture against radio, the press, and television, especially in the area of news.

Work within organizations and with their leadership are also important communicative tasks for social communicators. There cannot be a project of educational production and promotion that does not take into account a communicative strategy. This takes on greater meaning when we recognize the profound relationship that exists between social issues and gender. Understanding this connection can allow us to see potential in these movements of social change for the transformation of gender identities (Buxo Rey, 1988).

The political culture of women must be subjected to a real process of enrichment; it does not change spontaneously with the rise of the individual in the popular organization and political life. This change does not neces-sarily lead to women integrating their experiences, constructing a new subjectivity or cultural ideology. It is necessary to work with these experi-ences and to relate them to one's own life and to the macrosocial so that they become significant in achieving transformation. It requires, for example, the redefinition of the popular women "us" through a subjective acceptance of flexibility, tolerance, and the existence of other individuals who need change. Training must affect the world of personal and collec-tive subjectivities, bringing them forward to be processed.

The work and commitment of popular communication to the personal and internal worlds of women is then a new orientation in search of con-crete tools. The support and advice of psychology is ever more important in communicative work that has already been so marked by the perspec-tive and methodology of sociology.

The importance of educational confrontation between men and women is also key. Concentrating only on the dialogue between women is not enough, since it does not deal with the question or relationship between men and women or change how it works. Confrontation is an instance that not only educates but also demonstrates how much one has advanced. It permits then an identification of what to correct and how to proceed.

The Contributions and Setbacks of Feminism

Latin American feminists have evolved in their communication work and in the relation established with women of the popular classes. Feminism has been able to transcend a vision of society based only on gender differences to include other social and cultural differences in women's lives. Proposals for change have become more flexible, with a vision of women as both social subjects and objects of change linked to a more integral development.

The feminist emphasis on women as social subjects and on the impor-tance of subjectivity are crucial contributions to consider today. Further-more, we note the feminist consideration of daily life as the symbolic place for the construction of identities and social relations and the view that the validation of women's identity requires the acknowledgment of individual selfhood and of their larger intersubjective solidarity with other women. It is not possible to think about this development without seeing the transformation of relations between men and women and the changes in autonomy for both.

The importance of women's access to media has been another contribution of feminism. Given the acceptance of this issue by the logic of the marketplace, such access has increased in recent years. However, little research has been done on the impact of women's entrance into the mass media and the kinds of symbolic figures that are being represented as new prototypes of a "woman." This concern takes relevance today with the growing appearance of women in media as models and *vedettes*; central characters in soap operas or humorous dramatizations; news readers and reporters; and as histrionic program hosts of shows of parody, especially in television. Analysis of these new cultural forms is needed. Media research must take into account the complexity of these images of the feminine and the theoretical advances from studies of consumption. This research must overcome emphasis on just ideological factors that focus on the manipulatory influence of media.

Regarding women's leaders, the importance of work on self-esteem and on a renewed emphasis on identity, connects experiences of social leadership with those of gender. This allows the construction of another ideology, another praxis about roles of women and men, from a perspective of equality. These issues of women's political participation pose problems of access and participation to the power of the wider society, issues that must be tied to equality in the domestic and cultural arenas.

But there are some issues that require clarification. In the first place, we need to know what is happening with men's gender identity, what new models of masculinity are being advocated, and how men feel affected by sexual inequality. Also it is important to understand the complicity of women in gender inequality and their resistance to change. Oppression is not all external, it is necessary to investigate the changes that are needed and the real possibilities of implementing them.

There has not been sufficient analysis of the relationship among society, the social subject, and the media. Explanations about the way that power and ideologies act on people are still based on stereotypes and simplifications, as are explanations about the relationship between mass media and social and cultural organization. There has been an emphasis among feminists to denounce the media, grouping it totally to the ideology that is oppressive to women. This is a discourse repeated with little modification, especially at the level of publicity. The media are assumed to be omnipotent, and the consumer to be passive; there has been little integration of new research on this point.

Feminist alternative communication, as a consequence, works toward acceptance through the creation of a set of messages to be broadcast or publicized; however, they work with the same mechanistic logic as in the feminist media analysis noted above. Their view of democratization of communications is to counter ideology with ideology. The alternative does not recognize the real importance of the communication process, nor of the role of the listeners and viewers and their thoughts and feelings. This posture is one of vanguardism.

In the seminar "Communicative Identity and Alternative Proposals for Women," six Latin American studies were presented that evaluated alternative/popular communication from the point of view of the receptors. It was shown that in many communicative texts made from a feminist perspective no attempt was made to construct a complex male character: There was no internal tension in the male characters. Men were stereotyped as terrible and dangerous and as unchanging manikins with no appealing characteristics. In other cases, male characters did not exist, suggesting a society of women even playing the roles of men. In general, the narratives of these productions were not attractive or pleasurable; they did not propose any positive alternatives to being women and men or enrich the social construction of new gender identities. They did not succeed in overcoming dominant media messages that show inequality as something natural. Their messages portrayed women as victims, who can be rapidly transformed into heroines by becoming conscious of their oppressive conditions. The symbolic reality constructed in these productions lacked spontaneity and viability for the viewers. Perhaps that explains the lack of academic production in this area. Alternative communication is still rooted in an instrumental vision, preoccupied with critiquing the mass media because of its ratings or lack of creativity. The correct way to introduce a gender perspective is then only a technical problem via the alternative media. Understanding how gender identity is constructed from the perspective of receptors in daily interaction with media is not a theme for analysis. As a result, our workshop in Peru in 1992 was a pioneering activity, the beginning of outlining the general characteristics for a redefinition.

The Journey of Calandria

Our collective of social communicators, Calandria, has been actively involved in the process described. Our institutional goal is to contribute in a concrete manner to the development of popular actors and their articulation in Peru. We need to comprehend the communicative processes in the heart of what we call popular cultures.

The first steps of Calandria were marked by the passion of discovery of the potential of loudspeakers and radio soaps to empower the voice of women of the popular classes (Alfaro, 1985, 1988a). Following this, we learned about the complexities of Peruvian reality and of women's relations with media and the popular world (Alfaro, 1988b). Later, we encountered a number of conflicts at the organizational and interpersonal level that could not be solved through better communication but through an active commitment to grassroots development and all its political repercussions (Alfaro, 1990).

Our work began in a popular barrio and then entered into the multiplicity of microworlds found in the huge and disordered city of Lima, so brutally affected by crisis and violence. Our work and services were requested by many others, and we traveled the country and beyond throughout Latin America. We began by using a tape recorder and working with a group of grassroots women, later we extended our work to radio and the support of popular organizations. Then we moved on to other educational adventures with video, graphic media, and the analysis of media consumption, culture, subjective worlds, and politics. Today we have three departments: media (radio, video, graphics), communicative promotion or direct work with the community (women and community, district development, street commerce), and research and documentation as well as a team of communicators that includes sociologists and social psychologists.

Popular women have helped us become communicators and understand the complexities of peoples' lives and that there are not simple solutions. Reflection, research, and evaluation prepare us to define a more effective service, despite the complexities and conflicts present in our Latin American realities. Although a gender perspective is now a respected institutional line of work, it has brought with it many internal and external problems. We struggle against a vision of our world that reduces the subordination of women and gender inequality to a technical and production problem. Today we can say that our communication proposals are helping to enrich some feminist views, making them more flexible. It is also fair to say that the women of Calandria are incredible, without devaluing the men, and have put a great deal of passion into this organization. We color the management style with a certain dose of matriarchal feeling, which humanizes the place and makes it challenging. With our male colleagues, we are building a real concern for equality between men and women.

New Perspectives of Analysis

All the preceding analysis highlights the importance of generating empirical and theoretical studies capable of responding to the problems we see today. If we are in the initial moments of theoretical and methodological renewal, then our area of study requires greater precision and diversification. Alternative communication is rich today because it permits us to refine questions and makes concrete contributions to analysis.

It is important to call attention to some significant topics. The first is the relationship between consumption and the domestic world. The second is the relation between communicative genres and the identities of men and women. These topics are a necessary part of the consideration of the subjective construction of gender identity in relation to the media. Reception is a strategic place to understand how gender identities and inequalities are constructed. Women are leading public actors not only because of their participation in the social and political life of the country but also because they are media consumers. The women's movement must be analyzed from this space as well, which is vital in the construction of cultural and social relations.[10]

Relations between women, culture, and democratic institutions, within a larger examination of women and politics, is another topic, but one associated with the comparison of the daily life of women and that of politics. It is also necessary to question the autonomous institutions and educational processes that women have created. The personalization of politics promoted by mass media has generated a relational perception of politics that is opposed to an institutional perception of it. This perception relates to a gender identity that is not necessarily associated with control of power but rather to a bidirectional dialogue between individuals.

Alternative communication must develop a better approach to conflict and leave behind those romantic simplifications based on the passion of commitment without sufficient dialogue with reality. The developing of women as social and participative agents is a complex process that involves more than we ever imagined. Today we can understand that these problems are inherent to processes of change. The challenges presented by such developments are very complex and require a closer and more fruitful dialogue between research and action.

I want to affirm that despite the difficult times in which we in Peru are living, we continue to learn. And even if some unjust deaths have bent us, our hope has not gone. We regain it whenever it briefly disappears. In these days, we know we need faith to define other social models that bring together justice, democracy, and progress. Communication (alternative, feminist, and popular) represents a way of contributing to the building of a plural country, and the envisioning of a continental solidarity. We do not want to erase human sensibility, words, and music from our new communication proposals.

Notes

1. Calandria was formed by a group of university professors and seniors seeking professional alternatives to link socially committed research and the search for alternatives to Peru's crisis.

2. The term *popular* is used here to describe the subordination and cultural differences of specific groups in society with respect to dominant groups. See Chapter 6 for an elaboration of the term *popular women*.

3. Other groups and centers participating in this research process are *Centro Gregoria Apaza para la Promoción de la Mujer* in Bolivia, *Cine Mujer* in Colombia, *CEPAM* and *Taller de Comunicación Mujer* in Ecuador, and the *Circulos Femeninos* in Venezuela.

4. Henriquez and Alfaro (1991) referred to the complexity of this crisis in Latin America today:

For several years [in Latin America and particularly in Peru] we have referred to the confluence of several crises. The historical crisis revealed in broken identities and weak national integration, and the economic crisis including the economic recession since 1975 and the hyperinflation and shock since 1988. (p. 11)

5. In Peru some examples of this type of experiences are the radio programa *Our Lives* run by Calandria and *Warmicunan Rimanchis* of the association AMAUTO in Cuzco. Both programs used radiosoaps and testimonials based on women's life stories.

6. Research done by Calandria on assemblies gave much data on this path toward the formalization and hardening of communication in women's organizations. This change could never be totally handled or assimilated as in the case of men.

7. This was evidenced by the popular support for the coup carried out by President Fujimori in May 1992.

8. Women very early must assume major domestic and reproductive responsibilities, which hinder the development of relationships with other men and women. In Latin America, much education is segregated by sex. The affective world of women is centered on her spouse, which has as a correlate a more cold and calculating man. This relationship enhances subordination and power. The lack of value given to women builds a deficient sense of gender identity, and that added to their poverty creates knots in their personal development that are difficult to untie.

9. The program Between Women of the ICAE and NGOs such as Manuela Ramos, Flora Tristan, and Calandria have been organizing these competitions.

10. Calandria has done some empirical research on this topic. We have found that the ways men and women consume media have some common elements. Women, however, tend to relate to media from two main logics: utility and pleasure. Women share domestic work

with media consumption, while men tend to overlap moments of leisure with media consumption. Women tend to look for romantic music, melodrama, and romantic consultories, while men tend to look for information and sports. However, these patterns of consumption also depend on the individual's age and the educational level.

Glossary

Alternative. In communication, alternative refers to communication initiatives or media productions that are oppositional to mainstream media and cultural industries. Alternative communication identifies with a social project that is a reaction against the dominant order (Ambrosi, 1991). According to Puntel (1992), the alternative does not lie in the means of communication per se but in the *way* such media are used, within a horizontal and participatory communication process. Roncagliolo (1991) concluded that alternative implies greater access and participation in the production and transmission of messages on the part of an increasing number and variety of groups. Alternative, therefore, introduces pluralism to the communication flow.

Class. From a sociological and economic framework, class may be defined in quantitative terms as a group of individuals with a particular relationship to productive work (blue collar, white collar). Class may also be defined as a historical formation: a product of the individual's experiences of economic and social relations in a particular historical period. Class formations are identified through the observation of social processes and the characteristic responses of groups of individuals to specific situations. This includes the creation of institutions and cultures with class connotations. This is the definition used in various chapters in this book and is based on the work of British historian Thompson (1984).

Clientelism. In Latin America, clientelism describes a relationship between politicians (patron) and their constituencies (clients) that is mediated by an exchange of services and favors (e.g., the exchange of a vote for a recommendation to a job or a place in school).

Coalition. This is defined by Albrecht and Brewer (1990) as "groups or individuals that have come together around a particular goal. These groups operate autonomously and are usually not connected to each other;

most organizations have different agendas as well. Upon completion of the shared goal, coalitions often dissolve and organizations go back to their own work" (p. 3). Alliances are seen as longer-standing relationships in which people "struggle together on a number of progressive fronts, not just on a single issue" (p. 4).

Communication. As a social system of shared symbols and meanings, communication binds people together into a group, a community, or a culture. The relationship between communication as a symbolic process and as activator of identities is explored in several parts of this book (Chapters 2, 7, 13).

Communication competency. This refers to the ability—skills, knowledge, and attitudes—of individuals to respond to any communicative interaction (among individuals, media consumption, story telling, or a group situation). Communication competencies are grounded in the cultural realm in both indigenous knowledge and industrial or mass culture. The knowledge and skills derived from these sources constitute a competency that individuals unconsciously use in any communicative interaction (see Chapter 6).

Community. Community identifies geographical (e.g., village, city) or sectorial links (e.g., professional, cultural, ability, sexual orientation). As a community, these individuals share some common interests and recognize common bonds (Downing et al., 1990). The sense of community is described by the presence of a collective identity that in the terms of Dervin and Clark (1989) has existence and meaning only in communication.

Community communication. Developed in the North, this framework advocates the rights of citizens to access the media as a public resource and their participation in decision-making processes (see Chapter 1).

Conscientization. As defined by the Brasilian Freire (1973) conscientization refers to the ability to group in critical terms both individual and group experiences; that is, the dialectical unity between self and object. Freire saw that conscientization is a critical process that does not occur outside of practice, outside of the theory-practice, reflection-action unity.

Consumption. Consumption refers to "a social and cultural process in which products are appropriated and used" (Valles, 1991, p. 29).

Democracy. As related to communication, democracy involves the right to acquire and produce information, and the opening of spaces for all groups' cultural expression. Democracy requires the continuing distribution of power.

Democratization of communications. Democratization of communications is understood here as a process whereby (a) the individual becomes an active subject and not a mere object of communication, (b) various messages are democratically exchanged, and (c) the extent and quality of social representation or participation is augmented. This concept of democratization was articulated into the institutional field by the MacBride report *Many Voices, One World* (quoted in Puntel, 1992). The discussion of a new world information and communication order has relied heavily on institutional agendas and on expectations that democratization can be achieved through policy regulations and institutional change at the national and international level. In this book, we argue that an adequate debate on the democratization of communications can only be carried out successfully if all the various dimensions, components, and actors are taken into consideration at all levels, including the local and grassroots (see Chapters 1 and 2).

Development communication. Literature on development communication and community participation is concerned with how communication and, specifically media, constitute crucial elements for developing alternatives for participation. The role of communication is associated with the processes of empowering the powerless. However, literature on development communication and community participation has failed to look at the communicational and holistic perspectives of grassroots communication initiatives. The literature has also not dealt with gender as an analytical dimension in their frameworks. References to gender are limited to identifying the gender of the participants and to describing the subordinate position of women in their communities and societies. Neither the ways in which gender influences the nature of participation and communication production nor the mediation of gender in women's and men's experiences of subordination have been taken into consideration. Chapter 1 presents a detailed review of this framework.

Empowerment. Chapter 2 presents the various understandings of this term by the various frameworks addressing the relationship among women, participation, and communication.

Ethnicity. This is belonging or being perceived by others as belonging to an ethnic group. Ethnicity is seen here as a changing feature that according to the cultural and social environment does not refer so much to static survival from the historical past but rather to the modern and modernizing feature of a contrasting strategy (Sollors, 1989).

Feminism. Feminism is understood here as a movement for the "redefinition and redistribution of power" (Maguire, 1987, p. 79). Feminism is both a social theory and a political framework that recognizes the oppression of women and the commitment to end such oppression. Feminist principles advocate the defense of women's rights and the need to build alternative paradigms for social theory and research. Movements for the defense of women's rights have been part of the struggles of many communities both in the north and the south. Feminism, according to this view, encompasses women's social movements worldwide and recognizes the specific roots in local/regional civil rights and social struggles. The contemporary social and political agendas of such feminisms are influenced by the specific regional circumstances.

Feminist anthropology. This field has developed a framework to look at "the complex ways in which gender, race and class intersect and cross cut each other, as well as the way in which all three intersect with colonialism, the International Division of Labour and the rise of the modern state" (Moore, 1988, p. 10). If the feminist anthropological task is defined as one of studying differences, the field has been concerned with exploring how gender identities are constructed and the various culturally mediated perceptions of what it is to be a "woman" or a "man." Although the field is concerned with issues of identity, personhood, and representation, which are all intrinsically embedded in communication, the role that communication plays in shaping identities and in defining relations between individuals has been disregarded. At the same time, there has not been any attempt to apply the insights of feminist anthropology to the field of communication (Burton, 1985; Moore, 1988; Ortner & Whitehead, 1981; Strathern, 1987, 1990). The journal *Signs* frequently includes articles by feminist anthropologists. See also Chapter 2.

Gender and development (GAD). This framework looks at gender as a constitutive principle of social life. GAD literature has focused on an analysis of gender as a socially constructed relationship, shaped and sanctioned by values held by the members of society (Young, 1988). GAD identifies the social construction of production and reproduction as the basis of women's oppression (Rathgebher, 1989b). However, communication relations and practices have not been systematically included in this analysis. Communication, as the basic dimension/experience shaping social relationships, has not been taken into account as a central factor in the structuring of gender and cultural definitions of women (see Benería & Sen, 1986; ISIS, 1984; Rathgebher, 1989b; Stamp, 1989; Young 1988).

Grassroots communication. See Preface.

Group media. This term describes media production and broadcasting in small groups with the specific goals of education and social action. Sometimes it is used with alternative and low-scale technologies (see Chapter 1).

Indigenous knowledge. This is accumulated specific knowledge among a community with shared cultural practices. Indigenous knowledge includes the concepts, belief structures, explanatory systems, and analytical perspectives that define a community. It includes skills and practices on the environment and the natural resources, health, communication, and work skills critical to survival (Bernard, 1991).

Mestizaje. As understood in Latin America, mestizaje does not represent any particular ethnic essence but recalls the mixing of indigenous, black, rural, and urban cultural influences. Mestizaje does not embody cultural purity, but rather imitation, altered readings, and an energy that underlies ways of talking, telling, and perceiving. Over the time *mestizo* has come to signify a mixed population, the product of many generations of intermarriage (indigenous, Spanish, black).

Minorities. Wilson and Gutiérrez (1985) offered a contrasting definition:
> When used in its statistical sense, the term "minorities" refers to groups that are small in number, less than the majority. It has often been applied to people of Color in the United States because as individual groups, Blacks, Latinos, Asians, and Native American do not constitute

a large percentage of the national population. It has become a convenient umbrella under which to put any group that is not white. But it is also a misleading label. It misleads the person using the term to think of those who carry the label as small not only in number, but in importance. It also can make the interests and issues raised by "minorities" appear to be less meaningful than those of the majority. And, finally, it is no longer a statistically accurate term in many cases. (p. 13)

Modernization. As applied to development theories and policies, modernization initiatives argue for the *updating* of structures and practices in Third World countries. Modernization attempts in the Third World to promote development, the welfare of the community, and its homogenization through the introduction of technological innovation, external models of industrialization, control of urbanization, and cultural diffusion.

Participation. The uses of the word *participation* in the communication field are discussed throughout this book. In the framework presented here, participation generally refers to control and ownership rather than to physical presence (see also Chapter 1).

People of Color. Hurtado (1989) defines people of Color as comprising various ethnic groups that are all minorities such as Chicanos, Asians, Native Americans, and blacks. *Color* is capitalized here because it refers to specific ethnic groups.

Popular. In North America, the popular tends to be associated to wide consumption or acceptance, thus with mass cultural industry. Popular, however, also means as related to people. This is the use of the term in this book. The term popular as associated to people denotes a movement of emancipation. *People* is distinct from the "mass" of the mass media or mass consumption. People refers to those who are powerless and who are involved in gaining control of their own lives (Puntel, 1992).

Popular communication. Framework originated in Latin America to describe communication initiatives and media production controlled by powerless groups (see Chapter 1).

Public. Stamp (1989) and March and Taqqu (1986) have shown the conceptual confusion and variety of meanings attached to the word *public*. March and Taqqu provided the two primary competing ideas:
(1) "*the* public" that is, a conception of collectivity in whose name action is undertaken; and (2) "public" in the sense of "out in the open," or no secret, as in the "public eye." . . . The concept of "public" then, subsumes two major facets: the nature of the collectivity involved, and the nature of the space or style in which that collectivity operates.

Race. Gilroy (1992, pp. 38-40) defined race as an analytical, relational, and political category. Race does not correspond to any biological or epistemological absolutes, but to the power that collective identities acquire by means of their roots in tradition (see also Chapter 5).

Role. Role is understood as a dynamic concept describing a complex and varied set of functions and interactions that are defined by power relations and occur in a given context and at a specific time. Stamp (1989), Burton (1985), and Moore (1988) argued that an excessive emphasis on the role of women reinforces the belief that women are more central to gender relations than men. Furthermore, the concept of role might reinforce an idea of given and assumed social functions of women, missing the power dynamics and relations of control in which men's and women's activities and functions are negotiated (see Chapter 2).

Social actor. This term has been used in social movements theory as an alternative concept that places the research emphasis on the subjects and their own perspectives and perceptions, rather than on the researcher and his or her own framework. The term emphasizes the activity of the subjects in defining and directing the cultural and social orientation of their social actions.

Social movement. Jelin (1990) and Sénécal (1991) saw social movements as nontraditional, nonconventional, or noninstitutionalized forms of participation. A social movement groups individuals by a common goal of social action such as the defense of human rights, land claims, housing, food supply, urban services, and racial discrimination. Most important, a social movement represents a new view of engaging in politics (e.g., the feminist approach that the personal is political) and new forms of social relations and social organization (more horizontal relations, solidarity networks, alternative lifestyles, etc.). Sénécal (1991) summarized:

Their otherness is not foreign to the discourse of feminists, ecologists, populists, pacifists, homosexuals, etc. Each of these movements leaded for a variety of social actors seek to create a new social reality, a new culture, a new logic for all aspects of life, including the technology and skills of audio-visual communications. (p. 213)

South. As used here, South refers to countries in the Southern Hemisphere that are economically dependent on and, from a model of industrial capitalism, seen as less developed than those countries in the North. The word has been used to avoid negative connotations that terms such as *developing countries* or *Third World countries* may have.

Third World feminism. Included here is an extensive and very rich body of literature and feminist agendas carried out by various groups of women in the Third World. Although there is a wide regional variation in these approaches, there are some common concerns relating to the need to build alliances that recognize the multifaceted experiences of class, gender, sexual identity, and race (Anzaldúa, 1990a; hooks, 1989, 1990).

Third World women. Acknowledging that the term *Third World women* is a much maligned and contested one, Mohanty, Russo, and Torres (1991) used it to refer to the "colonized, neo-colonized or decolonized countries (of Asia, Africa and Latin America) whose economic and political structures have been deformed within the colonial process, and to Black, Asian, Latino, and indigenous peoples in North America, Europe and Australia" (p. ix).

Woman/women. Mohanty (1991, p. 53) clarifies the conceptual distinction between woman "as a cultural and composite Other constructed through diverse representational discourses" and women "as real collective subjects of their collective histories." As the focus of this book is on practical experiences, we will refer mostly to women.

References

AAVV. (1987). *Palabra de mujer. La experiencia de ser promotora popular de comunicación.* Lima, Peru: Calandria-Tarea.

Albrecht, L., & Brewer, R. (Eds.). (1990). *Bridges of power: Women's multicultural alliances.* Philadelphia: New Society.

Aldana, C. (1991). *Diagnóstico de la organización del vaso de leche.* Unpublished manuscript. Lima, Peru: Calandria.

Alfaro, R. (1985). *Del periódico al altoparlante. Materiales para la comunicación popular.* Lima, Peru: IPAL.

Alfaro, R. (1988a). Producers of communication: What is the proposition? *Group Media Journal, 7*(2), 10-15.

Alfaro, R. (1988b). *De la conquista de la ciudad a la apropiación de la palabra. Una experiencia de educación popular y comunicación con mujeres.* Lima, Peru: Calandria.

Alfaro, R. (1990). *Cultura de masas y cultura popular en la radio peruana. Diagnóstico para construir una alternativa radial.* Lima, Peru: Calandria.

Alfaro, R. (1992). *Informe de la investigación sobre la emisora radial La voz de la selva.* Unpublished manuscript. Lima, Peru: Calandria.

Ambroise, R. (1987). Towards a dynamic group media training strategy. *Group Media Journal, 6*(3), 9-10.

Ambrosi, A. (1991). Alternative communication and development alternative. In N. Thede & A. Ambrosi (Eds.), *Video the changing world.* Montreal: Black Rose.

Amoros, C. (1990). *Mujer, participación, cultura política y estado.* Buenos Aires: Editorial de la Flor.

Annis, S. (1990, March). *An information revolution at the grassroots: What it means for the poor.* Paper presented at the World Conference on Education for All, Jomtiem, Thailand.

Ansah, P. (1992). The right to communicate: Implications for development. *Media Development, 39*(1), 53-56

Anzaldúa, G. (1990a). Bridges, drawbridge, sandbar or island: Lesbians-of-color *Hacienda Alianzas.* In L. Albrecht & R. Brewer (Eds.), *Bridges of power: Women's multicultural alliances* (pp. 216-231). Philadelphia: New Society.

Anzaldúa, G. (Ed.). (1990b). *Making faces, making souls: Creative and critical perspectives by women of color.* San Francisco: Aunt Lute Foundation.

Anzola, P., & Cooper, P. (1985). *La investigación en comunicación social en Colombia.* Lima, Peru: DESCO.

Apetheker, R. (1989). *Tapestries of life: Women's work, women's consciousness, and the meaning of everyday life.* Amherst: University of Massachusetts Press.

Arizpe, L. (1990). Foreword: Democracy for a small two-gender planet. In E. Jelin (Ed.), *Women and social change in Latin America* (pp. xiv-xix). London: Zed Books.

Arnold, S., & Nitecki, A. (1980). *Culture and development in Africa.* Trenton, NJ: Africa World Press.

Aubin, B. (1992). Sublime leftovers. In J. Seigel (Ed.), *Mutiny and the mainstream: Talk that changed art 1975-1990.* New York: Midmarch Arts.

Baehr, H. (1980). Women and media. *Women's Studies International Quaterly 3*(1), 1-133.

Baehr, H. (1987). *Boxed-in women and television.* London: Pandora Press.

Balarubrahmanyan, V. (1988). *Mirror image. The media and the women's question.* Bangalore: Centre for Education and Documentation.

Balka, E. (1991). *Womentalk goes on line: The use of computers in the context of feminist social change.* Unpublished Ph.D. dissertation, Simon Fraser University, Burnaby, Canada.

Banerjee, S. (1990). Having the last laugh: Women in the XIXth century Bengali forces. *Manushi, 59,* 15-20.

Barkley-Brown, E. (1990). A framework for conceptualizing and teaching African-American women's history. In *Black women in America.* Chicago: University of Chicago Press.

Bates, B. (1988). *Communication and the sexes.* New York: Harper & Row.

Belbase, S. (1988). Video survey: Do rural people learn from video? *Media Asia, 15*(2), 108-112.

Belbase, S. (1989, February). *Participatory communication for development: How can we achieve it?* Paper presented at the Seminar on Participation: A Key Concept for Change and Development. University of Poona, India.

Beltran, H. (1986). People power, popular culture, and the February revolt. *Group Media Journal, 5*(4), 18-22.

Benería, L., & Sen, G. (1986). Accumulation, reproduction and women's role in economic development: Boserup revisited. In E. Leacock & H. Safa (Eds.), *Women's work: Development and the division of labour by gender* (pp. 141-157). South Hadley: Bergin.

Benjamin, W. (1991). *Para una crítica de la violencia.* Madrid: Taurus.

Bernard, A. (1991). Learning and intervention: The informal transmission of the knowledge and skills of development. In IRDC (Eds.), *Perspectives on education for all* (Manuscript Report 295e, pp. 30-766). Ottawa, Ont., Canada: IDRC.

Bhasin, K., & Agarwal, B. (Eds.). (1984). *Women and media: Analysis, alternatives and action.* New Delhi: ISIS International.

Bidegain (1986). Contemos otra historia. In M. C. Laverde & L. Gomez (Eds.), *Voces insurgentes* (pp. 299-309). Bogota, Colombia: SCCS.

Blasi, A., da Silva, A., & Weigert, A. (Eds.). (1978). *Toward an interpretative sociology.* Washington, DC: University Press of America.

Blondet, C. (1990). Establishing an identity: Women settlers in a poor Lima neighbourhood. In E. Jelin (Ed.), *Women and social change in Latin America* (pp. 12-44). London: Zed Books.

Boafo, S. T. Kwame (Ed.). (1989). *Communication and culture: African perspectives.* Nairobi, African Region: WACC.

Boafo, S. T. Kwame (1992). Mass media in Africa: Constraints and possible solutions. *Media Development, 39,* 53-56.

Bourdieu, P. (1988). *Distinction.* Cambridge, MA: Harvard University Press.

Bourdieu, P. (1991). *El sentido practico.* Barcelona: Taurus.

Brown, R. (1991, June 23). Tar beach [book review]. *New York Times Book Review.*

Brunner, J. (1987). *Ciencias sociales y el tema de la cultura: Notas para una agenda de investigación.* Santiago: FLACSO.

Building Zimbawe together. (1989, June). *Group Media Journal* [Special Issue], 29-30.

Bunster, B. X. (1977). Talking pictures: Field methods and visual mode. *Signs: Journal of Women in Culture and Society, 3*(1), 278-293.

Burke, R. (1987). Getting the mixture right: Non formal education through community radio in the Bolivian altiplano. *Convergence, 20*(2), 69-81.

Burkert, C. (1989a, November-December). Videoletters in an ancient land. *Development Forum,* 14.

Burkert, C. (1989b). Videoletters. *Development Communication Report, 1*(64), 13.

Burton, C. (1985). *Subordination: Feminism and social theory.* Sydney: George Allen & Unwin.

Butler, J. P. (1990). *Gender trouble: Feminism and the subversion of identity.* New York: Routledge.

Buxo Rey, M. (1988). *Antropología de la mujer. Cognición, lengua e ideología cultural.* Barcelona: Anthropos.

Calandria. (1989). *La videodramatización popular: Retos para la comunicación participativa.* Unpublished manuscript. Lima, Peru: Calandria.

Calda, A. (1988). The woman dimension of grassroots communication [Editorial]. *Group Media Journal, 7*(2), 2.

Calle, M. A. (1990). Así se hizo Sahuarí. *CHASQUI, 33,* 87-89

Calvelo, J. (1989a). Popular video for rural development in Peru. *Development Communication Report, 66,* 3.

Calvelo, J. (1989b). Video y televisión: Dos instrumentos diferentes. In M. Gutierrez (Ed.), *Video, tecnología y comunicación popular* (pp. 89-118). Lima, Peru: IPAL.

Carey, J. (1989). *Communication as culture: Essays on media and society.* Boston: Unwin Hyman.

Centro Para la Mujer Gregoria Apaza. (1991) *Informe evaluación taller de radio novela.* La Paz, Bolivia: CPMGA. (Unpublished)

Chadwick, W. (1990). *Women, art and society.* London: Thames & Hudson.

Chambulikazi, E. (1983). *Report on Msoga popular theatre workshop.* Unpublished manuscript. University of Dar es Salaam, Tanzania.

Champagne, L. (1990). *Out from under: Texts by women performance artists.* New York: Theatre Communications Group.

Charnley, K. (1990). Concepts of anger, identity and power and the vision in the writing and voices of first nation women. In D. Gregoire (Ed.), *Gatherings: The En-owkin journal of first North American people* (pp. 10-22). Penticton, B.C., Canada: Theytus.

Chitnis, S. (1988). Feminism: Indian ethos and Indian convictions. In R. Ghadially (Ed.), *Women in Indian society: A reader.* New Delhi: Sage.

Clifton, L. (1991). *Quilting, poems 1987-1990.* New York: BOA.

Cocks, J. (1991, November). The empire strikes back. *Times Magazine,* p. 98.

Collier, J. (1978). *The making of jazz.* New York: Dell.

Communication and social change: The Philippine experience. (1986). *Group Media Jounral* [Special Issue], *5*(4).

Communications Research Trends. (1988). *Popular Theatre, 9*(1-2), pp. 1-24.

Corral, T. (1990). News and development networks raise profile of Third World women. *Group Media Journal, 9*(2), 11-12.

Cottingham, J. (1989). ISIS: A decade of international networking. In R. Bush & D. Allen (Eds.), *Communication at the crossroads: The gender gap connection* (pp. 238-250). Norwood, NJ: Ablex.

Creedon, P. (Ed.). (1989). *Women in mass communication: Challenging gender values.* Newbury Park, CA: Sage.

Davis, A. Y. (1990). *Women, culture and politics.* New York: Vintage.

Daze, C. (1991). *Rap rock.* Premier Cards.

Del Pino, N. (1990). *Saliendo a flote, la jefa de familia popular.* Lima, Peru: Tacif-Fundación Naumann.

de Oliveira, R., & Harper, B. (1980). As mulheres em movimiento. Ler a própia vida, escrever a própia história. In P. Freire, R. de Oliveira, & C. Ceccon, *Experiencias do IDAC em educacao popular* (pp. 39-67). Sao Paulo: Brasiliense.

Dervin, B. (1987). The potential contribution of feminist scholarship to the field of communication. *Journal of Communication, 37*(4), 107-120.

Dervin, B., & Clark, K. (1989). Communication as cultural identity: The invention mandate. *Media Development, 36*(2), 5-8.

Deshler, D., & Sock, D. (1985). *Community development participation: A concept review of the international literature.* Paper presented at the International League for Social Commitment in Adult Education, Sweden.

Deza, A. (1989, February). *Media production and the process of becoming in the context of community-building.* Paper presented at the Seminar on Participation: A Key Concept for Change and Development, University of Poona, India.

Diaz-Bordenave, J. (1989, February). *Participative communication as part of the building of a participative society.* Paper presented at the Seminar on Participation: A Key Concept for Change and Development, University of Poona, India.

Dickson, K. B. (1969). *A historical geography of Ghana.* London: Cambridge University Press.

Dixon-Mueller, R., & Anker, R. (1990). *Assessing women's economic contributions to development.* Geneva: ILO.

Douglas, A. (1991). *Women and men in broadcasting in the 1990s.* Geneva: European Broadcasting.

Downing, J., Mohammadi, A., & Sreberny-Mohammadi, A. (Eds.). (1990). *Questioning the media: A critical introduction.* Newbury Park, CA: Sage.

Ellsworth, E. (1992). Why dosen't this feel empowering? Working through the repressive myths of critical pedagogy. In C. Luke & J. Gore (Eds.), *Feminisms and critical pedagogy* (pp. 90-119). New York: Routledge.

Eyoh, H. (1986). *From hammocks to bridges.* Yaounde: BET.

FASE. (1989). A comunicaçao como mediadora do conhecimiento: Uma imagem em movimento. *PROPOSTA, 43,* 11-21.

Fernández, M. (1988). *El centro de promocion Gregoria Apaza.* La Paz: CPMGA.

Ferris, W. (1983). Pecolia Warner, quilt maker. In G. K. Ferris (Ed.), *Afro-American arts and crafts.* Boston: Hall.

Flexner, E. (1975). *Century of struggle: The women's rights movement in the United States.* Cambridge, MA: Harvard University Press.

Ford-Smith, H. (1986). Sistren women's theatre, organization and conscientization. In P. Ellis (Ed.), *Women of the Caribbean* (pp. 122-128). Jamaica: Kingston.

Ford-Smith, H. (1989). *Ring ding in a tight corner. A case study of funding and organizational democracy in SISTREN, 1977-1988.* Toronto: International Council for Adult Education.

Foucault, M. (1988). *Un diálogo sobre el poder y otras conversaciones.* Madrid: Alianza.

Frank, A. G. (1980). *Crisis in the world economy.* New York: Holmes & Meier Publishers.

Fraser, C. (1990). México: Video rural. *CHASQUI, 33,* 78-81.

Freire, P. (1970). *Pedagogy of the oppressed.* New York: Continuum.

Freire, P. (1973). *Education for critical consciousness.* New York: Seabury.

Freire, P. (1983). *Pedagogy of the oppressed.* New York: Continuum.

Fuentes, C. (1985). *Gringo viejo*. New York: Farrar Straus Giroux.

Fuglesang, A. (1982). *About understanding: Ideas and observations on cross-cultural communication*. New York: Decade Media.

Fuglesang, A., & Chandler, D. (1986). The open snuff-box: Communication as participation. *Media Development, 2,* 2-4.

Gallagher, M. (1988). Women and NWICO. *Group Media Journal, 7*(2), 3-9

Gallagher, M. (1992). Women and men in the media. *Communication Research Trends, 12*(1), 1-36.

García-Canclini, N. (1982). *Las culturas populares en el capitalismo*. Mexico: Nueva Imágen.

García-Canclini, N. (1989). *Culturas híbridas: Estrategias para entrar y salir de la modernidad*. Mexico: Grijalbo.

Ghadially, R. (Ed.). (1988). *Women in Indian society*. New Delhi: Sage.

Ghosh, A. (1986). Demystifying media with rural women. In *Powerful images: A women's guide to audiovisual resources* (pp. 33-36). Rome: ISIS International.

Gilbert, S., & Gubar, S. (1985). *The Norton anthology of literature by women*. New York: Norton & Norton.

Gilroy, P. (1992). *There ain't no black in the Union Jack: The cultural politics of race and nation*. Chicago: University of Chicago Press.

Gogin, G. (1990). De los distintos modos de hacer radio en el Perú. In R. Alfaro, R. Tellez, H. Pinilla, & G. Gogin, *Cultura de masas y cultura popular en la radio peruana. Diagnóstico para construir una alternativa radial* (pp. 161-213). Lima, Peru: Calandria-Tarea.

Golding, P. (1991). Whose world, what information, which order? Rethinking NWICO in the 1990s. *Media Development, 38*(3), 46-49.

Gómez, R. (1990). *Popular video in the democratization of communication*. Unpublished manuscript. University of Montreal.

Goncharov, L. V. (1977). On the drain of capital from African countries. In P. C. W. Gutkins & P. Waterman (Eds.), *African social studies*. Budapest: Center for Afro-Asian Research of the Hungarian Academy of Sciences.

Goulet, D. (1989). Participation in development: New avenues. *World Development, 17*(2), 165-178.

Green, R. (1990). American Indian women, diverse leadership for social change. In L. Albrecht & R. Brewer (Eds.), *Bridges of power: Women's multicultural alliances* (pp. 61-73). Philadelphia: New Society.

Griffiths, M. (1990). How to improve child well-being? First increase mother's self-confidence. *Development Communication Report DCR, 79*(3), 7-8, 18.

Gunn-Allen, P. (Ed.). (1989). *Spider Woman's granddaughters. Traditional tales and contemporary writing by Native American women*. New York: Fawcett.

Guzman, V., Portocarrero, P., & Vargas, V. (Eds.). (1991). *Una nueva lectura: Género en el desarrollo*. Lima, Peru: Flora Tristan, Entre Mujeres.

Hartmann, A. (1990). Video: Primo pobre del septimo arte. *CHASQUI, 33,* 69-72.

Heeren, J. (1970). Alfred Schutz and the sociology of common-sense knowledge. In J. Douglas (Ed.), *Understanding everyday life* (pp. 45-56). London: Douglas.

Heller, A. (1977). *Sociologia de la vida cotidiana*. Barcelona: Peninsula.

Hemenway, R. E. (1980). *Zora Neale Hurston: A literary biography*. Urbana: University of Illinois Press.

Henaut, D. (1991). The challenge for change/societe nouvelle experience. In N. Thede & A. Ambrosi (Eds.), *Video the changing world* (pp. 48-53). Montreal: Black Rose.

Henriquez, N., & Alfaro, R. (1991). *Mujeres, violencia y derechos humanos.* Lima, Peru: IEPALA, Calandria.

Hill, R. E. (1991). *The black women's oral history project.* Westport, CT: Mackler.

Holub, R. (1984). *Reception theory.* London: Methuen.

hooks, b. (1989). *Talking back: Thinking feminist, thinking black.* Boston: South End.

hooks, b. (1990). *Yearning: Race, gender, and cultural politics.* Toronto: Between the Lines.

Hornik, R. (1988). *Development communication. Information, agriculture and nutrition in the Third World.* New York: Longman.

Houston, M. (1992). The politics of difference: Race, class, and women's communication. In L. Rakow (Ed.), *Women making meaning* (pp. 19-45). New York: Routledge.

Hurtado, A. (1989). Relating to privilege: Seduction and rejection in the subordination of white women and women of color. *Signs: Journal of Women in Culture and Society, 14*(4), 833-855.

ICAE & the Nicaraguan Association of Rural Workers. (1989). *The moon has her own light. The struggle to build a women's consciousness among Nicaraguan farmworkers.* Toronto: ICAE.

Illich, I. (1990). *El género vernáculo.* Mexico: Joaquin Mortiz, Planeta.

Innis, H. (1951). *The bias of communication.* Toronto: University of Toronto Press.

Innis, H. (1952). *Changing concepts of time.* Toronto: University of Toronto Press.

International Women's Tribune Centre. (1984). *Women using media for social change.* New York: IWTC.

Iser, W. (1989). La estructura apelativa de los textos. In R. Warning (Ed.), *Estética de la recepción* (pp. 133-164). Madrid: La Balsa de Medusa.

ISIS. (1984). *Women in development: A resource guide for organization and action.* Philadelphia: New Society Publishers.

Jakubowicz, K. (1989). Media communities replace local communities: A sign of the times? *Media Development, 36*(3), 2-4.

Jankowski, N., Vos, K., & Brouwer, W. (1989). Training Dutch citizen groups in video production techniques. *Media Development, 4,* 22-26.

Jansen, R. (1984). *Vivienda y luchas populares en Bogota.* Bogota, Colombia: Tercer Mundo.

Jelin, E. (Ed.). (1990). *Women and social change in Latin America.* London: Zed Books.

Jelincic, M. (1986). Making the best use of audiovisuals. In ISIS (Eds.) *Powerful images: A women's guide to audiovisual resources* (pp. 9-11). Rome: ISIS International.

Jiggins, J. (1988). The problems of understanding and communication at the interface of knowledge systems. In S. V. Poats, M. Schmink, & A. Spring (Eds.), *Gender issues in farming systems research and extension* (pp. 49-59). Boulder, CO: Westview.

Johnson, S. (1987). *Going out of our minds: The metaphysics of liberation.* Freedom, CA: Crossing.

Johnson-Reagon, B. (1990). Women as culture carriers in the Civil Rights Movement: Fannie Lou Hammer. In D. C. Hine (Ed.), *Black women in American history: The Twentieth Century.* Brooklyn, NY: Carlson.

Joseph, G., & Lewis, J. (1981). *Common differences: Conflicts in black and white feminist perspectives.* Garden City, NY: Anchor.

Jumani, J. (1988). *Getting an opportunity. Self employed women's association SEWA.* Unpublished manuscript. Ahmedabad, India.

Jumani, J., & Jumani, U. (1991). *Creating a people's alternative in video.* Ahmedabad: Jumani Foundation.

Jumani, J., & Jumani, U. (1993). *People's video and training.* Ahmedabad: Jumani Foundation.

Jurmo, P. (1980). Participation: Do villagers really want it? *Reports Magazine, 21,* 20-22.

Kaplún, M. (1984). *Comunicación entre grupos. El método del cassette foro.* TS45. Ottawa: IDRC.

Karl, L. (1989). ISIS network links women worldwide. *Group Media Journal, 3*(3), 15-18.

Kennedy, T. (1982). Beyond advocacy: A facilitative approach to public participation. *Journal of the University Film and Video Association, 34*(3), 33-46.

Kennedy, T. (1989). Community animation. An open-ended process. *Media Development, 36*(3), 5-7.

Kidd, D. (1992). *Alternate media, critical consciousness and action: The beginnings of a conversation about women and grassroots media.* Unpublished manuscript. Simon Fraser University, Burnaby, Canada.

Kidd, R. (1982). *The popular performing arts, non-formal education and social change in the Third World. A bibliography and review.* The Hague, The Netherlands: Essay-CESO.

Kidd, R. (1983, March). From outside into inside out: The Benue Workshop on Theatre for Development. *Media in Education for Development.*

Kidd, R., & Coletta, N. (Eds.). (1980). *Tradition for development: Indigenous structure and folk media in non formal education.* Berlin: German Foundation for International Development and International Council for Adult Education.

Kilusang, M. P. (1986). *Policy proposal on agriculture and countryside development.* Unpublished manuscript. Quezo City, Philippines.

Kindervatter, S. (1979). *Non-formal education as an empowering process.* Amherst: Center for International Education, University of Massachusetts.

Kishwar, M. (1990). Why I do not call myself a feminist. *Manushi, 61,* 2-8.

Koppman, D. (1991, October). Odyssey of faith: Faith Ringgold—A 20 year survey. *Women's Art Journal.*

Kranich, K. (1989). Celebrating our diversity. Women of color periodicals: 1968-1988. In M. Allen, *1989 directory of women's media* (p. 86). Washington, DC: Women's Institute for the Freedom of the Press.

La Belle, T. (1987). From consciousness raising to popular education in Latin America and the Caribbean. *Comparative Education Review, 31*(2), 201-217.

Lardinois, I., & Van Dijk, N. (1990). Environmental crisis exacts heavy toll on women. *Group Media Journal, 8*(1), 10-14.

Laverde, M., & Sánchez, L. (Eds.). (1986). *Voces insurgentes.* Bogota, Colombia: Fundación Universidad Central and SCCS.

Leacock, E. (1978). Women's status in egalitarian society: Implication for social evolution. *Current Anthropology, 19*(2), 247-275.

Lent, J. (1991). Women and mass communications: A selected international bibliography. *Media Development, 38*(2), 30-32.

León, R. (1990). Bartolina sisa: The peasant women's organization in Bolivia. In E. Jelin (Ed.), *Women and social change in Latin America* (pp. 135-149). London: Zed Books.

Leonard, A. (1989). *Seeds: Supporting women's work in the Third World.* New York: Feminist Press.

Levine, R. (1966). *Dreams and deeds.* Chicago: Chicago Unviersity Press.

Lewis, P. (Ed.). (1984). *Media for people in cities. A study of community media in the urban context.* Paris: UNESCO.

Lihamba, A., & Mlama, P. (1986). *Women and communication. Popular theatre as an alternative medium. The Mkambatani project in Tanzania.* Daka: Association of African Women for Research and Development.

Lippard, L. (1991/1992). The hands of memory in some Africian-American and Latina art. *IKON Journal, 12/13.*

Litwin, H. (1984, July). Video work in community organization: Boom or boondoggle? *Community Development Journal, 19*(3), 134-141.

Lobo, S. (1984). *Tengo casa propia.* Lima, Peru: IEP.

Lomnitz, L. (1978). Mechanisms of articulation between shantytown settlers and the urban system. *Urban Anthropology, 7*(2), 185-205.

Lozare, B. (1989, February). *Power and conflict: Hidden dimensions of communication, participative planning and action.* Paper presented at the Seminar Participation: A Key Concept for Change and Development, University of Poona, India.

Maguire, P. (1987). *Doing participatory research: A feminist approach.* Amherst: University of Massachussetts.

Mahoney, E. (1991). Women, development and media. *Media Development, 38*(2), 13-17.

Mainardi, P. (1982). Quilts: The great American art. In M. Broude & M. D. Garrard (Eds.), *Feminism and art history* (pp. 209-225). New York: Harper & Row.

Making our voices heard. (1989, August). *Voices Raising,* 24-26.

March, K., & Taqqu, R. (1986). *Women's informal associations in developing countries: Catalysts for change?* London: Westview.

Martín-Barbero, J. (1987a). *De los medios a las mediaciones.* Barcelona: Ed. G. Gili.

Martín-Barbero, J. (1987b). La telenovela en Colombia: Televisión, melodrama y vida cotidiana. *Dia-logos de la Comunicación, 17,* 46-58.

Martín-Barbero, J. (1989). Repossessing culture. The quest for the popular movements in Latin America. *Media Development, 36*(2), 21-24.

Mascarenhas, O., & Mbilinyi, A. (1983). *Women in Tanzania: An analytical bibliography.* Uppsala: Scandinavian Institute of African Studies.

Mata, M. (1983). Formación e interrelacionamiento. La experiencia del programa de comunicación de CELADEC. *Chasqui, Ciespal, 8,* pp. 76-79.

Mata, M. (1985). *Radio Enriquillo en diálogo con el pueblo* (Serie Investigaciones No. 3). Quito, Ecuador: ALER.

Mata, M. (1989). Radio Enriquillo: Una experiencia de acceso y participación en la comunicación masiva. In A. Tealdo (Ed.), *Radio y democracia en America Latina* (pp. 171-199). Lima, Peru: ALER.

Mata, M. (1990). Radios populares: Pensando en los receptores. *Media Development, 37*(4).

Mata, M. (1991). *Radios populares Latinoaméricanas. Realidades y desafios.* Unpublished manuscript. Argentina: ALER.

Mattelart, M. (1986). *Women, media crisis: Femininity and disorder.* London: Comedia.

McAnany, E., & Storey, D. (1989, May). *Development communication: A reappraisal for the 1990's.* Paper presented at the International and Intercultural Division of the 39th Annual Conference of the International Communication Association, San Francisco.

McKee, N. (1988). *Social marketing in international development: A critical review.* Unpublished master's thesis, Florida State University.

McLellan, I. (1987, December). Video and narrocasting: TV for an ordinary people. *Media in Education and Development,* pp. 144-149.

Mda, Z. (1987). Towards an alternative perspective of development. *Union of African Performing Artists Newsletter, 16.*

Meena, R., & Mbilinyi, M. (1991). Women's research and documentation project, Tanzania. *Signs: Journal of Women in Culture and Society, 16*(4), 852-859.

Mies, M. (1986). *Patriarchy and accumulation on a world scale: Women in the international division of labour.* London: Zed Books.

Mishler, E. (1986). *Research interviewing: Context and narrative.* Cambridge, UK: Cambridge University Press.

Mlama, P. (1973). *Music in Tanzania traditional theatre.* Unpublished masters thesis. University of Dar es Salaam, Tanzania.

Mlama, P. (1983). *The pedagogical function of traditional African theatre: The Kaguru as a case study.* Unpublished Ph.D. dissertation. University of Dar es Salaam, Tanzania.

Mlama, P. (1989a). Culture, women and the media. In S. T. Kwame Boafo (Ed.), *Communication and culture: African perspectives* (pp. 11-18). African Region: WACC.

Mlama, P. (1989b). *Women and communication for development. The popular theatre alternative. The Namionga child durvidal and development project.* Unpublished manuscript, Dar es Salaam, Tanzania: UNICEF.

Mlama, P. (1990). *Communication and social mobilisation for child survival and development.* Unpublished manuscript, Dar es Salaam, Tanzania: UNICEF and University of Dar es Salaam.

Mlama, P. (1991). Women's participation in communication for development: The popular theatre alternative in Africa. *Research in African Literature, 2.*

Moemeka, A. (1981). *Local radio, community education for development.* Zaria: Beleo University Press.

Moemeka, A. (1989). Communication and African culture: A sociological analysis. In S. T. Kwame Boafo (Ed.), *Communication and culture: An African perspective.* African Region: WACC.

Mohanty, C. (1991). Cartographies of struggle: Third World women and the politics of feminism. In C. Mohanty, A. Russo, & L. Torres (Eds.), *Third World women and the politics of feminism* (pp. 1-50). Bloomington: Indiana University Press.

Mohanty, C., Russo, A, & Torres, L., (Eds.). (1991). *Third World women and the politics of feminism.* Bloomington: Indiana University Press.

Moore, H. (1988). *Feminism and anthropology.* Minneapolis: University of Minnesota Press.

Moore, S. (1986). Participatory communication in the development process. *The Third Channel, 2*(2), 587-623.

Moraga, C., & Anzaldúa, G. (Eds.). (1981). *This bridge called my back: Writings by radical women of color.* Watertown, MA: Persephone Press.

Moser, C. (1989). Gender planning in the Third World: Meeting practical and strategical needs. *World Development, 17*(11), 1799-1825.

Moser, C., & Levi, C. (1988). Género, capacitación y planificación. In M. Barrig (Ed.), *De vecinas a ciudadanas: La mujer en el desarrollo urbano* (pp. 43-68). Lima, Peru: Centro & Sumbi.

Mouffe, C. (1984). *Por una teoría para fundamentar la acción política de las feministas.* Madrid: Jornadas de feminismo socialista.

Muller, K. (1987). The group media in the next five years. *Group Media Journal, 6*(3), 20-21.

Muñizaga, G. (1983). *Algunas problematizaciones en torno al tema de la democratización de las comunicaciones.* Santiago de Chile: CENECA.

Muñoz, S. (1988). *La politica en la cotidianeidad de las mujeres populares.* Cali: CLACSO.

Muñoz, S. (1990). *Mundos de vida y modos de ver.* In J. Martín and S. Muñoz (Eds.), *Melodrama y televisión en Colombia.* Bogota, Colombia: Tercer Mundo.

Muñoz, S. (1992a). *Barrio e identidad.* Mexico: Trillas.

Muñoz, S. (1992b). *El ojo, el libro y la pantalla: Análisis del consumo cultural de la ciudad de Cali.* Universidad del Valle, Cali, Columbia.

Nair, K., & White, S. (1987a). Participation is the key to development comunication. *Media Development, 3,* 36-40.

Nair, K., & White, S. (1987b). *Participatory message development: A conceptual framework.* Paper presented at the International Seminar on Development Communication, National Institute of Rural Development, Rajendranagar, Hyderabad, India.

Nair, K., & White, S. (1987c, July). *A conceptualization of development communication concepts.* Paper presented at Communication and Change: An Agenda for the New Age of Communication. East-West Center, Honolulu, Hawaii.

Neverdon-Morton, C. (1978). The black woman's struggle for equality in the South: 1895-1925. In S. Harley & R. Terborg-Penn (Eds.), *The Afro-American woman: Struggles and images.* London: Kennikat.

Nguni wa, T. (1982). Women in cultural work: The fate of Kamiriithu People's Theatre-Kenya. *Development Dialogue,* 1-2.

Ngwanakilala, N. (1981). *Mass communication and development of socialism in Tanzania.* Dar es Salaam: Tanzania Publishing House.

Nyong'o, P. (Ed.). (1987). *Popular struggles for democracy in Africa.* Tokyo: The United Nation's University.

O'Connor, A. (1989). People's radio in Latin America—A new assessment. *Media Development, 2,* 47-51.

Ogan, C. (1989). Video's great advantage—Descentralized control of technology. *Media Development, 4,* 2-5.

Ortner, S., & Whitehead, H. (Eds.) (1981). *Sexual meanings: The cultural construction of gender and sexuality.* Cambridge: Cambridge University Press.

Otro Modo de Ser. (1991). Mujeres Mexicanas en movimiento. Mexico: Centro de Comunicación Alternativa, Alaida Foppa, Interaktion.

Pareles, J. (1992, May). Hip hop makes a sharp turn back to melody. *New York Times,* D24.

Pearson, J. (1985). *Gender and communication.* Duburque, IA: Brown.

Peck, S. (1987). *The different drum: Community making and peace.* New York: Simon & Schuster.

Pedersen, C. (1988). *Nunca antes me habían enseñado eso.* Lima, Peru: Lilith Ediciones.

Penn, O. (1986, March). *Jazz: American classical music as a philosophic and symbolic entity.* Lecture presented in the Fifteenth Anniversary of African and African-American Studies Program. Atlanta: Emery University.

Pigozzi, M. (1982). Participation in non-formal education projects: Some possible negative outcomes. *Convergence, 15*(3), 6-16.

Pike, F. B. (1973). *Spanish-American 1900-1970: Tradition and social innovation.* New York: Norton.

Pinilla, H., Macassi, S.,& Alfaro, R. M. (1990). Autoevaluación del programa nuestra vida: Informe de investigación. Unpublished report. Lima, Peru: Calandria

Prado, E. (1985). Televisión comunitaria en Cataluña. *TELOS, 2,* 53-58.

Protz, M. (1987). *Visual education media for rural development: A comparison of professional and participatory materials in St. Lucia.* Unpublished Master's thesis, University of Guelph, Ontario, Canada.

Protz, M. (1991). *Seeing and showing ourselves: A guide to using small-format videotape as a participatory tool for development*. New Delhi: Centre for Development of Instructional Technology.

Puntel, J. (1992). *The Catholic church and the democratization of communication in Latin America*. Unpublished Ph.D. dissertation. Simon Fraser University, Burnaby, Canada.

Rahnema, M. (1990). Participatory action research: The last temptation of Saint Development. *Alternatives, 15*, pp. 199-226.

Rakow, L. (Ed.). (1992). *Women making meaning. New feminist directions in communication*. New York: Routledge.

Rattray, R. S. (1923). *Ashanti*. London: Oxford University Press.

Rattray, R. S. (1929). *Ashanti law and constitution*. London: Oxford University Press.

Rathgebher, E. (Ed.). (1989a). *Women's role in natural resource managment in Africa* (Manuscript Report 238e). Ottawa, Ont., Canada: IDRC.

Rathgebher, E. (1989b). *WID, WAD, GAD: Trends in research and practice*. Ottawa, Ont., Canada: International Development Research Centre.

Riaño, P. (1990). *Empowering through communication: Women's experiences with participatory communication in development process* (Manuscript Report 278e). Ottawa, Ont., Canada: IDRC.

Riaño, P. (1991). Myths of the silenced: Women and grassroots communication. *Media Development, 38*(2), 20-22.

Ricard. A. (1970). *Literature and cultural pluralism*. Paper presented at the University of California, Los Angeles.

Ringgold, F. (1992). *Tar beach*. New York. Scholastic.

Rivera, M. (1991). La historia de las mujeres y la conciencia feminista en Europa. In L. Luna (Ed.), *Mujeres y sociedad. Nuevos enfoques teóricos y metodológicos* (pp. 127-138). Barcelona: University of Barcelona.

Rivera-Cusicanqui, S., & Andean Oral History Workshop. (1990). Indigenous women and community resistence: History and memory. In E. Jelin (Ed.), *Women and social change in Latin America* (pp. 151-180). London: Zed Books.

Roach, C. (1990). Limitations and new possibilities. *Media Development, 37*(3), 28-30.

Robson, E. (1991, March). *Sketching a better life in urban Peru*. New York: Source, UN Development Program.

Rodríguez, C. (1989). *Turning a TV screen into a mirror. A chronicle of participatory video production*. Unpublished manuscript. University of Ohio, Athens.

Rodríguez, C. (1990). Media for participation and social change: Local television in Catalonia. *CommDev News*, 4-10.

Rodgers, C. (1969/1975). *how i got over: IT IS DEEP*. New York: Doubleday.

Romero, J. (1979). *Latinoamérica. Las ciudades y las ideas*. Mexico: Siglo XXI editores.

Romero, L. (1987). *Los sectores populares en las ciudades Latinoaméricanas: La cuestión de la identidad*. Buenos Aires: CISEA.

Roncagliolo, R. (1982). El NOMIC: Communicación y poder. *Chasqui, 3* 26-33.

Roncagliolo, R. (1991). Notes on "the alternative." In N. Thede & A. Ambrosi (Eds.), *Video the changing world* (pp. 206-208). Montreal: Black Rose.

Roncagliolo, R. (1992). Latin America and the NWICO: Neither widows nor orphans. *Media Development, 39*(2), 9-10.

Rosaldo, M. (1980). The use and abuse of anthropology: Reflections on feminism and cross-cultural understanding. *Signs: Journal of Women and Culture, 5*(3), 389-417.

Ruby, J. (1990). *Eric Michaels: An appreciation.* Philadelphia: Center for Visual Communication. (A revised version of *In the Belly of the Beast: Eric Michael and the Anthropology of Visual Communication*)

Rueda, J. (1989). Tendencia demograficas en Colombia. In A. Camacho (Ed.), *La sociología hoy* (pp. 245-263). Bogota: CISDE, CEREC.

Ruiz, C. (1987). Palabro de mujer. *Cuadernos de Communicaión Alternativa, 5,* pp. 23-40.

Rush, R., & Allen, D. (Eds.). (1989). *Communication at the crossroads: The gender gap connection.* Norwood: Ablex.

Salinas, R. (1988). Agonizan las radios mineras. *CHASQUI, 27,* 46-49.

Santisteban, F. (1989). Dimensión subjetiva y organización de la mujer. Presentation to the seminar Estrategias de promoción y organización de la mujer. Lima, Peru: Calandria.

Saravia, J., & Sandoval, G. (1991). *Jacha Uru. ¿La esperanza de un pueblo?* La Paz: ILDIS, CEP.

Schutz, A. (1962). *The problem of social reality: Collected papers I.* The Hague, The Netherlands: Nijhoff.

Scott, J. (1986). Gender, a useful category of historical analysis. *The American Historical Review, 91,* 23-32.

Sen, G., & Grown, C. (1987). *Development crisis and alternative visions.* New York: Monthly Review.

Sénécal, M. (1991). The alternative search of its identity. In N. Thede & A. Ambrosi (Eds.), *Video the changing world* (pp. 209-218). Montreal: Black Rose.

Servaes, J. (1989, February). *The role and place of research in participatory communication projects.* Paper presented at the Seminar on Participation: A Key Concept for Change, University of Poona, India.

Sistren, & Ford-Smith, H. (1987). *Life-stories of Jamaican women.* Toronto: Sister Vision.

Smith, E. (1975). *The evolution and continuing presence of the African-American oral tradition in Black America.* Unpublished Ph.D. dissertation. University of California, Irvine.

Smitherman, G. (1977). *Talking and testifying: The language of Black America.* Boston: Houghton Mifflin.

Sojo, A. (1988). *Mujer y política. Ensayo sobre el feminismo y el sujeto popular.* San Jose de Costa Rica: DEI

Sollors, W. (1989). *The invention of ethnicity.* New York: Oxford University Press.

Speak Magazine. (1992a, August). Ellen Kuzwayo. Vol. 42, pp. 5-7.

Speak Magazine. (1992b, October). Walls can shout! Vol. 44, p. 11.

Spellman, A. B. (1968). *Not just whistling Dixie-Black fire: An anthology of Afro-American writing.* New York: William Morrow.

Stamp, P. (1989). *Technology, gender and power in Africa* (Technical Study 63e). Ottawa, Ont., Canada: International Development Research Centre.

Starhawk. (1988). *Dreaming the dark.* Boston: Beacon.

Starhawk. (1989). Ritual as bonding. In J. Plaskow & C. Christ (Eds.), *Weaving the visions.* San Francisco: Harper & Row.

Stein, D. (1988). *The women's book of healing.* St. Paul, MN: Llewellyn.

Stein, S. J., & Stein, B. (1970). *The colonial heritage of Latin America.* London: Oxford University Press.

Steiner, L. (1992). The history and structure of women's alternative media. In L. Rakow (Ed.), *Women making meaning. New feminist directions in communications* (pp. 121-143). New York: Routledge.

Strathern, M. (1972). *Women in between: Female roles in a male world.* London: Seminar.

Strathern, M. (1987). An awkward relationship: The age of feminism and anthropology. *SIGNS, 12*(2), 276-292.

Strathern, M. (1990). *The gender of the gift.* Berkerly: University of California Press.

Stuart, S. (1987). The village video network: Video as tool for local development and south-south exchange. *Convergence, 20*(2), 62-68.

Stuart, S. (1989a). Access to media: Placing video in the hands of people. *Media Development, 36*(4), 8-11.

Stuart, S. (1989b). *Participation and video. Putting media tools in service of the people.* New York: Martha Stuart Communications.

Sunkel, G. (1985). *Razón y pasión en la prensa popular.* Santiago: ILET.

Taylor, D. (1976). Black English in black folklore. In S. Harrison & T. Trabasso (Eds.), *Black English: A seminar.* Hillsdale, NJ: Lawrence Erlbaum.

Taylor, S. (1990). *Co-creating community. Report for the Canadian Research Institute for the Advancement of Women.* Ottawa: Department of Health and Welfare and Secretary of State.

Thede, N., & Ambrosi, A. (Eds.). (1991). *Video the changing world.* Montreal: Black Rose.

Thompson, E. P. (1984). *Tradición revuelta y conciencia de clase.* Barcelona: Editorial Crítica.

Tomaselli, K. (1989). Transferring video skills to the community: The problem of power. *Media Development, 4,* 11-15.

Turnbull, T. M. (1963). *The lonely African.* New York: Simon & Schuster.

Turner, T. (1991, January-February). Visual media, cultural politics, and anthropological practice: Recent uses of film and video among the Kayapo of Brazil. *The Independent.*

UNESCO. (1985). *Communication in the service of women. A report on action and research programmes, 1980-1985.* Paris: UNESCO.

Uribe, H. (1992). The NWICO as a victim of neo-liberal right-wing politics. *Media Development, 39*(2), 3-4.

Valdeavellano, P. (1989). America Latina está construyendo su propia imágen. In P. Valdeavellano (Ed.), *El video en la educación popular.* Lima, Peru: IPAL.

Valdes, T. (1988). *Vendid, benditas de mis padre: Las pobladoras, sus rutinas y sus sueños.* Santiago: FLACSO

Valles, S. (1991). *The place of culture between processes of communication and popular movements.* Unpublished manuscript. Simon Fraser University, Burnaby, Canada.

Video animation and conscientization [Editorial]. (1989). *Media Development, 4,* 1.

Viezzer, M. (1977). *Si me permiten hablar. Testimonio de Domitila, una mujer de las minas de Bolivia.* Mexico: Siglo XXI.

Wahlman, M. (1983). *Ten Afro-American quilters.* The Center for the Study of Southern Culture, University of Mississippi.

Wahlman, M., & Scully, J. (1983). Aesthetic principles in Afro-American quilts. In G. K. Ferris (Ed.), *Afro-American folk art and crafts.* Boston: Hall.

Waltrous, P. (1991, August). When the queen speaks, people listen. *New York Times,* D4.

Warning, R (Ed.). (1989). *Estética de la recepción.* Madrid: La Balsa de Medusa.

Watchel, N. (1973). La visión trágica de los vencidos. In I. Prado (Ed.), *Ideología mesianica en el mundo andino. Antología* Lima, Peru: Prado.

WEDNET. (1991). *Background information on WEDNET.* Unpublished manuscript. Nairobi, Kenya: Environment Liaison Centre International.

White, R. (1987, October). *From group communication to comunicación popular.* Discussion paper prepared for the Board of Consultants of Sonolux, London, Centre for the Study of Communication and Culture.

White, S. (1989, February). *Participation: A key concept in communication for change and development.* Background document to the Seminar on Participation. University of Poona, India.

White, S., & Patel, P. (1988). *Strategies for message development: Using participatory video.* Paper presented to Intercultural & Development Communication Division, International Communication Association, New Orleans.

Williams College Museum of Art. (1991). *Stitching memories: African-American story quilts.* Author.

Williamson, H. A. (1991). The Fogo process: Development support communication in Canada and the developing world. In F. L. Casmir (Ed.), *Communication in development* (pp. 270-288). Hillsdale, NJ: Ablex.

Wilson, C., II & Gutiérrez, F. (1985). *Minorities and the media: Diversity and the end of mass communication.* Newbury Park, CA: Sage.

Witheford, N. (1992). *Autonomous Marxism and the Information Society.* Unpublished manuscript. Simon Fraser University, Burnaby, Canada.

Wood, J. (1991). Politics, gender and communication: A review of contemporary texts. *Communication Education, 40,* 116-123.

Yacoob, M. (1990). Women and water: The bucket stops here. *Development Communication Report, 70*(3), 6, 17.

Young, K. (1988). *Gender and development: A relational approach.* Toronto: Institute of Development Studies.

Zimbawe producing a popular text. (1989, August). *Voices Raising,* 18-21.

Index

About the Authors

Rosa María Alfaro is the Director of the Association of Social Communicators of Peru, Calandria, and Professor at the University of Lima. She has published *Palabra de Mujer, De la Conquista de la Ciudad a la Apropiación de la Palabra,* and *Cultura Popular y Cultura de Masas en la Radio Peruana,* as well as several articles in Latin American and European journals.

Susan Y. Dyer-Bennem is a Feature Writer for the *Women's Art Magazine* of the Women Artists Slide Library in London and has published several essays in *Anthology of African-American Women Artists.* For the past five years she has been a Domestic Violence Counselor for the M.E.N. program in Rochester, New York, working with men who batter women.

Jennifer Kawaja is a Caribbean Writer and Video Film Producer. She works and lives in Toronto. She has had extensive experience in participatory media and has worked with groups of immigrants, women, and youth.

Dorothy Kidd is completing her Ph.D. in Communications. Her research examines how women use community radio for social change. Since the 1960s, she has also worked in a number of different grassroots media, involving women's groups and other social movements.

Libby Lloyd is the *Speak* magazine Radio Audio Programme (RAP) Coordinator in South Africa. She also worked as Assistant Editor of *Speak* magazine. She has experience as a Trade Unionist, Media Activist, and Media Worker, and she has been involved in the broad struggle for justice in South Africa.

Marita Mata has conducted research in the area of communication at the Research Centre of the Faculty of Philosophy and Humanities at the National University of Cordoba. As a trainer and researcher, she has collaborated with the Latin American Association for Radio Education (ALER) for the last ten years.

Rose Mensah-Kutin is the Program Officer-in-Charge of the Social Impact Assessment (SIA) program of the Ministry of Energy in Ghana. She received her master's degree in Development Studies from the Institute of Social Studies in the Hague, The Netherlands, and her graduate diploma in journalism and mass communication from the School of Communication Studies, University of Ghana. For nine years, she has been a journalist and has been involved in several NGOs in Ghana.

Penina Mlama is a Professor of Theatre Arts at the University of Dar es Salaam in Tanzania. She has worked extensively in Theatre for Development in rural communities in Tanzania and other parts of Africa and has also been involved in the study of women and communication for development. She has published eight plays and the book *Culture and Development: The Popular Theatre Approach in Africa.*

Sonia Muñoz received her Ph.D in the Science of Communication and Information from the Autonoma University in Barcelona and is Professor at the University of Valle in Cali, Colombia. Her research has focused on popular cultures, communication, women, and the city. Her publications include *Barrio and Identity: Everyday Communication Among Women in the Popular Barrios, Politics in Every Day Life of Popular Women, Television and Melodrama* (co-author), and *The Eye, the Book, and the Screen.*

Maria Protz is a Rural Communications Consultant in Jamaica for the CIDA and the InterAmerican Institute for Cooperation on Agriculture. She recently conducted a Caribbean regional workshop on participatory communication methodologies for rural women and has also published a training manual on the use of participatory video techniques with CENDIT, in New Delhi, India. She has worked with the University of Guelph in Canada and with TV Ontario, Canada.

Pilar Riaño is an anthropologist and communicator. She worked in Colombia for ten years implementing programs in popular communication, participatory research, and community participation. Her research has focused in the areas of popular culture, gender and communication, and participatory research. She is a consultant on community development, gender, and communication in development and a trainer on antiracism and multicultural issues.

Clemencia Rodríguez is Assistant Professor at the University of Texas at San Antonio. She taught communication research at the University Centroamericana in Managua, Nicaragua, and at the University Javeriana in Bogota, Colombia. For several years, she worked in Colombia in the area of popular communication and conducted research on television and melodrama. Her present research involves community-based television in Catalonia. Her publications include "Media for Participation and Social Change" and *When the Screen Became an Electronic Mirror.*

Carmen Ruíz is a Communicator and the Director of the Centre Gregoria Apaza for the Promotion of Women in La Paz, Bolivia. She is responsible for the project radio Pachamama, is a correspondent for the Women's Special Service (SEM), and is an active member of the Women's Directory and the Association of Institutions for Promotion and Education. Her publications include *Women's Voice* and *Notes for a Discussion on Productive Units.*

Sharon Taylor is a Professor of Social Work at Memorial University of New Foundland, specializing in women's economic development issues. She initiated the organization Single Moms Against Poverty in Newfoundland, Canada; developed innovative teleconferencing techniques in work with native women's groups across Canada; and facilitated workshops in women's community-based economic development with faculty, graduate students, and rural women from Canada and Thailand. She is Vice-President of Canada World Youth and is an Associate of the Participatory Development Project at the East-West Center in Honolulu, Hawaii.